Linguistic Field Methods

Linguistic Field Methods

Bert Vaux
University of Cambridge

Justin Cooper
Orrick, Herrington & Sutcliffe LLP

Emily Tucker
Oregon Graduate Institute

Wipf & Stock
PUBLISHERS
Eugene, Oregon

Wipf and Stock Publishers
199 W 8th Ave, Suite 3
Eugene, OR 97401

Linguistic Field Methods
By Vaux, Bert and Cooper, Justin
Copyright©2007 Vaux, Bert and Cooper, Justin
ISBN 13: 978-1-59752-764-4
ISBN 10: 1-59752-764-5
Publication date 11/14/2006

Authors' Preface

The present volume addresses the need for an up-to-date and accessible introduction to the elicitation of linguistic data from native speaker informants. The material, following introductory chapters surveying the general enterprise of field research, is organized into eight major areas of current linguistic interest: Phonetics, Phonology, Morphology, Syntax, Semantics, Pragmatics, Sociolinguistics and Dialectology, and Historical Linguistics. Each chapter presents basic structures to be elicited, and provides cautionary tales drawn from the experiences of seasoned fieldworkers who have attempted to elicit these structures. These, in turn, are followed by suggested readings and illustrative exercises for each chapter. Emphasis is placed not on developing a theory of fieldwork (though it should be clear to the careful reader that one underlies this book), nor on learning linguistic theory, but rather on providing enlightening suggestions and entertaining anecdotes designed to inspire students to make their own brilliant linguistic discoveries. Though we are theoretical linguists by training, this is not a book of linguistic theory; we believe that the fundamentals of linguistic theory are best covered in the introductory phonetics and phonology, syntax, morphology, and general courses offered by most linguistics departments. This book is designed to be accessible to those who have no background in linguistics and may not even be interested in pursuing a degree in linguistics. Those who *are* interested in pursuing further linguistic study should consider this book as the jumping-off point for theoretical study of each topic. For example, we consider stress systems in chapter 7, but we do not look at the theories that have been developed by phonologists such as Morris Halle and Bruce Hayes to account for the behavior of stress systems.

We focus on how to collect the relevant data successfully; the question of why the data look the way they do is amply treated in textbooks on phonological theory, such as Kenstowicz 1994. We have tried to lead the interested beginning reader to these sources in our suggested readings at the end of each chapter.

Though the pace of the text is designed for an undergraduate-level introductory Field Methods course and requires no prior knowledge of linguistics, more advanced students and scholars may find many portions of the book useful as well. We have made a conscious effort to present the material in a conversational manner devoid of unnecessary technical terms and rhetorical devices; we hope that this departure from the norms of academic writing style will not prove jarring to our readers.

We thank the following colleagues for help with this book: Maki Asano, Peter Bakker, Ernie Barreto, Andrew Carnie, James Clackson, Dan Everett, Amanda Fortini, Ken Hale, Morris Halle, Kevin Herwig, Sabbir Kolya, Terri McClain, Lynn Nichols, James Russell, Seth Sanders, Engin Sezer, Michele Sigler, Höskuldur Thráinsson, Cassia van der Hoof Holstein, Calvert Watkins, and Lindsay Whaley.

We would like to dedicate this book to the memory of Ken Hale (1934-2001), an inspiring theoretical and field linguist, and (unknown to many) a great armenologist and abkhazologist.

Bert Vaux
Cambridge, England
October 2006

Contents

1 Introduction

Judgements about oneself are as fallible as any others.

Noam Chomsky
Language and problems of knowledge

The field of linguistics has become a bit schizophrenic in the last fifty years. On one hand, most cutting-edge research in the field for the past forty years has been based on the Chomskyan premise that the primary focus of linguistic inquiry should be on the grammatical competence of the individual, regardless of the particular language (s)he speaks. This has engendered a great deal of insularity in the linguistic community, as theoretical linguists have increasingly concentrated on their own language (normally English), and quite often only their own idiolect. This approach is of course justified in many respects, for no two individual grammars are the same, and conflation by the linguist of multiple grammars can lead to all sorts of confusion and error. Furthermore, there is—contrary to popular belief—more than enough material of linguistic interest in a single individual's grammar to keep a linguist busy for an entire career.

However, linguistics is simultaneously moving in the opposite direction as well. The same research program which validates devoting one's whole professional life to elucidating the grammar of a single individual also mandates (by virtue of its belief in Universal Grammar, an innate linguistic endowment common to all humans) investigation into the full range of linguistic possibilities allowed by natural languages. It is therefore in the interest of theoretical linguists to have at their disposal descriptions and analyses of the widest possible variety of languages. At the same time, there is an ever-increasing need to document and analyze the rapidly decreasing pool of human languages. Fortunately, in spite of

1

the current dominance of theoretical linguistics in the United States and Europe, there are still many professional and aspiring field linguists who are committed to carrying out the work that remains to be done.

The state of the field, then, is that we have widespread interest in both theoretical linguistics and empirical linguistics. Unfortunately, the intersection of the set of theoretical linguists, who wish to elucidate the structure of human language as a whole, and the set of field linguists, who wish to study new and exotic languages, is relatively small. Theoretical linguists often condemn fieldwork as a misguided use of time better spent on reflection on and analysis of a constrained corpus of data, whereas field linguists generally find theoretical linguistics to be excessively narrow in scope and would prefer to be out in the field collecting new data. How do we strike a compromise between these disparate ways of looking at language?

This textbook is an attempt to mediate between these two linguistic camps: we endeavor to make it possible for theoretical linguists to conduct research in the field, and for field linguists to organize their efforts in a theoretically enlightened manner. We also hope to encourage fieldwork on the vast variety of languages that remain entirely or partially unstudied, and to imbue this work with a modicum of theoretical sophistication. This last point is very important for, as Morris Halle often points out, data on their own are meaningless; it is the theoretical framework that dictates what facts are interesting and what facts are not. The theory, moreover, tells us what questions to ask; without a well-articulated linguistic theory, the fieldworker (like most pre-nineteenth century scholars) is limited to disconnected anecdotal observations. We therefore ground our selection of topics and questions to be presented in this book in the general framework of modern (generative) linguistic theory. However, we are careful not to overemphasize here the machinery of generative linguistics, as it would be distracting to students at the level for which this textbook is designed.

We have also attempted to address the lack of a comprehensive textbook that presents the rudiments of field methodology in all of the major areas of linguistic inquiry. Though a number of books and articles dealing with various aspects of fieldwork already exist (see for example Payne 1951, Longacre 1964, Samarin 1967, Brewster 1982, and the extensive list of sources provided in the References), each is fairly limited in scope, and most are now outdated in terms of the theoretical machinery they employ or assume. Consequently, we cover not only the core disciplines of Phonology, Morphology, and Syntax, but also Pragmatics, Sociolinguistics, and so on.

1. Why do fieldwork?

The skeptic may ask why one should do fieldwork at all, given that

- there are no professorships of field methods, nor of most of the languages of the world,
- life in the field is often fraught with personal, political, intellectual, and intestinal difficulties,
- it is (normally) easier to deal with oneself in familiar surroundings than it is to devote the time and energy necessary to go into the field, locate informants, befriend them, learn their language, and so on,
- most of the languages on which fieldwork is or needs to be conducted will in all likelihood soon be dead (cf. Hale et al. 1992).

There are in fact many counters to this daunting list of objections. Let's take the last objection first. The fact that a language is endangered makes it no less interesting linguistically. In fact, there is a certain fascination in working with a language that may be dead in fifty or a hundred years—how many of us would give everything we have to hear a living speaker of Hittite, Egyptian, Prussian, or any of thousands of other extinct languages? Furthermore, with many endangered languages the fieldworker can actually play a role in saving the language, by developing a writing system, fostering speakers' interest in passing on the language to their children, and so on. I have found my own work on developing a writing system and the beginnings of a literary tradition for the Homshetsik of northeastern Turkey to be much more rewarding on a personal level than any of my work in theoretical linguistics.

Fieldwork can also bring a great deal of personal enrichment associated with visiting exotic locations and meeting new and unusual people. Documenting an unstudied language also instills the satisfaction of creating something new and adding knowledge to the world. Ideally one's fieldwork will also benefit the linguistic community being studied, by demonstrating to speakers that their language is of interest to outsiders. Sometimes it is even possible to validate the speakers' language by creating literature or by training native speakers as linguists so that they can conduct further research on their own. These points may not seem important to Western readers, who speak languages that are officially recognized in their countries, are taught in schools, and have millions of speakers. However, many minority languages are not even acknowledged to exist in the countries where they are spoken, much less taught in schools or allowed in publications. For example, the Homshetsik mentioned earlier are not recognized by the Turkish government, though their population numbers in the hundreds of thousands. Their language, Homshetsma, is not allowed to be taught in the local schools or to be spoken in public areas. For the many ethnic minorities like the Homshetsik located throughout the world, the attention of a non-native linguist can therefore be laden with significance that Americans might not appreciate at first.

There are also a number of reasons for theoretical linguists to carry out fieldwork. Fieldwork is obviously required for syntacticians and phoneticians who are not working on their native language, since grammaticality judgements and phonetic data cannot be culled at will from published materials. Fieldwork also provides the linguist with access to a broader range of data than can be culled from published sources, and these data are generally more reliable than what one finds in many publications dealing with theoretical linguistics, where the data cited are often taken from secondary sources. Modern linguistics also dictates that it is important to collect what *can't* be said as well as what *can* be said, and published sources such as dictionaries and grammars generally state only the preferred way of pronouncing a given item or saying a given phrase. For example, grammars of English might well state that sentences like "who do you think that John saw?" are possible, but few of these would mention that "who do you think John saw?" is also possible, and even fewer (or perhaps none) would include the fact that the seemingly similar sentence "who do you think that saw John?" is *not* possible. Along similar lines, theoretical linguists often need to know not only what can and can't be said, but also nuances of acceptability and optionality that are never mentioned in traditional grammars and dictionaries. Dictionaries of English, for example, invariably fail to mention that both [hɪtʰ] and [hɪʔt˺] are acceptable pronunciations of "hit", and that in American speech the latter is preferable, whereas the former sounds somewhat awkward and affected, though it is more common on television programs. Linguists who need access to this sort of detailed information must perforce garner it from field research.

Finally, fieldwork instills an appreciation of the complexity of language which linguists can easily miss if they work only on their native languages. The most convincing demonstration of this comes when novices are asked to transcribe a simple utterance in a language with which they are not familiar, and invariably find it impossible to identify even the most "basic" linguistic elements, such as word boundaries and phonemes.

2. Selecting an informant

I found the best informants to help me get a grasp of Jamaican Creole were children of eleven or twelve, old enough to know their language thoroughly but young enough not to be affected by the sense of linguistic shame and embarrassment that characterized adult speakers.

John Wells
Linguistics in Britain: Personal Histories

So far we have seen that there are many reasons for learning field methods and conducting research in the field. The next challenge is to track down and begin working with one or more speakers of the language you have chosen to work on. This is not as easy as it might appear at first, unless of course you are taking a Field Methods course, in which case the teacher will normally have selected an informant (or "linguistic consultant", as some prefer[1]) in advance.

When selecting an informant, there are many factors to be taken into consideration. We will begin with suggestions that apply to individuals searching for a native speaker, and then conclude with some tips for selecting informants for Field Methods courses.

---

[1] We generally use the term "informant" to refer to the native speakers with whom we carry out fieldwork, but many people find this term to smack of espionage and skullduggery, and prefer to use more neutral terms such as "linguistic consultant" or even "raconteur".

2.1. Selection for an individual linguist

Fieldwork can be extremely rewarding if one selects the right informant(s), and equally painful if one selects the wrong informant. However, there are certain steps one can take to reduce the risk of picking unwisely.

First of all, it is generally a good idea to select an informant who is of the same gender as the fieldworker. Of course, in a society where more than two gender types are recognized, this maxim should be adjusted accordingly; the basic point here is that fieldworkers should avoid selecting informants who might become sexually interested in them (see section 3.1.2.1 for discussion of what can be done when this happens). Relationships of this type inevitably disrupt the working relationship between fieldworker and informant, and often lead to personal trauma as well. A further advantage of selecting an informant of the same sex is that he or she will be more likely to feel comfortable interacting with the fieldworker, particularly when discussing potentially touchy issues such as terms for body parts, incontinence, and so on.

One should naturally try to find a fluent native speaker of the language being studied. However, this is not always possible. The Algonquian language Miami, for example, has no native speakers left; one can now only work with elders who remember isolated words and may be able to understand passages of older texts. At least in this situation, though, it is possible to distinguish easily between what is Miami and what is English. Other cases can be much more complicated. For example, most of the nonstandard dialects of Armenian are only spoken by individuals who also speak standard Armenian and freely mix the two. In cases like this, where the dialects, registers, or languages spoken by the informant are very similar, it can be extremely difficult to be sure which category a given form belongs to, and the informant generally does not indicate which is which. When working on the Armenian dialect spoken in the Iranian city of Isfahan, I once came upon a dialectal form that was glossed in Armenian as ʃikʰ. Not knowing this word offhand, I checked through all of the biggest and best Armenian dictionaries, without any success. After many hours of torment, I realized that the author was not providing an obscure Armenian lexical item, but rather was invoking the French word *chic*!

For these reasons, it is generally better to pick an informant who is monolingual. However, this option can also present complications. The most obvious difficulty is that monolingual informants are much harder for the fieldworker to communicate with, unless he or she happens to speak that language as well. Monolingual informants are also less likely to be familiar with the notion of grammatical categories, variability in the semantic fields covered by different lexical items, and so on, since they have not had to confront the differences between their own and another language.

There is no general rule for determining the age of the optimal informant, because all ages have advantages and disadvantages in a given situation. As a general rule, younger informants are more likely to defer to the fieldworker (though extremely young informants are of course prone to having short attention spans and can become uppity); they are also more likely to be willing to provide saucy vocabulary, less likely to be sensitive to touchy social and political issues, and may be quicker to grasp the subtleties of the linguistic enterprise, which can be useful if one is interested in training native speaker linguists. Older informants may be preferable for researchers interested in archaisms in language, folklore, and so on.

As for the number of informants that the fieldworker should strive to obtain, the answer is again unclear. Some linguists prefer to have only one informant, and some prefer to have many; there are advantages to each scheme. If one works with a lone informant, one obtains relatively consistent data, whereas when working with two or more informants, differences in idiolect, dialect, and so on inevitably appear. For generative linguists interested in studying the linguistic competence of a single individual, working with two or more informants is in many ways counterproductive. Finally, with only one informant it is easier to establish a working relationship, simpler and faster to obtain the information one wants, easier to arrange meetings, and cheaper (assuming one pays the informants).

Conversely, by working with many informants one obtains a better overall picture of the language (though many generative linguists would claim that languages do not exist—only individual grammars...). Interaction with multiple informants takes some of the social and mental pressure off of each individual in the group (though a certain type of social skill is required on the part of the fieldworker to mediate among the members of a large group). When multiple informants are present simultaneously, it becomes possible to record natural conversations. Technically this is possible with single informants as well, but most individuals find it difficult and strange to conduct a conversation with themselves! Multiple informants can also exercise quality control on each other and trigger each other's memories of elusive forms and constructions. In one Homshetsi couple I work with, the wife comes up with forms her husband can't remember or corrects the forms he does produce, even though in general he is much more familiar with the language than she is (both are bilingual in Turkish, which she speaks almost exclusively). One final advantage of consulting multiple speakers of a given language is that some of them may not possess the linguistic feature in which the fieldworker is interested. Once, after reading a grammar of a dialect of Armenian which the author claimed to have 44 vowels, I made a concerted effort to find speakers who could produce these vowels. Each speaker of the dialect that I met, however, turned out to speak a subdialect with significantly fewer vowels; it took several years and numerous informants to find a single person who spoke the relevant subdialect. (I later found out that the former president of Armenia speaks the same subdialect, but it has been somewhat difficult to arrange a meeting with him.)

It is also important to consider the amount of schooling that the potential informant has had. Informants with a great deal of education can be useful in the sense that they may have a better idea of why it is important to carry out field research. Individuals with less exposure to academia, conversely, sometimes find intellectual enterprises such as linguistic fieldwork to be self-indulgent, obscure, pointless, and devoid of "product" (words drawn from the mouth of my grandfather upon hearing that I was becoming a linguist).

However, I have found that schooling is normally counterproductive when dealing with informants. Schools generally teach students a broad range of fallacies about language in general and their language in particular, such as the idea that certain literary forms that no one actually says in real speech are "correct", and the forms that people actually use are "wrong". This sort of misinformation can have a significant effect on people's linguistic performance, particularly in situations where they feel their linguistic competence is being tested, such as a data gathering session with a linguist. I have often found it very difficult to elicit certain forms (that I knew existed) from my informants, because they insisted that certain other forms were "correct", though they never actually used them in spontaneous discourse.

Another product of education that can be problematic in informants is knowledge of orthography. Surprisingly often, as we will see in more detail in chapters 2 and 7, speakers try to alter their pronunciation to match what they know to be the spelling of a given word, particularly in careful speech registers. Even when they do not alter their pronunciation, informants are generally reluctant to acknowledge that their pronunciation differs from the sequence of letters in the official orthography. Consequently, it is generally preferable (at least for phoneticians, phonologists, and morphologists) to pick informants who have not learned to spell or who speak a language that has no writing system.

One final tip about selecting an informant: some informants are better than others. Informants, after all, are not just grammars; they are regular people with likes and dislikes, quirks, and eccentricities (though probably not as many as the average linguist). Consequently, they are unlikely to be content sitting in a room churning out mundane vocabulary items and what to them are obvious grammaticality judgements. It is important, therefore, to select an informant who is patient, friendly, and likely to be interested in or at least tolerant of linguistics. Whether or not the informant is interested in linguistics is partly in the hands of the fieldworker, of course; it is his or her responsibility to make the data gathering sessions interesting to the native speaker. But more on this subject later.

2.2. Selection for a class

The factors to be considered when selecting an informant for a class are by and large the same as those discussed above. However, some of the caveats we issued in the previous section are less important in a classroom situation, since the individual student is more sheltered from the informant on a personal level. By the same token, though, fieldwork in a classroom situation is generally less rewarding, because one has less time to develop a relationship with the informant and one must subordinate one's own lines of research to the interests of the class as a whole.

When selecting an informant for a Field Methods class, we recommend finding a speaker of a language that has not been studied and/or is endangered. Such a language is more likely to engage the interest of the class, and will also make it possible for the teacher and students to make novel contributions to the field by compiling the data collected in class.   The drawback of picking an unstudied language is that it will raise the hackles of the large number of students who demand that background reading materials be made available for the course.   A typical example of this problem arose recently when I taught a Field Methods course on a completely unstudied language spoken in Azerbaijan.   One of the students insisted at the end of the course that he could have done a much better job on his final project if I had provided reading materials for him to study.   This of course misses the point that conducting fieldwork is not like writing a research paper; one wants to discover new   facts   and   generalizations,   not   reanalyze   old   ones. Unfortunately, students with this particular philosophy often appear in required Field Methods classes, so the teacher should consider selecting a language on which a modicum of literature has been written.

The teacher furthermore can choose between what I call *Blind* and *Easy* fieldwork. Blind fieldwork involves working with an informant who does not share a common language with any member of the class; Easy fieldwork involves the less challenging task of dealing with an informant who understands a language spoken by the members of the class. While Blind fieldwork is certainly more intellectually challenging, and presents a whole range of hurdles that do not arise in Easy fieldwork, I do not recommend it for an introductory-level Field Methods course. For this reason, we do not cover the techniques peculiar to Blind fieldwork in this textbook; interested readers may consult Loving 1962, Anderson and Cox 1970, Cowan 1970, Healey 1970, and Suharno 1976. (The famous field linguist Kenneth Pike was famous for teaching a Blind fieldwork course; there are four videos of this course available at the University of Michigan. See http://www.sil.org/klp/klp-mono.htm for further details.)

Finally, when preparing a Field Methods class, the teacher should try to find a language that is exotic (at least to the students), but not *too* exotic. The first time I taught a Field Methods course, I exuberantly brought in a speaker of Abkhaz, a Caucasian language known for its wild inventory of 60 consonants and 2 vowels, expecting the students to share my excitement with this new linguistic challenge. The good news was that they shared my excitement, but the bad news was that they were completely unable to distinguish most of the phonemes reliably, even by the end of the semester. The lesson to garner from this is that it is probably better to choose a language that has no more than a few sounds that will be unfamiliar to beginners. Conversely, if one selects a language with no unusual sounds, the students in the course who are of a phonetic or phonological bent may become alienated. Try, then, to pick a language with a goodly sprinkling of unusual features in each linguistic domain—phonetics, phonology, morphology, syntax, and so on.

3. Working with an informant

Once the fieldworker selects an informant, a whole new set of conditions must be satisfied if the two are to interact pleasantly and efficiently. Some of these conditions involve personal interactions, and some are purely linguistic; we consider each in turn.

3.1. Interacting with the informant on a personal level

The main guidelines for getting along well with an informant are fairly simple:

- Become friends.
- Watch out for personal space!
- Don't underestimate the importance of food and drink.

We'll return to these points in more detail in the discussion that follows.

First, though, we would like to discuss some more delicate matters. It is very important to be sensitive to issues of ethnicity when working with informants. Members of majority cultures often do not realize, for example, that ethnic and linguistic identity can be a source of embarrassment or even danger for many minority groups. This can have a range of psychological effects even when members of these groups have relocated to a country where they are not persecuted. When individuals have grown up in a society where they are ridiculed, beaten, or jailed merely for belonging to a certain group or speaking a certain language, they can become extremely sensitive to even the mention of their ethnic or linguistic identity.

I once came upon a checkout worker in a computer store who was clearly from Africa. Being interested to find out what language(s) she spoke, I asked her what her native language was. "French," she replied. Since her accent indicated that French was not actually her native language, I asked what other languages she spoke. "None." At this point the interview was in danger of ending, so I tried another tack, asking where she was from. "Ivory Coast".. Since no further information was forthcoming, I fell back on one of the most important lessons of fieldwork, namely that sometimes one can only get the right information by asking the right question. "Do you speak Bambara?" I asked, guessing one of the larger languages of the area. "Yes! How did you know??" she replied, suddenly becoming interested.

Several lessons can be drawn from this story. It is risky to press individuals too closely about their language and ethnicity, unless one knows the right questions to ask and how to ask them. This should only be done when one is sure that it will not make the informant feel uncomfortable or annoyed. Furthermore, as we shall see in more detail later, one cannot always take what the informant says at face value.

On another occasion, I ran into a worker at a convenience store who appeared to be from Ethiopia. Having recently taught a Field Methods course on Tigrinya, a Semitic language of Ethiopia, I decided to ask him what language he spoke. He indicated that he spoke Amharic, the official language of the country. Knowing from experience that ethnic identity in Ethiopia is a highly charged political issue, and that many Ethiopians therefore say that they are Amharic when they actually belong to a minority tribe, I tried to think of a way to ascertain his true identity in an inoffensive way. In the end, I decided to try out some Amharic phrases I knew on him. This had the desired effect, as he became very friendly, gratified that someone was interested in his country, and subsequently revealed that he actually was a native speaker of the Cushitic language Oromo.

A similar situation arose with a friend of mine from the Homshetsi community mentioned earlier. This particular man identified himself upon moving from his village to Istanbul as either Turkish or Laz, another ethnic minority of northeastern Turkey. By doing so he avoided being identified as a member of the Homshetsik, who are related to the Armenians, one of the primary enemies of the Turks. I found that on the first few occasions that I met with him, my friend became very sensitive when the colleague I was working with at the time mentioned parallels between his language and Armenian, and when he pointed out how the Homshetsik were related to the Armenians. Ironically, my Homshetsi friend (who owns a rug store) later developed a working relationship with a repeat customer who identified himself as Jewish and refused to pay by check or credit card, insisting instead on paying in cash (thereby not having to reveal his name). This man then entered the store one day when I was having a session with my friend and his wife, and I immediately recognized him as a member of the local Armenian community! It turned out that he had tried to hide his Armenian identity from my Homshetsi friend because he had heard him speaking Turkish with his wife, and therefore assumed that he was Turkish and would not want to deal with an Armenian.

The fieldworker should also be aware of cultural differences, especially those involving issues such as gender, politeness, and personal space. The latter issue is one that few people are aware of, yet causes more problems than almost anything else. As any visitor to a Mediterranean or Middle Eastern country can tell you, not all cultures have the same standards of personal space. Americans, for example, need to maintain a certain distance (at least two feet) between themselves and their interlocutors; any distance smaller than this can create surprising amounts of discomfort and emotional trauma. An Italian male, on the other hand, typically prefers a much smaller personal space and is more likely to make direct physical contact than an American is. All too many times I have seen this sort of discrepancy in standards of personal space and physical contact lead to major problems, normally involving American fieldworkers coming to believe that their informants are sexually harassing them. Since accusations of sexual harassment are very serious in many countries, fieldworkers should be extremely careful to avoid confusing disparity in standards of personal space with sexual harassment. My informants from Turkey and Armenia frequently grab my arm or leg, hug me, and do various other things which in their own countries are indications of friendship but in countries like the United States would be construed by women as sexual harassment.

Some colleagues have expressed to me the opinion that informants from other countries should be required to conform to the social mores of the country in which they are living at the time and should be punished if they do not.[2] Though I certainly agree that this is the safest course for visitors to take when visiting or moving to a foreign land, I feel that the situation is slightly different with fieldworkers. When one decides to conduct field research, one commits to interacting with informants on their own terms. Fieldwork is not about forcing informants to conform to our standards; it is about learning what one can about their language and culture. Fieldworkers therefore should be prepared to deal with a wide variety of potentially disquieting social and cultural discoveries, even if they are only trying to collect syntactic data.

One can make it easier to appreciate differences of this type by trying to develop an appreciation of the informant's culture. Fieldworkers can in fact kill two birds with one stone by asking informants about their religion, history, local geography, personal and place names, local customs, and so on. In doing so, you not only learn about the informants' culture, but also demonstrate to them that you are interested in them as more than objects of linguistic curiosity. This is very important in developing a friendship with the informant, which is one of the cornerstones of successful fieldwork.

---

[2] In 2002 this issue rose to international prominence when military pilot Martha McSally successfully sued U.S. defense secretary Donald Rumsfeld over the dress code. She contended that the policy on abayas, a form of head-to-toe gown in Saudi Arabia similar to the burqa worn by many women in Afghanistan, discriminates against women and violates their religious freedom by forcing them to adopt the clothing of another faith. In January of 2002 the Defense Department dropped its requirement that female military personnel in Saudi Arabia put on black, head-to-toe gowns when leaving their base, though as of this writing it still prohibits them from driving, sitting in the front seat of vehicles, and leaving base except in the company of men. Interestingly, the Saudi government has never requested that American females wear the abaya, at least not formally; even more intriguingly, *men* in the U.S. military are *forbidden* from wearing Saudi religious apparel.

Perhaps the most important element in befriending an informant, though, is food and drink. Food and drink provide the fastest way to a person's heart, and failing to take advantage of this fact can make one's road long and hard. Many times while in Armenia I wished for an iron stomach as I was plied with vodka, köfte loaf, and boiled lamb chunks, and had to say no. As someone who dislikes both meat and alcohol, I am all too aware that consumption of the two constitutes a central bond between guest and host in most countries of the world. Declining to partake in these communal feasts can drive a hefty wedge between the fieldworker and the informant. Scholars of delicate gastronomical inclination can sometimes avoid offending their hosts by announcing their dietary restrictions in advance, so that it does not appear later on that vegetarianism for example has been trotted out as an excuse for not eating something that is perceived as cheap or poorly prepared. Unfortunately, though, this strategy often does not work. The problem is that people assume the set of foods and drinks that they like corresponds exactly to the set of foods and drinks that are Good in absolute terms; therefore, *everyone* should like these items, if they just try them. In this philosophy, vegetarians are just picky; if they were to try boiled lamb chunks, they would like them.

Regrettably, most humans[3] subscribe to this philosophy, which social psychologists call the *Status Quo Bias*, a tendency to see our own views as objective and reasonable, while those of others are perceived as biased by their ideology (Keltner and Robinson 1997), and it is therefore difficult to avoid some awkward moments during the course of one's fieldwork. The best that the fieldworker can do in situations like this is to come prepared; it is useful to know if working with Ethiopians, for example, that in Ethiopia hosts are

---

[3] A particularly egregious example being the administration of George W. Bush (2000-2008).

allowed to force-feed guests who they feel have not eaten enough. You should also expect to have to broaden (or at least suspend) your tastes somewhat in these situations; it may not be possible to keep kosher in the field, for example.

One should also avoid condemning foreign cuisine too hastily. I once heard from a colleague that he had thrown out something fermented in the communal refrigerator in his dormitory, only to find out later that it was actually a Korean delicacy, whose owner was outraged that some gourmet thief had spirited away his special treat!

Another touchy topic is that of payment: should the fieldworker pay the informant, or not? The obvious answer would seem to be yes; however, this is not always correct. In many cultures, it is considered offensive to offer someone money for what they feel to be a favor for a friend. Furthermore, accepting payment can be interpreted as a sign of being poor or greedy, which many members of non-Western cultures would prefer to avoid. For these reasons, almost all of the informants I have worked with have refused payment. However, it is a good idea to try to pay your informants nonetheless, since they are sacrificing their time and energy to help you. I have found that one way to convince my informants to accept payment is to indicate that the money is being provided by my university. Since the university is an abstract entity rather than a concrete person, many informants are willing to accept payment when it is offered in this way. Another way of getting around the payment problem is to offer your informants appropriate gifts, such as dictionaries of their language. Treating them to lunch or dinner—or, even better, having them over to your place for a meal—can be helpful as well.

Finally, beware of publishing the results of your field research. Informants, like all people, are easily offended by what you say about them. There are three principal reasons for this:

- Informants invariably know more about themselves than you do, so they will easily identify any mistakes or oversights that you have committed when describing them and their language.

- People rarely like hearing themselves on tape, watching themselves on television, and so on. If you aren't careful, they can interpret what they perceive to be flaws in the presentation of themselves as the result of negligence or inaccuracy on your part. My grandfather, for example, was apparently resented by the Native American tribe about which he wrote a book, because (despite the fact that all of his research was rigorously documented) in their minds he had not represented them fairly, had revealed too many personal facts, and so on.

- As we mentioned earlier, people can be very sensitive about their own language and ethnicity. My Homshetsi informant, for example, became very worried and agitated when he saw the name of himself and his village in an article I was preparing. He was concerned (perhaps rightly) that the Turkish government would hear about the article and crack down on his village.

For these and many other reasons, it is wise to be as discreet as possible in preparing publications based on one's fieldwork. It is always a good idea to go over all such material with the informant(s) before putting it in print.

3.1.1. The Parrot Syndrome

One unfortunate problem that has been fueled by the advent of generative linguistics and the decline of field methods in linguistics and anthropology curricula is that all too many linguists now treat informants as grammars rather than people. This problem, which I call the "Parrot Syndrome", surfaces in a variety of subtle and not-so-subtle ways.

In case study number one, an anthropologist initiated a study of the sex lives of Parsi women in India. An observer, noting that her stream of personal questions was making the women uncomfortable, suggested that the anthropologist relate something about her own sex life to the group. "I can't—I'm an anthropologist!" she replied. Fieldworkers should try to avoid developing this notion that they are somehow superior to the informants, like a biologist studying flies through a microscope or a zoologist collecting butterflies.

Case study number two involves a linguist who worked with a speaker of an endangered language for two years. The work, in which the informant collaborated for free, was geared towards preparing a proposal for a government grant of several hundred thousand dollars to support the creation of a grammar of the informant's language. Upon successfully obtaining the grant, however, the linguist promptly ceased speaking with the informant, who thereafter had no input on the book and received no windfall from the grant. This sort of behavior is again all too common—scholars feel that their informants play no part in the creative process and can be picked up or discarded as needed. Having spoken with several individuals who were treated in this way by wayward linguists and anthropologists, I can attest that they did not share these scholars' assessment of the working relationship. (It was in fact the unfortunate informant just mentioned who inspired the phrase "Parrot Syndrome" after he complained to me that all of the linguists he had previously worked with—including the newly wealthy linguist—treated him like a parrot, expecting him to squawk out phrases on their command. It took several months' worth of meetings to convince him that not all linguists behaved that way.)

Our final case study involves a student behavior pattern that teachers must nip in the bud. Since the teacher generally runs the class, students in Field Methods courses tend to develop a certain dependency on him or her. Every year I have taught Field Methods, this has led to the students directing their questions towards me, rather than towards the informant. As one might imagine, this can be intensely annoying to the informant, who is made to feel unimportant, excluded, and inferior to the teacher. Students should therefore make an extra effort to look at the informant when asking questions and to tailor the content of their questions for the informant as well—questions like "what would she say for snail?" are to be avoided at all cost. Teachers may also want to consider minimizing their role in the elicitation process as much as possible.

The best way to avoid succumbing to the Parrot Syndrome is to treat your informants as friends, rather than objects of curiosity or sources of information. If you interact with informants in the same way that you would with any other friend, you are much more likely to establish a good working relationship conducive to collecting the information you want efficiently and painlessly. (For further discussion, see Nida 1981.) If, on the other hand, you simply pump your informants with obscure linguistic questions, anything could happen.

A good lesson for potential fieldworkers can be found in the story of Frau Holle, as told by the brothers Grimm. A woman had two daughters, an evil one whom she loved, and a good one whom she despised. She sent off the good daughter to earn some money to support the evil daughter. The good daughter wandered off, and ended up coming across Frau Holle, who offered to pay her for performing certain chores around the house. The chores were extremely difficult, but the good daughter performed them without complaint. At the end of her time Frau Holle sent the girl back to her family. On her way home the daughter passed under an archway, and when she did so gold showered down upon her. She brought the gold home to her mother and sister, who grabbed it and demanded to know where she had obtained so much money. Upon finding out, the mother sent her favorite daughter to work for Frau Holle. Work for Frau Holle she did, but in an insolent and sloppy manner. Before she had even finished her chores, she demanded gold from Frau Holle. She was told to return home, passing underneath the same arch as her sister had earlier. When the evil sister passed underneath the arch, however, she was showered not with gold, but with coal. The moral of the story is of course that the fieldworker should treat the informant like the good daughter treated Frau Holle; one gets no rewards if one fails to treat the informant with civility.

3.1.2. *When the informant is not (yet) interested*

As amply demonstrated by the recent rash of eliminations of linguistics departments in the United States, not everyone finds the study of language as fascinating and important as linguists do. Ideally, fieldworkers can dissuade a recalcitrant informant from such skepticism by means of their erudition. Few things impress and engage informants more than a linguist who can accurately reproduce their pronunciation; it is also effective to begin speaking whole sentences in the target language as soon as possible. If this is not possible, however, and in fact even if it is, it is important to take all possible steps to insure that the informant is not bored to tears by your linguistic attentions. Many a human will not be amused at being asked ten times to repeat the word for 'nit'.

I once met a man who mentioned that his wife spoke a dialect of Armenian that I and other Armenologists had assumed to be dead. Needless to say, I was very eager to meet and work with the man's wife. He was very supportive of this plan and soon introduced me to his wife. Upon hearing of my interest, though, she insisted with a somewhat distressed look that she spoke only

Standard Armenian. I was still inclined to believe her husband at this point, because it was highly unlikely that he would have fabricated the fact that his wife spoke an obscure dialect of Armenian. Suspecting that she denied speaking the dialect because she considered it provincial or uneducated, my challenge was then to find some way of convincing her to help me with the dialect without embarrassing her. I decided in this case to mention offhand some wacky idioms in the dialect and see how she reacted. Sure enough, her eyes lit up and she let loose a stream of comments on their meaning, not suspecting that speakers of Standard Armenian would not be able to make head or tail of these idioms, much less comment on subtleties of their usage.

When this linguistic strategy is not enough, I have sometimes found it useful to bring along a friend who is able to interact with the informants about their culture, history, and so on. Having along such a person, who clearly is not using the informant as a language parrot, can help convince the informant of the sincerity of the fieldworker's intentions.

Even after you have convinced the desired individual to act as your informant, it remains a constant challenge to maintain his or her interest. One technique that can be useful is to mention to informants the prospect of publishing the results of their joint efforts with the fieldworker. This is a double-edged sword, though, because it commits fieldworkers to actually publishing their results!

3.1.3. *When the informant is too interested*

Sometimes the informant is *too* interested in the fieldworker. Cases like this call for a different set of strategies. What does one do when the informant starts asking too many questions or being too affectionate?

3.1.3.1. Sexual interest

The most problematic scenario arises when the informant conceives a sexual interest in the fieldworker. Sadly, this happens more often than one might expect. Typical manifestations include asking the fieldworker if she[4] is married, squeezing more than just her arm, observing that she is pretty one time too many, making suggestive comments, and so on. Problems of this type are of course best avoided by choosing informants who are not interested in the sexual category to which the fieldworker belongs. This is easier said than done, though. A Field Methods class, for example, normally contains students of both male and female genders, one or more of which the informant may conceive an interest in. Furthermore, it is not always possible to ascertain discreetly the sexual preferences of a potential informant in advance.

Some readers may find it strange and disconcerting to discuss speculation on the sexual preferences of informants. This is certainly a valid concern, since individuals are free to be of whatever sexual inclination they choose. However, in the context of fieldwork such discussion is justified, since it is imperative to protect both fieldworkers and informants from the trauma of sexual harassment and accusations thereof.

If a sexual problem does arise, it is normally possible for the fieldworker to simply withdraw from the situation, either by steering clear of the informant (if in a classroom situation) or by leaving the village (if in a field situation). If these steps aren't possible, it can be very effective to bring a friend along to every session. If the oppressed fieldworker is a student in a classroom situation, he or she should make sure that the teacher is made aware of the problem; it is

---

[4] We use the paradigm of a male informant and a female fieldworker here, because all cases we have observed have been of this type. It goes without saying that sexual problems can involve any combination of canonical and/or non-canonical genders.

sometimes possible for the teacher to speak with the informant and make him aware that he is not allowed to make advances towards students.

3.1.3.2. *Nonsexual interest*

There is another inconvenient kind of interest that an informant can take in a fieldworker, and this does not involve sexual attraction. In many field situations, the fieldworker is at least as exotic to the informants as they are to the fieldworker; therefore it is quite possible that they will be more interested in asking the fieldworker questions than vice versa. This can be quite unnerving and disruptive to the data collection process. For example, a colleague studying the Yezidis of eastern Anatolia once encountered a Yezidi sheikh who cryptically answered every question with "yes", quickly followed by a pointed question about the scholar's own activities. Situations like this can be very difficult, because one does not want to have a one-sided relationship with the informant where only the fieldworker asks questions and receives information, yet at the same time one doesn't want the relationship to be lopsided in the other direction. If matters get to the point where the informant is clearly expressing too much interest, several maneuvers can be employed. The simplest is to ride out the questions, providing equitable but not overzealous or hostile responses. Oftentimes this strategy will bring the informant down to a more manageable level of interest. Another effective trick is to raise a topic that one already knows to be of interest to the informant. Most people enjoy talking about themselves; switching to a topic concerning the informant's activities is therefore likely to be successful.

3.2. *Interacting with the informant on a linguistic level*

Now that we have dispensed with the touchy personal issues, we can move on to some less controversial linguistic concerns. The basic problem is how to engage the informant's interest in a way that will elicit the maximum possible amount of reliable data in the minimum amount of time. There is no simple solution to this problem, though, because different informants respond to different techniques: some will work well with word lists, some will prefer conversation, and so on. It is a good idea to try several methods of interaction and elicitation with the informant to see which works best. Beware, though, that a given technique may not always work equally well. I have often found that an informant is in the mood for storytelling one day, but on another day prefers to work with a word list or translate a text, and so on. Varying strategies in this way not only accommodates fluctuations in the informant's mood, but also can help relieve the informant's potential boredom.

No matter which strategy you use, it is essential to know how to frame the questions you pose to the informant. Question asking is a complicated and subtle art, but there are a few general guidelines that should help.

- Don't ask leading questions. All too often I have heard students ask an informant "this means __, doesn't it?" Informants are already inclined to answer "yes" to any question you might ask, partly out of desire to give you the answer you want, and partly from desire to finish the question session as quickly as possible. Leading questions, particularly those which contain the answer within the question, only push informants further along the road to becoming linguistic yes men. This must be avoided at all costs, since the data gathered from yes men are obviously useless. However, it is sometimes necessary to employ leading questions, such as when the informant will not otherwise be able to think of the appropriate word, construction, etc. Resort to this strategy only when it is absoloutely necessary to get the information that you need. It can also be dangerous to give informants too much of an idea of what you are working on or what sort of findings you are looking for; information of this type can influence their responses. You also need to be careful not to go too far in the other direction by intentionally keeping the informant in the dark about the goals of your linguistic activities. (For further discussion of leading and how to avoid it in interviews, see Labov 1972b and Hohulin 1982.)

• Try to infuse your questions with interesting semantic content; this is an effective way of maintaining the informant's interest. Employing quirky vocabulary items, amusing scenarios, and local personal and place names collected from the informant is generally successful.

• Avoid using too much linguistic terminology with and in front of the informant. It can give the fieldworker a satisfying feeling of power and superiority to casually drop fancy terms like "quantifier raising", "hypercorrection", and other linguistic concepts the informant is not likely to be familiar with, but this in no way enhances the quality of the data collected and almost certainly cows or irks the informant. On top of these negative side effects, you never know what the informant may do with your highfalooting phrases. The first time that I taught a Field Methods course, for example, the informant decided that "schwa", which she heard me use frequently in my side discussions with the class, meant 'reduplication'.

• Don't overload the informant. If you present informants with too much data or too many tasks at once, they may be put off. The key, as with writing a thesis, is to break your tasks into tiny, manageable chunks. For example, don't announce to your informant one day that you are going to begin collecting all of the items in a 5000-word list. It is much more effective to break the list into thematically related smaller groups, like body parts, animals, and so on.

- Beware of priming and satiation effects. It is well known among syntacticians that informants can become highly unreliable in their judgements after they have been presented with too many examples of the same type of sentence. Typically they begin at this point to find all sentences of a given type acceptable, even if, when presented with one of the sentences out of the blue on a separate occasion, they might find it unacceptable. They may also lose their ability to make any judgements about a word, construction, etc. that they have heard too many tokens of. (See Snyder 2000 for further discussion.)

Finally, when working with informants we recommend that you attempt whenever possible to train them to carry out their own work on the language. This makes the informants feel like they are integral parts of the fieldwork process, helps them appreciate the work you are doing, and enables them to work on their language after you are gone. It is not always possible to train one's informants as linguists, of course, but fieldworkers should at least try to teach their informants the transcription scheme they are using. This allows the informants to follow what is being written on the board in class or in the notebook in field sessions, and to correct your transcriptions when necessary.

3.3. *What to believe*

If all has gone well so far, you will now be collecting data from your informants. Your data will not necessarily correspond to the set of correct facts about the language, however. One of the more important lessons in life is that you cannot believe everything a person says. This is not to say that informants intentionally lie about the data they provide; rather, various factors discussed below can lead them to unwittingly provide inaccurate or unreliable data. This became a serious problem during the late structuralist period, when fieldwork still played a central role in the practice of linguistics. As Sampson 1980:64 states, "when, rather later, the behaviorist method had entered linguistics via Bloomfield's writings, it manifested itself in slogans such as 'accept everything a native speaker says in his language and nothing he says about it'". This is too harsh, but it is certainly true that one should be extremely careful in interpreting what one's informants say about their language, and this includes their grammaticality judgements.

Noted philosopher of language Ludwig Wittgenstein was similarly skeptical of individuals' intuitions about the meanings of words in their language. In his book *Philosophical Investigations*, he repeatedly catches his interlocutors falling prey to their overconfident intuitions about what their words mean when they carry out thought or inner speech. On these occasions he states, "the decisive moment in the conjuring trick has been made, and it was the very one that we thought quite innocent" (p 87).

Along similar lines, Chomsky observes that "it is quite apparent that a speaker's reports and viewpoints about his behavior and his competence may be in error" (1965:8), and "the greatest defect of classical philosophy of mind...seems to me to be its unquestioned assumption that the properties and content of the mind are accessible to introspection" (1968:22).

Labov 1987 adds that "the opposition between the idealist and materialist position on data resources is a long-standing one in linguistics, long antedating generative grammar. Among the leaders of American linguistics in the first half of this century, Boas and Sapir favored the basic strategy of 'ask the informant.' Bloomfield, Harris and Voegelin (1951) distrusted the subjective bias of this procedure, and argued that the invention of the magnetic tape recorder should make it possible to base linguistic work on spontaneous speech production [...] The most obvious hiatus in the foundations of modern linguistics is the absence of a concern for the reliability and validity of the introspective judgments that form the main data base of grammatical research. Much linguistic research must be carried out by the direct elicitation of data, especially in the initial stages of investigation, and in the study of syntactic forms of low frequency. One approach to resolving the opposition between subjective and objective approaches is embodied in the following 'working principles for continued exploration of grammatical judgments' (Labov 1975:30):

I.   **The Consensus Principle:** If there is no reason to think otherwise, assume that the judgments of any native speaker are characteristic of all speakers of the language.

II. **The Experimenter Principle:** If there is any disagreement on introspective judgments, the judgments of those who are familiar with the theoretical issues may not be counted as evidence.

III. **The Clear Case Principle:** Disputed judgments should be shown to include at least one consistent pattern in the speech community or be abandoned.

As Newmeyer points out (1983:65) these principles assume that the object of investigation should be the speech community, rather than the individual, an issue which still divides the idealist and materialistic approach. In any case, there are no accepted experimental methods that would resolve disputed judgments. Linguists are building on sand until they can answer basic questions: what are the test-retest reliabilities of judgments of grammatical acceptability? Under what conditions do introspections match speech production? What are the sources of bias? Many hundreds of authors have published articles based on introspective data, but only a half dozen have been concerned with this issue. In Anthropology, on the other hand, we find a long-standing and serious concern with informant accuracy (Freeman, Romney and Freeman 1987)."

Most people believe—incorrectly—that language consists of a set of *consciously* memorized words and grammatical rules. By this reasoning, it should in theory be possible for informants to recall with perfect accuracy all of the words and rules that constitute their language.   However, individuals' knowledge of their language actually consists of a set of *unconsciously* learned lexical items, rules, principles, and assorted other linguistic structures. Since this knowledge is in the main acquired unconsciously, it is to be expected that speakers will not necessarily be able to verbalize it. However, certain steps can be taken by the fieldworker to facilitate this process for the informant.

Two factors that can lead the informant to provide inaccurate information are the leading and priming that we discussed earlier. If you lead informants to believe that you are looking for a particular answer, they may well provide it. Similarly, if you ask them for acceptability judgements for ten sentences of similar structure and then ask about an eleventh sentence that appears to be of the same type (but actually is not), they may well give the same judgement as for the previous sentences.

If they are feeling impatient, informants sometimes give the quickest answer, even if it is not correct. A student of mine once conducted a study of color foci with an informant who was fairly uninterested in the project, due to the student's gender. The informant played along at first, thinking for a while before he identified the focus of each color. After a while, though, he became bored and began to simply point to the middle exemplum of each color zone, without considering the others. All of the data he provided after this point were therefore unreliable. Fieldworkers must learn to recognize when informants have passed over the threshold of boredom; this is best accomplished by getting to know their behavior patterns and keeping an eagle eye on them at all times. Informants can be kept clear of the boredom threshold if the fieldworker follows the suggestions given earlier, such as employing entertaining example sentences, breaking up tasks into small portions, and so on.

Informants can also be led to error on the basis of what they learned about their language in school, which is usually linguistically inaccurate. If your informant is literate, then you must constantly be on the lookout for grammar book answers. These are normally betrayed by their prescriptive bent, such as "you can't say ___", "the noun always comes before the verb", "sentences can't end in a preposition", and so on.

Some informants come into the field process with wacky personal linguistic analyses of their own. One should generally avoid working with informants of this type, but this is not always possible. Sometimes one can demonstrate to these informants that they should think twice before forming linguistic generalizations. For example, I once had an informant who insisted that all words in his language stressed a particular vowel when it was present. Beginning fieldworkers must be very careful about generalizations of this type, which are all too easy to accept at face value. In this particular case, I knew independently that the informant's generalization was incorrect, and I was able to produce some forms that demonstrated this fact to him. This had the desired effect, as he was more careful about making linguistic generalizations from then on.

How can novice fieldworkers smoke out falsehoods like this, though? A good strategy is to note down all claims made by the informant, and then to test all of them against one's corpus of data.

If the relevant data have not already been collected, it is often possible to test the informant's hypothesis on the spot with a few well-chosen questions. The same informant was fond of detailing the linguistic origin of each word he provided: "this word is Persian" or "this is from Turkish", he would say. In cases like this, one can easily check the informant's claims in a dictionary or similar reference tool.

Another source of unreliability in informants' responses is register (cf. chapter 11). Informants typically provide answers in what we can loosely call "careful speech register". This is of course a natural consequence of the fieldwork context, unless spontaneous dialog is being collected. Careful speech register is just as interesting and linguistically valid as other more casual registers, and has the added advantage of mirroring more closely the speaker's linguistic competence, being less influenced by pragmatic and other performance factors. However, the fieldworker must be careful not to come to the conclusion that what the informant produces in careful speech is all that the language contains. When informants are accessing their careful speech register, they will typically ignore or deny the existence of fast speech phenomena and allophonic rules. English speakers, for example, are typically unaware of (and if asked would deny) the existence of low-level rules such as *s*-retroflexion (*street* → [ʂtɹiːt]; Shapiro 1995, Lawrence 2000) and obstruent aspiration (*pat* → [pʰæt]). Similarly, though a hefty percentage of Americans pronounce *else* as [ɛlts], very few of them admit that they do this, even when it is pointed out to them.

One should also be careful of informants leaping to conclusions. A Spanish speaker once produced the form *rendí* 'I subdued', prompting a friend of mine to inquire whether the infinitive of this verb was *render* or *rendir*. The informant replied that it had to be from *rendir* because of the *i*, forgetting for the moment that *i* in verbal forms can also come from -*er* verbs in

Spanish. In this case the friend knew from her Spanish education that the informant's reasoning was faulty, but fieldworkers will not always have access to this kind of independent knowledge. For this reason, it is very important to take everything that your informant says with a grain of salt and verify it whenever possible.

Despite the warnings we have issued so far in this section, the data you collect from an informant will by and large contain trustworthy linguistic intuitions. Don't shrug off these intuitions—they almost always contain at least a grain of truth and are often more correct than the intuitions of the fieldworker. When I was developing a spelling system for the Homshetsik, for example, I decided for orthographic convenience to render the palatal affricate [tʂ] as <ts>. The informant jumped on this decision, observing that it was a single sound, not a combination of [t] and [s]. In this he was quite right, though he had no linguistic training to tell him so, only his intuitions as a native speaker of the language. The same speaker (and, in fact, at least one other speaker who is from a different village and does not know the first speaker) systematically failed to distinguish between two other phonemes in his language (χ and ʁ), though, demonstrating that fieldworkers must always be on their toes, even with reliable informants.

One would think that in a language with no writing system, the speakers, free from the shackles of a rigid orthography, would render exactly the sounds of their language once provided with the necessary transcription symbols. This is not always the case, though: another speaker of Homshetsma whom I have worked with writes all voiced and voiceless stops as voiceless, even though the two are phonemically distinct in both Homshetsma and Turkish, the two languages she speaks. We can conclude from our discussion, then, that fieldworkers must draw on both their own intuitions and those of the informant. Combining these with the tips given so far should enable the fieldworker to obtain fairly reliable data.

3.4. How to get the most out of a data-gathering session

The fieldworker's next challenge is to run the data-gathering session efficiently, collecting as many data as possible within the time allotted without alienating the informant. The key to success in this arena is to prepare the informant properly. The techniques already discussed in this section will help towards this end; we add here a few additional tips and warnings.

Be aware that some days are better than others for the informant. One of my informants, for example, can't remember anything useful on some days, but on others he knows all of the words I ask him, and furthermore volunteers stories, sayings, recipes, and so on. For this reason, you should not despair when your first few meetings with informants do not go well. Give them some time to warm up and get in the right mood, and give yourself some time to try out the different techniques outlined earlier.

When informants finally get on a roll, I've found it useful to let them go off on whatever tangents strike their fancy; interesting things often pop up, such as stories that you can later ask them to narrate for transcription. If you are too quick to nip their tangents in the bud, informants are likely to become resentful and feel that you do not care about them except for their linguistic knowledge.

Some informants do have to be kept in check, though, if you want to be able to collect any linguistic data at all. It should be fairly clear when you are dealing with a person like the one I just mentioned, whose tangents are useful, and when you are dealing with a person who will ramble on about politics, his version of history, and so on for as long as you give him the bully pulpit.

4. Collecting and organizing the data

The next step in the process of collecting data during a field session is deciding how one should put the data in a permanent and manageable format. This process should normally consist of two components: recording the session in real time on audio and/or videotape, and transcribing the linguistically relevant portions of the session in a field notebook.

4.1. Recording

I cannot emphasize strongly enough the importance of *recording all of your field sessions* if humanly possible. There are all sorts of obstacles to doing this: it can be difficult to lug recording equipment to every session, and one can easily forget to bring it on any given day; procuring tapes and recording equipment can be very expensive; one feels at the time that nothing worth recording is coming out of a given session. Experience dictates, though, that at a later date you will wish for recordings of your sessions—your informant may die or move away, you may suddenly need to check some of the data that you transcribed in your notebook, you may want to make acoustic studies of their pronunciation, and so on. Making recordings of each session gives the fieldworker the additional advantage of being able to review and analyze the session later at a more leisurely pace, without having to worry about entertaining the informant. Field sessions are generally very hectic, and one often misses some of the things that the informant says. All too often I have paid the penalty for not recording a session, when my informant proceeded to reel off a string of interesting stories which I was unable to transcribe on the spot. Somehow it always seems that informants save their best material for the times you do not bring your recorder along! Remember also that your informants may be offended or distracted if you scribble away furiously, your nose buried in your notebook, as they try to interact with you. Recording your sessions leaves you free to maintain eye contact with your informants (if that is valued in their culture), nod, respond, and ask questions at appropriate times, and generally behave as if you were having a normal conversation rather than studying a lab animal.

If possible, you should use an unobtrusive DAT (digital audio tape), minidisk, CD, or direct-to-computer recording system, together with a good microphone, in a soundproof room. It is important to make the equipment as unobtrusive as possible, because informants often tense up when they see that they're being recorded. Every step you take to make them less aware that they are being recorded will make it more likely that they will be able to produce good data. As for the microphone, remember that you get what you pay for, or less. It is advisable to get the best microphone that falls within your budgetary constraints. Of course, it is not always possible to follow all of the suggestions made here, but try to follow as many of them as you can. (For further information on the type of recording setup to use, see chapter 6 and Ladefoged 1997.)

Remember that it is also possible to make fairly good recordings over the telephone if necessary; most of the frequencies necessary for basic speech analysis can be conveyed over phone lines. If you are affiliated with a university, it is a good idea to check with the campus radio station, which is likely to have high quality equipment for recording phone conversations. My favorite long-distance recording technique is Skype (skype.com), which allows one to carry on high-fidelity conversations for free with anyone in the world who has a computer, the free Skype program, and an internet connection.

Once you have made your recordings, be sure to label all of your tapes immediately, and cross-reference these labels with the entries in your field notebooks. Beware of the unlabelled photograph syndrome: it is easy to fall into the trap of thinking that you remember all of the relevant information about the session, but even a few weeks later you may find it impossible to remember the exact day on which you met, what each tape contains, and even the name of the informant you met with. Furthermore, each day that you put off labelling your tapes makes it less likely that you will ever do it, and before you know it you will be dead, and the person in charge of your *Nachlass* will have no idea of the significance of the unlabelled tapes in your office and throw them out.

4.2. Transcription

When transcribing the data you obtain in a field session, several points should be borne in mind. It is important to get into the habit of using notebooks designated specifically for the purpose of transcribing your field notes. Don't write on old pieces of paper or any other medium used for other purposes, such as a notebook from another class, empty pages of a grammar of the language you are working on, etc. Arbitrary materials of this kind are far too easily misfiled, lost, or forgotten. Make sure that the paper in the notebooks you use will last, and that the ink you write with is legible and won't smear or fade. Don't use pencil, because it is too tempting to erase things that you have written. One often needs to correct earlier transcriptions, but it is better to cross them out with a single line, so that they can be read later but it is clear that they are no longer correct. The reason to leave all of your transcriptions in legible form is that you may later realize that something you wrote earlier is in fact correct, or at least useful in some way.

Make sure that you label all of your notebooks, and clearly indicate where each session begins and ends. Try to avoid going back to earlier sessions to add or modify entries, as this can make unclear what was collected when. If you must make modifications of this sort, be sure to mark them in some way, and indicate the significance of this marking in the margin, including information such as when the modifications were made and (if different) when they were collected. Always include in your notebook the time, date, and location for each session, and indicate who was present at the meeting. The latter bit of information not only serves as an index of who is speaking at any given point during a session (both on tapes and in your field notes), but can also be useful later in identifying external factors that may have exerted an influence on the responses of the informants. If, for example, you find out at a later date that a different register is used with males than with females, it may be useful to know whether only males were present at an earlier session, in order to classify the data from that session according to register.

Write down as much as possible of what the informants say during the session. This includes not only hard linguistic data such as vocabulary items and sentences, but also any metacomments the informant might make, such as "I've heard that form, but I would never use it myself". One never knows when seemingly less significant information like this may turn out to be of vital importance, so it is a good idea to note down everything that you can. When this is not possible, you should augment your notes later with material garnered from the recordings of the session.

The way in which you write down your notes is also very important. Don't take the significance of seemingly obvious symbols for granted; for example, a question mark "?" can have a wide variety of interpretations, such as:

- Informant doesn't understand the question.
- Informant doesn't know the meaning of the word he was asked.
- Informant doesn't know any word in his language for the word he was asked.
- Informant can't remember the word in his language but knows it.
- The fieldworker skipped this word for some reason.
- The writing (if copying from another set of notes) or recording was unclear.

These distinctions may seem obvious now, but in the heat of a session it is easy use an ambiguous symbol like "?" without realizing how difficult it will be to reconstruct its significance later.

Finally, make sure to use a set of symbols that you have explicitly defined in your notebooks (we propose a sample set in the next chapter). If you do not do so, it will be difficult for you and other linguists to interpret your notes at a later date.

5. Introductory procedures

With these preliminaries in mind, we now turn to the question that occupies most of the remainder of this book, namely what to ask the informant. During your first meetings, it is a good idea to collect basic background information about each informant, such as:

- Gender.
- Date and place of birth (also indicate how old the informants are at the time of your session).
- All of the places they have lived in, and when and how long they lived in each.
- What languages they speak or have been exposed to, and which languages they are able to read and write.
- Their profession(s), both past and present.
- The social class to which they belong, both in their own assessment (if they are willing to answer such a question) and in your assessment.

Some readers may wonder why we have included in this list seemingly nonlinguistic factors such as social class. We have done so because sociolinguistic factors of this type have been shown to exercise significant influence on linguistic performance (cf. chapter 11), and therefore must be taken into consideration when evaluating data collected from a given informant.

You should try to collect the information in the list above for the informant's parents as well, either from the parents themselves, or from the informant if they are not available. It is important to do so, because the speech of the parents may have a significant impact on that of the children.

When you begin eliciting actual linguistic data, bear in mind the following points:

• Prepare for your sessions as much as possible. This includes preparing specific questions for the informant and learning as much as you can about the language in advance. You will often have to modify your questions or come up with new ones on the spot, but it is much better to come into a session with a good idea of what you are going to ask than it is to come in cold and have to make up everything on the spot. In the heat of the moment, it is all too easy to forget topics that you had wanted to cover.

• Elicit sentences rather than words as soon as possible. This is generally not feasible at first, since it is too difficult to keep track of what the informant is saying. Once you are sufficiently proficient to process them, however, sentences provide much more information per unit of time and also are more likely to maintain the informant's interest.

• Remember that it is almost as important to know what *can't* be said as it is to know what the *best* way of saying something is. When possible, try to elicit all of the possible ways of saying the desired word or phrase, together with an assessment of their relative acceptability.

• Try to double check your data blindly whenever possible. If you have collected a word for 'dog', for example, try eliciting that word again later in a different context (asking the informant to repeat a word right after you have elicited it does not quite count). Also, check your transcriptions with the informant if possible.

As we mentioned earlier, there are various techniques to choose from when eliciting data from an informant. Word lists, conversations between the informant and the interviewer or another native speaker, collection of grammaticality judgements, reading of a prepared text, and recitation or performance of songs, stories, jokes, and so on each have their own place in the set of useful elicitation strategies. Some of these will work for certain kinds of linguists, and others will not; few people other than linguists would be interested in collecting grammaticality judgements of sentences for example (and conversely, theoretical syntacticians are generally uninterested in any of the strategies other than grammaticality judgements). Each strategy is designed to collect certain sorts of information, and you should choose the ones you employ according to your needs. Stories and other forms of connected speech, for example, are much more likely to contain phenomena associated with more casual speech registers. A good illustration comes from the Homshetsma language mentioned earlier, where the verb *gasa* 'he says' is inserted in narratives with astonishing frequency; in isolated sentences it is not used in this way.

Some of the strategies will work with some informants, and others will not. For example, many of my informants are not interested in singing, but with one of my other informants I collect only songs. She enjoys singing, and the only material she knows in the dialect I am interested in is contained in songs she learned from her mother as a child, so this is what we work on when we meet.

In addition to the strategies suggested here, you will probably want to come up with some of your own that are tailored to the particular circumstances of your field situation. It is important to maintain a certain degree of spontaneity and adaptability in your approach. However, don't make this an excuse for not preparing!

The suggestions and warnings presented in chapters 1-4 are designed to serve as general guides for fieldwork conducted in all areas of linguistics. In the remaining chapters of this book, we turn to the details of data collection in each of the main subfields.

Suggested Readings

Barnwell, Katharine. 1998. Preparing to be a consultee: How to get the best help from your consultant. Notes on Translation 12.4:42-45.

Hale, Ken. 2001. Ulwa (southern Sumu): The beginnings of a language research Project. In Paul Newman and Martha Ratliff, eds., Linguistic Fieldwork. Cambridge: Cambridge University Press.

Itkonen, Esa. 1981. The Concept of Linguistic Intuition. In Florian Coulmas, ed., A Festschrift for the Native Speaker, 127-140. The Hague: Mouton.

Labov, William. 1975. Empirical Foundations of Linguistic Theory. In Robert Austerlitz, ed., The Scope of American Linguistics, 77-134. Lisse: Peter de Ridder Press.

Miller, James. 1973. A Note on So-called 'Discovery Procedures'. Foundations of Language 10:123-139.

Nida, Eugene. 1946. Morphology: The Descriptive Analysis of Words, second edition. Ann Arbor: University of Michigan Press.

Nida, Eugene. 1947. Field Techniques in Descriptive Linguistics. International Journal of American Linguistics 13.3:138-46.

Nida, Eugene. 1981. Informants or colleagues? In Florian Coulmas, ed., A Festschrift for the Native Speaker, 169-174. The Hague: Mouton Publishers.

Ringen, Jon. 1981. Quine on Introspection in Linguistics. In Florian Coulmas, ed., A Festschrift for the Native Speaker, 141-151. The Hague: Mouton.

Samarin, William J. 1967. Field Linguistics: A Guide to Linguistic Field Work. New York: Holt, Rinehart, and Winston.

Schütze, Carson. 1996. The Empirical Base of Linguistics: Grammaticality Judgments and Linguistic Methodology. Chicago: University of Chicago Press.

Sutter, Judith and Cynthia Johnson. 1990. School-Age Children's Metalinguistic Awareness of Grammaticality in Verb Form. Journal of Speech and Hearing Research 33.1:84-95.

Ulvestad, Bjarne. 1981. On the Precariousness of Linguistic Introspection. In Florian Coulmas, ed., A Festschrift for the Native Speaker, 245-261. The Hague: Mouton.

Exercises

1. You need to find a speaker of Akan for your field research.

• Outline how you might go about ascertaining if there are any informants in your area (or if there are none, think about how to contact Akan speakers elsewhere, and discuss how you might conduct field research with them), how to meet with them, and what questions to ask them at your first meeting.

• How do you get around the problem of calling them out of the blue?

• How do you research their culture and language beforehand?

• Where is the best place to meet?

• How do you bring up the issue of payment?

2. You desperately need certain data from Karaim for an important paper you are writing, but there are only two Karaim speakers in your area, and you don't get along with either one of them. What do you do?

3. Ask your informant to produce a sentence. Have the entire class transcribe the utterance. Compare and discuss everyone's renditions of the sentence vis-à-vis the correct version.

4. The only available speaker of the language you are interested in is female, and you are male. Unfortunately, it is not acceptable in her culture for women to speak with foreign males. How might you get around this problem without seriously violating her cultural mores?

2 Transcribing what you hear

De la Condamine says of a small nation living on the Amazon River: "Some of their words could not be written, not even most imperfectly. One would need at least nine or ten syllables where in their pronunciation they appear to utter hardly three."

Johann Herder
On the Origin of Language

1. Introduction

For most beginning linguists, transcription probably causes more headaches than any other task. This is primarily due to the well-known fact that it is not possible to identify word boundaries in an unknown language, and it is often impossible even to identify individual sounds. As many ancient writing systems reflected in their orthography, connected speech generally does not contain many word boundaries; the only thing that enables speakers of a language to identify word boundaries is their knowledge of the words of the language. Unfortunately, beginning field linguists generally do not know the words of the language they are studying, and therefore face an uphill struggle when trying to break down a stream of connected speech into individual words. We believe that it is a good idea for the professor in a Field Methods course to have the students try to carry out this task, just so they get an idea of how speech processing actually works (and doesn't work). Once this demonstration is completed, though, the students (and, even more so, linguists conducting fieldwork on their own) are still faced with the challenge of identifying word boundaries that do not even exist in the speech signal.

There are several ways to make this task easier. For at least the first few sessions, collect words in isolation (for specific words to collect, see chapter 3; remember that what is one word in English

47

may correspond to more than one word in your informant's language, and vice versa). This puts off the problem of identifying word boundaries until you have a better grip on the vocabulary of the language. While you are building up a basic vocabulary in this way, look for any items that characteristically occur at word boundaries, such as specific word endings, particular intonation patterns, and word stress. Stress placement is especially instructive, because most languages place primary word stress on either the initial or the final syllable of every word, or on the second or second-to-last syllable. If your language employs one of these four stress types, it will be relatively easy to identify word boundaries. For example, in a language that stresses the penultimate syllable of every word, you know when you hear a stressed vowel that the end of the word is the following syllable. By the same token, you know that the beginning of the next word immediately follows. Other helpful tricks for getting a handle on word boundaries include asking the informant for help, and preparing for the session in advance by learning as many words and endings as possible.

Segmenting the speech stream into individual sounds is perhaps even harder than segmenting it into words. This is because speech is quantal; in other words, many bits of information are transferred simultaneously. The average human can process up to twenty individual sound blips per second; blips recurring at any frequency greater than this are heard as single sound. Speech sounds, on the other hand, can be processed at rates as high as 40-50 per second (Pinker 1994). If speech sounds were no more than random sound blips, this would not be possible. Linguists have deduced from this fact that humans must transmit and process sounds in chunks, enabling them to pack several speech sounds into each blip of sound that the ear can distinguish. The relevant aspect of this phenomenon for our purposes is that when humans speak, they do not produce a discrete string of speech sounds—for example, *heat* is not produced as a blip of sound corresponding to [h], followed by a blip of sound corresponding to [i], followed by a blip of sound corresponding to [t]. Rather, the information encoding the sequence [h i t] is crammed into a single burst of sound. If you cut this burst of sound into smaller slices, each slice will typically contain information about at least two of these sounds.

What this means for beginning fieldworkers is that it is quite hard to break a stream of speech into individual sounds, unless these sounds are sufficiently similar to ones in their own language, which their ears are already trained to segment into sequences of phonemes. Beginners are often surprised to find that even sound sequences in their own language are difficult to parse when produced out of context. Vowels are notoriously difficult in this regard, but in poor acoustic situations the consonants can be difficult to distinguish as well. For example, it is extremely difficult to tell the difference between English [s], [f], and [ʃ] over the telephone, because phone lines do not transmit the frequencies necessary to differentiate these three sounds. The effects that neighboring consonants have on one another can also add to this confusion. In English, for example, *r*, *l*, and *n* have particularly noticeable effects on preceding vowels. As a result, even native speakers of English can have trouble discerning whether the vowel in *sing* is [i] or [ɪ], whether the vowel in *thanks* is [æ] or [ɛ], and so on. Problems like this are of course compounded when one does not speak the language being studied. It can also be difficult to distinguish acoustically similar sounds, such as flapped [ɾ] vs. trilled [r] vs. [l]. Beware, too, of phonetic distinctions that are extremely subtle. Like individual sounds, different features can also be very similar acoustically: the Karabagh dialect of Armenian, for example, has a problematic feature that some people hear as consonant rounding (e.g. [vʷɛnːə] 'foot'), some hear as velarization [vˠɛnːə], and some hear as a central vocalic onglide [vᵊɛnːə]. Hopefully the phonetic distinctions in the language you choose to work on will not stymie you the way the Karabagh phenomenon (and a very similar one in Ponapean) has done to linguists (including myself), but you should be prepared nonetheless to listen very carefully for difficult distinctions of this type.

Further complicating matters is our tendency to perceive sounds that aren't there. When presented with a recording in which a medial phoneme of a word has been manually replaced by a cough, listeners report hearing the complete word followed or preceded by a cough (Warren 1970). Similarly, most humans hear the word "slit" as "split" if a silence of more than about 35 milliseconds is inserted between the s and the l (Bastian, Eimas, and Liberman 1961). Even without the assistance of digital trickery, a native speaker can be confused by the phonology of his own language. One of my students desribed an incident in which her Arabic teacher denied the existence of emphasis spreading, a well-documented phonological process in Arabic. Even when presented with evidence of the phenomenon in his own speech, the teacher had difficulty perceiving it.

The best way for fieldworkers to overcome these challenges is to prepare as much as they can in advance, concentrating in particular on learning the inventory of surface sounds in the language to be studied. Try to prepare a set of words containing each of the sounds in the language, and collect these from the informant. Typically informants will not know or use all of the words in your list, but if this problem arises you can ask them to come up with other words that contain the relevant sounds. Once you have a recording of all of the sounds, listen to them on your own as many times as possible until you feel that you can identify each sound in the language consistently. It is also a good idea to check your transcriptions with the informant in order to verify that you are hearing the sounds correctly.

One warning: be careful not to fall into the trap of only eliciting words that you already know how to transcribe. Students tend to do this in order to avoid revealing their lack of transcription abilities in front of their peers. If you do this, though, you will never learn to transcribe properly. You *can* learn to transcribe without props in a relatively short period of time, if you are willing to endure a bit of hardship and embarrassment for the first few sessions. Remember—no pain, no gain!

2. The transcription system

As you are learning how to identify words and sounds, you must also come up with a way of transcribing what you hear. We mentioned in chapter 1 that it is important to use a consistent transcription scheme, with all potentially unclear signs defined in at least one of your notebooks. Remember that you may know what all of your quirky symbols represent, but others who inherit your notebooks may not, and you yourself may forget!

The transcriptions from which linguists normally choose fall into four categories.

1.   The International Phonetic Alphabet (IPA).
2.   The official orthographic system already used for the language.
3.   An orthographic system based on the dominant language in the area.
4.   A standard system already employed by scholars who work on the language.

We strongly recommend using the IPA, because most linguists are familiar with it, and your work will therefore be able to reach the largest possible audience.[5] Using the IPA does have a number of drawbacks, though, which you should bear in mind when deciding

---

[5] Interested readers can consult the official web site of the IPA at http://www.arts.gla.ac.uk/IPA/ipa.html.

which transcription system to use. The set of symbols constituting the IPA (see the appendix) will almost certainly require some modifications to deal with the language you are studying, since it is incomplete in many ways and is not tailored for your language. In addition, it will be largely incomprehensible to your informants, since most of the symbols it employs are not used in standard spelling systems of the world's languages.

In some situations it may be most convenient to choose option (2), the official orthographic system employed for the language you are studying. This option is very favorable for informants, since they will immediately recognize all of your transcriptions if they are literate. Unfortunately, this option is also extremely bad for linguistic purposes, since official orthographies generally neglect to represent phonetic nuances of pronunciation, and can be inconsistent or misleading in their representation of morphophonemic and phonological alternations. Russian orthography, for example, fails to represent the fact that word-final voiced obstruents are pronounced as voiceless. Someone reading the spelling-based transcription <sad> for 'garden' could therefore mistakenly conclude that the word was pronounced [sad], and would miss the devoicing rule that produces the correct pronunciation, [sat]. It is especially unwise to use the official writing system for languages that employ syllabic and logographic systems, such as Japanese and Chinese, because these typically omit even more phonetic details. In sum, we only recommend option (2) for syntacticians, who as a rule are not concerned with phonetic details, and for languages with phonemic writing systems. (In the latter case, make sure that the orthography actually has a one-to-one correspondence between sounds and symbols; if it does not, try to modify the writing system slightly until this is achieved.)

The third option is to use an orthographic system based on the dominant language of the area. When working with

Homshetsma, for example, I found it useful to develop a transcription system based on Turkish orthography. This was the best option for several reasons: the phonemic inventories in the two languages are essentially identical; the Turkish system is pleasantly phonemic (i.e. it does not use arbitrary spellings like English does); the characters are easily rendered on a typewriter (most people in northeastern Turkey do not have computers); and the informants can easily read my transcriptions and use the system to write the language on their own, since all of them know how to write Turkish. When I take field notes on Homshetsma for myself, though, I use the IPA, since the Turkish orthography again misses certain phonetic nuances of Homshetsma pronunciation.

The fourth option is to use a standard system already employed by scholars who work on the language. For example, many linguists who work on Armenian use a transcription scheme called the Hübschmann-Meillet system, which differs both from official Armenian orthography (Armenian has its own script) and from the IPA. Most Armenologists who are not linguists employ the Library of Congress transcription system, which is more closely based on English orthography than on Armenian pronunciation. The fourth option, represented here by the Hübschmann-Meillet and Library of Congress systems, has the advantage of being familiar to other specialists who work on the language, but normally should be avoided, because it will inevitably be difficult and confusing for other linguists and for your informants.

To give you a better idea of the differences between these four strategies, we give here a transcription of the Homshetsma sentence 'the cow that the bear ate was very dangerous' in systems representing each of the four types:

(1)	IPA	ɑɹtʃonɑ gijɑdz govɛ ʃad zijonkʰaɹ ɛɹ
(2)	Armenian script	արջոնա կիաձ կովէ շատ qhoնքար էր
(3)	Turkish-based script	arçona giyadz gove şad ziyonkar er
(4)	Hübschmann-Meillet	arč'ona giyaj gove šad ziyonk'ar ēr
(5)	Library of Congress	archona giyadz gove shad ziyonkar er

Linguists often like to substitute symbols that are easier to write for symbols that are more accurate. Perhaps the most common example of this is the use of [ɣ] (voiced velar fricative) for [ʁ] (voiced uvular fricative). Try to avoid doing this, because people who read your transcriptions can easily be deceived into thinking that you are actually transcribing a velar fricative. If you must use substitute symbols, make sure that you indicate in your notes what these symbol actually represent. Do the same for any customized symbols of your own creation; remember that the explanations you provide will be vital for anyone who uses your notes in the future.

When entering field data in a notebook, it is very tempting to use different colors of ink or pencil, as this effectively distinguishes between different types of entries. Though this scheme is esthetically pleasing, we discourage using different colors. One reason for this is that it takes time to switch between pens, and when your informant is spewing out a continuous stream of interesting data you do not want to be wasting your time looking for a different writing implement. The main reason for not using different colors, though, is that the color distinctions will be lost if you photocopy your notes, and the reader will be unable to access the information encoded by your different colors. The need to photocopy notes actually comes up more often than you might think, primarily because you do not want to loan out your original field notebooks to colleagues who are interested in seeing them, lest they be lost. Thus, it is best to prepare for this eventuality by taking notes in one color only, preferably a dark black ink that shows up well on photocopies and does not smudge.

The question then becomes how to convey all of the distinctions that are so easy to make with different colors. We suggest that you try delineating marked information with boxes, underscores, and the like. It is also possible to contrast a thin pen with a noticeably thicker pen, though we do not recommend switching between these two during a session, since it can make you miss valuable pearls of wisdom from the informant. When adding notes at a later date, however, this technique is acceptable.

The last major notation problem involves conveying different types of prosodic boundaries, such as those that divide morphemes, clitics, words, phrases, and sentences. If you do not plan out in advance what symbols you are going to use for each of these boundary types, you are likely to confuse some of them in your notes in the heat of the moment. We suggest the following symbols:

symbol	boundary type
-	clitic
/	morpheme
∪	word (when you originally transcribed as two words what is actually a single word)
I	word boundary missed initially and added later
, or | or ||	phrase
.	sentence

You will also want to indicate whether a given boundary is your postulation, or was pointed out by the informant. It is very important to make this distinction, because for example you may at a later date have trouble remembering whether a given morpheme boundary was your idea or the informant's. Since informants do not normally mention linguistic boundaries of any sort, and when they do they interrupt the elicitation process to do so, we suggest that their suggestions be indicated with a special note nearby, as follows:

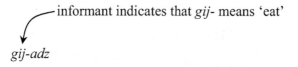

informant indicates that *gij-* means 'eat'

gij-adz

Our final notational challenge is sandhi, a process wherein the beginning of one word or morpheme alters the end of the previous word or morpheme, or vice versa. Sandhi rules can make it very difficult to indicate prosodic boundaries clearly. In the Armenian dialect of New Julfa, for example, the future tense prefix *k-* merges with a verb-initial *h-*, yielding the voiced aspirate g^h, as in /k-havadam/ 'I will believe' → [g^havadɑm]. How is one to represent the morpheme boundary between the *k* and the *h* here? It simply is not possible, unless one presents the underlying sequence of morphemes before it undergoes the merger rule. We suggest that you leave fused forms of this type unparsed, and simply make notations in the margin if necessary.

3. How to transcribe

3.1. Broad and narrow transcription

Even after you have come up with a reasonable set of symbols to use in your transcriptions, there are still many challenges to be faced when transcribing. The most complicated of these involves what are generally referred to as *broad transcription* and *narrow transcription*. Loosely speaking, broad transcription is relatively phonemic; in other words, it represents only the aspects of sounds that are needed to predict the actual pronunciation of words, and to distinguish these sounds from other sounds in the language. Features that do not play a role in distinguishing meaning, such as intonation, are not represented. Narrow transcription, on the other hand, represents more of the phonetic nuances of pronunciation, including some that are not essential in distinguishing meaning. The domain of broad and narrow transcription is obviously a continuum: there can be relatively broad transcriptions, extremely broad transcriptions, relatively narrow transcriptions, and so on, as exemplified in the following representations of my pronunciation of the sentence 'do you want to go to the store?'.

very broad	du ju wɑnt tu go tu ði stor
broad	də ju wɑnə go tə ðə stor
narrow	djə wɑɾə gowɾədə stɔɹ

very narrow	djəwɑ̃ɾəgəəɾədəstɔːɹ

The level of detail that you choose to include in your transcriptions will of course depend on the type of work you are interested in. Syntacticians, for example, will probably prefer fairly broad transcription, since subtle phonetic nuances are rarely relevant syntactically. (This is not always true, however—intonation contours and contraction of the *want to* → *wanna* type are syntactically relevant, for example.) Broad transcription can also be preferable when your informant is producing vital data and you are not recording the session, and therefore have to transcribe everything on the spot. Some other advantages of using broad transcription are that it is easier to avoid making transcription mistakes on phonetic subtleties, and it is much easier to check your transcriptions with informants, since the transcriptions will be more intelligible to them if devoid of complicated metanotation.

    Nevertheless, as a general rule it is better to use a maximally narrow transcription, including as many nuances as you are able, so that you and other linguists who might use your notes will have the most possible information at your fingertips. If you have the wherewithal, you should try to include in your transcriptions not only segmental information such as nasalization, aspiration, length, and so on, but also suprasegmental features such as stress, pitch and intonation, and creaky and breathy voice. Each of these plays a significant linguistic role in languages like English, for example, and you may be surprised at what you find out if you pay attention to features of this type.

When you are transcribing, be very careful to avoid phonemicizing; in other words, avoid the temptation to write down what you know the word "should" be. For example, if someone says [pʰɹɑbli] for 'probably', don't transcribe it as [pʰɹɑbəbli], the form of the word in careful speech. On the other hand, don't go too far the other way and wildly write down whatever comes into your head. If you think that you may have heard something incorrectly, double check it with the informant or your original recording of the session. You should also be careful about transcribing underlying forms instead of surface forms (an example of this would be writing <poteto> for 'potato' when someone actually says [pʰətʰeɪɾəw]). It is surprisingly tempting to do this, and you must make a conscious effort to avoid it.

3.2. Transcription tips

No matter how broad or narrow your transcription is, you should beware of the power of the symbol choices you make. Unfortunately, there is not a one-to-one mapping between sounds and symbols; rather, a given sound can be transcribed in many different ways depending on its linguistic function. For example, a sound that includes labial approximation, rounding, velar approximation, nasality, and voicing could be represented in at least four different ways depending on the context: if the sound is functioning as a vowel, it could be [ũ]; if it is functioning as an approximant, it could be [β̃ᵞʷ] or [w̃]; if it is functioning as a consonant, it could be [m^{YW}]. Normally the symbol you choose as the basis for your transcription (e.g. *m* in [m^{YW}]) will be one of the phonemes of the language, and the extra notations will be phonetic details that you have noticed in the pronunciation of this phoneme. If there is no preexisting phoneme list for the language, though, you will have to make your own judgement calls on how to represent each sound.

You can make your task much easier by learning in advance the set of phonemes and allophones in your informants' language. If you can, collect words illustrating each allophone, and try to elicit minimal pairs for each in order to get an idea of how each phoneme can be pronounced. If it is not possible to prepare a list on your own because you cannot find a dictionary or grammar of the language, try asking the informant to come up with a set of words illustrating each sound in the language.

When you are trying to figure out the sounds that your informant is producing, there are a few general tricks you can use to make your life easier. All of these rely on the fact that human languages show certain tendencies, and the language you are working on is very likely to manifest many or most of these. If you can familiarize yourself with these tendencies, then you can give yourself a head start in figuring out what your informant might be saying. Here are some common cross-linguistic tendencies:

- Voiced consonants (especially obstruents) are often devoiced at the end of a word, especially when not followed by a vowel-initial word.
- Clusters of obstruents tend to assimilate in voicing.
- The final member of a consonant cluster is generally released; non-final members are often unreleased (consider the pronunciation of English *apt*, for example, where the *p* is unreleased and the *t* is released).

- Languages with aspirated consonants often do not aspirate these consonants after *s* (contrast English *tar* [tʰɑɹ] and *star* [stɑɹ], for example).
- Nasal consonants tend to take on the place of articulation of a following stop consonant.
- Nasals also cause following stops to become voiced in many languages.

Keeping these tendencies in mind may well prove useful, but be careful not to force your expectations on the data, because a given tendency may not appear in the language you're studying.

4. Transcription traps

We conclude this chapter with a discussion of some common transcription traps into which both tyros and seasoned linguists often fall. The most common trap involves forcing the phonetic categories of your own language onto the language that you are trying to transcribe. English-speaking linguists, for example, often commit the following blunders:

- [β] (a bilabial fricative) is misheard as [v] (a labiodental fricative).
- [ç] (a palatal fricative, the German *ich-laut*) is misheard as [ʃ] (a postalveolar fricative).
- [c] (a palatal stop) is misheard as [k] (a velar stop), [kʲ] (a palatalized velar stop), or [tʃ] (an alveopalatal affricate).
- [t̪] (a dental stop) is misheard as [t̺] (an apical alveolar stop).
- Unaspirated voiceless consonants are misheard as voiced, and aspirated consonants are heard as unaspirated.
- [r̥] (a voiceless r) is misheard as [ʒ] (a voiced palato-alveolar fricative) or [ʃ] (a voiceless palato-alveolar fricative).

The same language transfer phenomenon that causes all of the above mistakes is also responsible for most features of foreign accents; part of the accent of French speakers trying to speak English, for example, results from the fact that they do not aspirate their voiceless stops, which is correct for French but incorrect for English.

Even when your language has the same sounds as the target language, it can still be very difficult to transcribe accurately what you are hearing. For example, Japanese /r/ is pronounced in a manner extremely close to the English flap [ɾ], but Japanese speakers typically both hear and produce our flap as a [d] or a [t] rather than their *r*. This is in part due to their knowledge of English spelling, of course, but there are many other examples where spelling cannot be the culprit. Korean, for example, has both an *l* and an *r*, but Korean speakers nonetheless have great difficulty distinguishing English *l* and *r*. In this case, the problem appears to stem from the fact that *l* and *r* are positional allophones in Korean, whereas they are separate phonemes in English. The liquids *l* and *r* can cause problems even when they are separate phonemes in both the informant's language and the fieldworker's language: I often mishear Armenian *l* as *r*, and vice versa, even though I have both sounds in my native language, English. The problem in this case presumably results from the fact that the Armenian liquids are pronounced very differently from the English liquids.

Many linguists also have difficulty distinguishing tense-lax vowel pairs, such as e vs. ε and i vs. ɪ. Speakers of languages that do not make these distinctions typically hear both e and ε as [e], both i and ɪ as [i], and so on, or else they hear e as [eː] and ε as [e], etc. Similarly, English speakers have difficulty distinguishing these pairs because we reinforce the contrast in our own language with length distinctions. The English vowel pair e : ε, for example, as in the words *sate* vs. *set*, is actually realized by most speakers as the long diphthong [eɪ] vs. the short lax vowel [ε]. For this reason, speakers of English typically have a devil of a time distinguishing short [e] from [ɛ] in other languages.

Another tricky phonetic contrast to beware of involves tones. Some languages have phonemic tone contrast, and others have distinctive prosodic tonal contours. Both of these types of tonal contrasts are very difficult to discriminate consistently for speakers of non-tonal languages such as English. For example, in one of his first meetings with a speaker of Igbo, a colleague transcribed three separate words as homophones. Upon checking these words with the informant, though, he discovered that they were not actually homophones, but rather were distinguished by three different tonal contours. The informant, by the way, was stunned that the linguist had not noticed this "obvious" difference between the three words. The best way to cope with tones is to practice; if you cannot practice with your informants or with recordings of their language, try at least to acquire recordings of another tone language, and familiarize yourself with their tonal contrasts.

One final transcription trap that you should be on the lookout for involves the distinction between consonantal and vocalic features, which we alluded to at the beginning of this chapter. Given that adjacent consonants and vowels typically exert an influence on each other, it can be very difficult to tease them apart and decide which acoustic features belong to which sounds. In the Karabagh dialects of Armenian, for example, it is extremely difficult to tell the difference between a sequence of a plain consonant followed by a front vowel (e.g. kö), and a sequence of a palatalized consonant followed by a back vowel (e.g. kʲo). Both are pronounced as something like [kʲö], but my informants insist (and I agree) that the two are slightly different. There are no hard and fast rules for resolving confusions of this sort, but it can help to ask the informant's opinion, and to examine recordings of the relevant sound sequences with sound analysis software on a computer (for more details, see chapter 6).

The tips and warnings we have dispensed in this chapter should greatly alleviate your initial suffering, if all goes well. Remember, though, that it is impossible to foresee every challenge that will arise, and even when you know what the challenges are, it is not always possible to produce a perfect solution in advance. It is therefore important for you to enter into each session with an open mind, and a willingness to adapt to the whims and vagaries of the moment.

Suggested Readings

Voegelin, Charles. 1960. Guide for Transcribing Unwritten Languages in Field Work. Manuscript, Harvard University.

Kelly, John and John Local. 1989. Doing phonology: observing, recording, interpreting. Manchester: Manchester University Press.

Exercises

1. Record a brief passage from your informant. Transcribe it broadly and narrowly, indicating as much detail as possible in the latter. Discuss any differences that appear between your two transcriptions.

2. Convert the following excerpt from an article on Robert Mitchum and David Caruso in *Spy* magazine from the IPA[6] into conventional English orthography.

ɹabɹtʼ mɪtʃm̩, ðə haliwʊd lɛdʒn̩d, ðə ɡɹeɪɾəst æktɹ ʌv hɪz dʒɛnəɹeɪʃn̩, ɪz dɛd. now lɒŋɡɹ wɪθ ʌs. deɪvəd kʰəɹɨwsow, ðə fɔɹmɹ ɛn waj pʰiː bliw staɹ, hɨwz haliːwʊd kʰəɹiːɹ tʰʊk ɒf lajk ə ɹakət dəɹɛktlij ɪntʰɨw ðə sajd ʌv ə mawnʔtʼʔn̩, ɪz miɹliː "owvɹ." kʰamən sɛns wʊd səɡdʒɛst ðætʼ ðə flɛɪmheɹd deɪvəd kʰəɹɨwsow, wʌɾɛvɹ bæɡədʒ hiː maytʼ biː kʰeɹɪjɪŋ fɹʌm hɪz kʰəɹiɹz kʰəlæps ænd hɪz owvɹ pʰʌbləsajzd dəsent ɪntʰɨw ælkəhalɪzəm, wʊd hæv æn iːzijɹ tʰajm ɡeɪnɪŋ vij aj pʰij æksɛs tʰɨw ə baɹ ɔɹ ɹɛstəɹantʼ ðæn ðə leɪtʼ ɹabɹtʼ mɪtʃəm. ɔɹ wʊd ɪtʼ ? æz pʰaɹɾ ʌv aɹ ɒnɡowɪŋ ɪnvɛstɪɡeɪʃən ɪntʰɨw ðə pʰɹəsajs kʰampəzɪʃən ʌv səlɛbɹəriː "hatʼnəs" ɔɹ "bʌz", wiː ɹæŋ əɹawndʼ mænhæʔtʼʔn̩ tʰə siː wɪtʃ wʌn—ðə dɛd wʌn ɔɹ ðə "fɪnəst" wʌn— ɪz kʰɹɹəntʼliː hɛftɪŋ də mowst "pʰəl".

ɹawnd wʌn: pʰɹəmiːɹ najtʼ spats "dʒɛtʼ lawndʒ" ændʼ "dʒɛtʼ lawndʒ iːst"

---

[6] The transcription, which is somewhat narrow, is based on the American dialect spoken by Vaux and contains some Midwestern and some Southern elements.

ɹabˌɪtˀ mɪtʃəm

AS: haj. ɹabˌɪtˀ mɪtʃəm wants tʰə biː pʰuɾ ɒn
                       jɹ lɪst fɹ tʰənajtˀ.

dʒetˀ lawndʒ iːst: jɹ sɔɹɾ əv læstˀ mɪnətˀ, bʌtˀ...haw mɛniː ?

AS: ɹabˌɪɾ ændˀ fɔɹ gɛsts.

dʒetˀ lawndʒ iːst: ʌm, owkʰeɪ, al pʰuɾ ɪtˀ dawn. mɪtʃəm
                       pʰlʌs fɔɹ.

dɛɪvəd kʰəɹɨwsow

AS: hɛlow, aj waɾ̃əd tʰə getˀ mɪstɹ
                       kʰəɹɨwsow ɒn ðə lɪst. ajm hɪz pʰˌɹsənəl
                       əsɪstəntˀ.

dʒetˀ lawndʒ: now, ðə lɪst ɪz fəl fɔɹ ðɪs iːvnɪŋ. ɪts
                       tʰɨw leɪtˀ.

AS: ðɪs ɪz dɛɪvəd kʰəɹɨwsow, ðə æktɹ, ðætˀ
                       wiɹ tʰɒkɪŋ əbawtˀ.

dʒetˀ lawndʒ: ajm saɹiː, ðə lɪst ɪz kʰlowzd.

AS: wʌɾ ɪf ɪts hɪm əlown ?

dʒetˀ lawndʒ: now. naɾ iːvən ðɛn.

ɹawnd tʰɨw: kʰansˌɹtˀ baj ðə aɹɹəst fɔɹmɹliː nown æz pʰɹɪns
ɹabˌɪtˀ mɪtʃəm

AS: haj, ðɪs ɪz ɹabˌɪtˀ mɪtʃəmz pʰˌɹsənəl
                       əsɪstəntˀ. mɪstɹ mɪtʃəm wud lʌv tʰə
                       gowrə ðə ʃow tʰənajtˀ.

baks ɒfəs: ðə pʰɹɪns ʃow? tʰənajtˀ ?

AS: jæː, hiːz ɹɪliː kʰwajɾ ə fæn.

baks ɒfəs: ʌm, owkʰeɪ. haw mɛniː tʰɪkəts dʌz hiː
                       wantˀ ?

AS: tʰɨw.

baks ɒfəs: ɹabˌɪtˀ mɪtʃəm. owkʰeɪ, ɡɹeɪtˀ !
                       al ɡeɾ əm sʌmθɪŋ ɡud !

dɛɪvəd kʰəɹɨwsow

ʌs: haj, ðɪs ɪz mɪstɻ dɛɪvəd kʰəɹɨwsowz
                  pʰɻsənəl əsɪstənt'. aj wəz howpɪŋ wi:
                  majt' bij ɛɪbl̩ ɾə skwi:z mɪstɻ kʰəɹɨwsow
                  ɪn tʰə ðə pʰɹɪns ʃow tʰənajt'.

baks ɒfəs: wɛl, jɻ kʰalɪŋ pʰɹɪɾi: lɛɪt', jə now. aj
                  mi:n, hi: kʰən dʒəst baj wʌn æt' ðə dɔɹ.

ʌs: jɨwʒəli: mɪstɻ kʰəɹɨwsow dʌznt' hæf tə
                  dɨw ðæt' sɔɹɾ əv θɪŋ.

baks ɒfəs: ɪt' lʊks lajk hi:z gowɪŋ tʰə hæf tʰɨw
                  tʰənajt'.

ʌs: aɹ jɨw ʃɻ ðɛɹz now wɛɪ wi: kʰən wɻk
                  ðɪs awt' ? ðɛɹ mʌst bi: sʌmθɪŋ jɨw kʰən
                  dɨw. ðɛɪvəd sow wants tʰə si: ðə ʃow.

baks ɒfəs: wɛl...aɹ ði:z tʰɪkəts gowɪŋ tʰə hɪm
                  pʰɻsənəli: ?

ʌs: ʌv kʰɔɹs.

baks ɒfəs: owkʰɛɪ, hold ɒn, al tʃɛk. [pʰɒz] now,
                  hi: kʰænt' gow.

ʌs: ðɛɹ mʌst bi: sʌmwʌn ɛls aj kʰən tʰɒk
                  tʰɨw. aj mi:n, ðɪs ɪz dɛɪvəd kʰəɹɨwsow.
                  ɛn waj pʰi: di: blɨw! dʒɛɪd! kʰɪs əv dɛθ!
                  kʰʌm ɒn.

baks ɒfəs: ɪf dɛɪvəd kʰəɹɨwsow wants tʰə gow ɾə
                  ðɪs ʃow, ðɛn hɪl bi: bajɪŋ ə tʰɪkəɾ æt' ðə
                  dɔɹ.

3. Transcribe the following text into the IPA, based on your pronunciation or that of a native speaker if you are not one. See appendix 2 for one solution.

What Is and Ain't Grammatical
by Dave Barry

I cannot overemphasize the importance of good grammar. What a crock. I could easily overemphasize the importance of good grammar. For example, I could say: "Bad grammar is the leading cause of slow, painful death in North America," or "Without good grammar, the United States would have lost World War II."

The truth is that grammar is not the most important thing in the world. The Super Bowl is the most important thing in the world. But grammar is still important. For example, suppose you are being interviewed for a job as an airline pilot, and your prospective employer asks you if you have any experience, and you answer: "Well, I ain't never actually flied no actual airplanes or nothing, but I got seven pilot-style hats and several friends who I like to talk about airplanes with."

If you answer this way, the prospective employer will immediately realize that you have ended your sentence with a preposition. (What you should have said, of course, is "several friends with who I like to talk about airplanes.") So you will not get the job, because airplane pilots have to use good grammar when they get on the intercom and explain to the passengers that, because of high winds, the plane is going to take off several hours late and land in Pierre, South Dakota, instead of Los Angeles.

3   Collecting Vocabulary

But sometimes these collectors were the innocent dupes of their informants and such errors were deliberately provided; Otto Duhmberg's 1870 wordlist of Siberian Romani for example has the entry kari *['penis'] glossed as 'grandson',* chamrimintsch *(i.e.* xa miri mindz *['eat my cooter']) as 'granddaughter' and* bremintsch *(i.e.* bari mindz *['big cooter']) for 'donkey'.*

Ian Hancock
The Concocters: Creating Fake Romani Culture

As we have already mentioned, it is a good idea to begin your fieldwork on a language by collecting individual vocabulary items. By doing so, you should be able to familiarize yourself with the sounds used in the language, become comfortable in transcribing these sounds, learn a bit of the morphology, and begin developing a basic feel for the language. Even if you are a syntactician who is only interested in grammaticality judgements, it is still a good idea to focus on vocabulary collection at the outset, because otherwise you probably will have tremendous difficulty figuring out what your informant is saying.

1. Approaches to vocabulary collection

There are two main ways to go about collecting vocabulary items. If you are in a Field Methods course or you are interested in core grammatical structures such as phonology, morphology, and syntax, it is best to start by eliciting words in isolation from a standard list of basic lexical items, such as the so-called Swadesh list (provided at the end of this chapter) or the Samarin list discussed in section 5. If the informant does not speak your language very well, you can also use a frequency-based word list from another language with which the informant is more familiar. Most commonly studied languages have dictionaries of this sort which arrange the words in order of frequency of usage; we have given a sample list of this type as list 2 at the end of the chapter. It is also a good idea to begin collecting personal and place names immediately; you can then make good use of these names in the sentences you ask your informants, as well as in your non-linguistic conversations with them.

If you are conducting fieldwork on your own, it is sometimes preferable to begin with a more customized word list. Fieldworkers interested in dialectology, folklore, lexicography, and so on may find it more efficient and useful to use a dialect survey-type questionnaire, as these are designed to elicit regional, archaic, and in general more folksy and traditional vocabulary, in contrast to the more run-of-the-mill, modernizing slant of frequency-based lists. The word lists used in dialect surveys typically include words for farm implements, natural phenomena, household items, and culture-specific concepts. We have found lists of this type to be very successful in eliciting both interest and useful vocabulary from non-urban informants. They can be particularly helpful for dialectologists in fighting informants' tendency to say that they "don't speak a dialect", since these word lists typically contain lexical items that immediately draw out dialectal and non-standard forms. Bear in mind, though, that word lists of this type normally do not fare well with younger informants who have grown up in cities, and they may not work well with informants who come from a different area of the world or cultural milieu than the one for which the particular word list was designed.

Readers who are interested in word lists of the dialect-survey type should consult a few linguistic atlases and dictionaries, such as Gilliéron and Edmont 1902-10, Redard 1960, Guillaume 1963-66, Avanesov and Orlova 1964, Australian Institute of Aboriginal Studies 1967, Wolff 1969, Pederson et al. 1974, Muradjan et al. 1977, König 1978, Stokoe and Kuschel 1979, Heine and Mohlig 1980, Johnston 1980, Breen 1981, Cassidy 1985, Lastra de Suárez

1986, and Upton, Sanderson, and Widdowson 1987. It is usually possible to find at least one linguistic atlas that provides a word list for a language in the area you are interested in.

2. Elicitation versus reference tools

> *The idiom of nomads contains an abundant wealth of manifold expressions for sword and weapons, and for the different stages in the life of their cattle. In a more highly cultivated language these expressions become burthensome and superfluous. But in a peasant's mouth, the bearing, calving, falling, and killing of almost every animal has its own peculiar term, as the sportsman delights in calling the gait and members of game by different names.*
>
> Jacob Grimm
> *History of the German Language*

When eliciting forms from a word list, a problem commonly encountered is the informant saying "Why are you asking me these words? They're all in the dictionary!" This is again a reflection of the popular notion that language is nothing but a limited set of consciously learned words and sentences. According to this line of reasoning, a dictionary is precisely a list of these learned words, and therefore the informants will not know any lexical items that you, the field linguist, cannot find in a dictionary of their language.

This is exorbitantly far from the truth, as anyone who has ever tried to translate a text using just a dictionary can tell you. The simple fact is that dictionaries are *always* incomplete; it is in fact impossible for them to be otherwise. Even basic information about a language is often missing: for example, if you examine any English dictionary (including the OED) you will fail to find the word 'sunshower', which is known by a significant percentage of English speakers. Regular dictionaries generally do not include slang and other "alternative" vocabulary either; there of course are slang dictionaries for larger languages, but most languages are lucky to have even one dictionary. Furthermore, dictionaries give only citation forms, and almost always neglect to mention vital information such as the case(s) a given verb or preposition takes, how the word is pronounced (lexicographers are particularly fond of omitting stress), what irregular forms it has, and so on.

Perhaps the most important reason for eschewing dictionaries in favor of data gathered from informants is the fact that informants often disagree with the information provided in a dictionary. For example, just a brief examination of the *American Heritage Dictionary of English* reveals that:

- The comparative and superlative degrees of *often* are supposedly *oftener* and *oftenest* respectively, yet I find both of these forms to be unacceptable. (Apparently I'm not alone: googling *oftener* on September 30, 2006 yielded ca. 654,000 hits, whereas *more often* got ca. 45.5 million hits.)
- The extremely common pronunciation of *mayonnaise* as [mænɛɪz] (i.e. "man-A's") is not mentioned. (My 2003 Harvard survey[7] revealed that of ca. 50,000 Americans surveyed, 45% preferred "may-uh-naise", vs. 41% for "man-A's".)
- The most common American pronunciation of *template*, [tʰɛmplɛɪt], is not mentioned.
- The most common American pronunciation of *something*, [sʌmpθɪŋ], is not mentioned.
- The word *sonorant*, which the dictionary specifically states to be a linguistic term, is said to be pronounced [sənɔɹənt], but in fact all linguists that I am aware of pronounce this word as [sownəɹənt] or [sɑnəɹənt].

---

[7] For maps and percentages of the word *mayonnaise*, see cfprod01.imt.uwm.edu/Dept/FLL/linguistics/dialect/staticmaps/q_16.html.

- Though about fifty percent of Americans pronounce *groceries* as [gɹowʃ(ə)ɹiːz],[8] only the pronunciation [grosəriz] is listed.
- *Butter* is listed with the pronunciation [bʌtər], though almost all Americans say [bʌɾəɹ].
- *Girl* is said to be pronounced as [gərl], but in fact is pronounced as [gəɹəl] by many speakers.
- There is no mention of the fact that *younger* is pronounced [jʌŋgɹ], not *[jʌŋɹ] as one might infer from the dictionary entry for *young*.

Even when the entries are technically correct, they often omit crucial information. For example, *Negro* is glossed by the *American Heritage Dictionary* as 'a person of Negro descent', with no mention of the fact that this is not currently an acceptable term to use to refer to African-Americans in the United States. Fieldworkers obviously need access to this sort of sensitive cultural information if they are to avoid offending their informants and hosts.

Dictionaries also contain heaps of words that are outdated or would never be used. Taking the American Heritage Dictionary as a scapegoat again, few English speakers would know that *slut* can mean 'female dog', or that *girn* means 'complain in a whiny voice'. This problem can become more serious when the word listed for a basic item is not used by anyone, and the word that they do use is not mentioned. For example, most Armenians use some form of the (originally Persian) word dʒigeɾ for 'liver', but very few Armenian dictionaries include this word, preferring to have an entry for ljaɾd, which is only used by highly-educated speakers.

It is important for fieldworkers to be aware of these shortcomings in dictionaries, because they are likely to surface at

---

[8] For maps and percentages for the word *groceries*, see: cfprod01.imt.uwm.edu/Dept/FLL/linguistics/dialect/staticmaps/q_36.html.

some point during their research. Once, for example, I was studying the pronunciation of Armenian words that end in a stop followed by a sonorant, so I collected from a reverse dictionary all of the words ending in sequences of this type. Imagine my surprise when I discovered that none of my informants knew more than four or five of the hundred or so words that I had collected! (This was not because they had small vocabularies; the words were simply not used in Modern Armenian.) You must prepare for shocks like this, because you want to avoid having to rely too much on dictionaries— they will almost always let you down.

One of my informants learned this the hard way. For our first few sessions, he insisted that it was fruitless for me to work with him because everything about his language (of which he is one of the last three surviving speakers) was recorded in a chapter of a book on his village. As our work progressed, he occasionally had to consult the chapter to refresh his memory about certain words. After several years of looking for and failing to find the words in question, and discovering moreover that he often knew words that the book either did not mention or listed with a different pronunciation, my informant finally had to admit that the book was woefully inadequate compared to his own knowledge of the language!

Bear these cautionary tales in mind when you begin collecting vocabulary from your informants. They should give you private satisfaction when your informants inevitably refer you to the dictionary, and they may save you some time that you would otherwise have to spend convincing the informants to help you.

3. Eliciting vocabulary effectively

Once you have convinced your informants to cooperate with you in collecting vocabulary, there are a few tips and tricks that you should keep in mind. It has been well known since William Labov's pioneering writings on working with inner-city informants in the

1960's that collecting data is not as simple as asking questions to informants and noting down their answers. Labov found, for example, that inner-city African-American children generally did not answer interviewers' questions, and when they did answer, the responses were one or two words at most, or "I don't know". Instead of attributing the children's minimalist responses to inferior intellect, as many previous researchers had done, Labov demonstrated that they actually resulted from the fact that the children were suspicious of the interviewers, and saw no reason to humor them. Labov showed that the African-American children were actually just as talkative as any other "normal" children, if they were simply put in the right environment.

What is of interest to us here is the way that Labov went about creating the right environment. Specifically, he and his colleagues would begin their sessions with the children by saying various taboo words and phrases, such as "my dad doesn't eat poo poo". By doing so, the fieldworkers broke down the social barriers between themselves and the children, while simultaneously piquing their interest. This technique proved very successful in getting the children to speak openly with the fieldworkers.

Taboo topics, then, can be a very powerful tool in the fieldworker's bag of tricks. However, this tool must be used with caution, especially with adult informants. The reason that field methods textbooks generally avoid taboo, despite its great efficacy, is that it can cause as much harm as benefit if not invoked properly. The basic problem is that even the mention of taboo items makes some informants uncomfortable. You should therefore be careful when asking questions that involve body parts, bodily functions and their byproducts, places in which bodily functions are carried out, sexual acts, religion, curses, insults, superstitions, and magic. The latter category is of course unlikely to faze urban informants, but it can be quite unsettling for people raised in traditional cultures.

Because taboo items can wreak so much havoc, one might conclude that it is best to steer clear of such subjects at all times. However, taboo vocabulary items are just as valid a part of the vocabulary as any other kind of word, and they are often more interesting, due both to their intrinsic meaning and to the fact that they are normally not discussed or even mentioned in grammars and dictionaries. Furthermore, informants who can stomach discussion of taboos are likely to be more entertained by this more than by elicitation of the numbers 61-69, for example.[9] Before you can begin eliciting taboo vocabulary, though, you must be sure that you have a sufficiently casual relationship with the informant; this typically requires at least a year of prior acquaintance. If the fieldworker and the informant are relatively young and of the same sex, it may be possible to broach the topic of taboo much earlier. If all goes well, you can even end up collecting juicy taboo vocabulary from people who in theory might seem unapproachable: for example, at a party a few years ago I was able to collect a fascinating set of Japanese verbs for vomiting from a female Japanese friend.

When collecting vocabulary you should also be on the lookout for dialect and register differences related to gender, class, age, and so on. For example, some languages such as Japanese and Thai use significantly different sets of vocabulary depending on the identity of the interlocutors: one set is used for a woman talking to an elder woman, another for a man talking to a younger woman, and so on. It may be hard to discover lexical strata of this type in advance,

---

[9] People tend to tire very quickly of reciting the numbers in their language; normally they stop at about twenty or thirty, and consider the remainder to be obvious. Since the higher numbers are not always self-explanatory, you should consider eliciting them subtly by including them in your carrier sentences. For example, if you are interested in collecting the word for *dog*, you might ask how to say "I bought seventy-eight dogs at the market last year".

but you should at least bear in mind that such differences often exist, and may influence the data you collect.

4. Elicitation traps

We pointed out in chapter 1 that you cannot take everything your informant says at face value. This fact plays an important role in the collection of vocabulary items, so you must be very careful about what you elicit and how you elicit it. Henderson and Harrington for instance offer a number of helpful warnings and suggestions concerning the collection of terms for fauna in their excellent 1914 treatment of the ethnozoology of the Tewa Indians; since this work is no longer readily available, we have excerpted relevant portions here.

Speaking of their methods for collecting vocabulary terms they provide the following guidelines:

"Most of the animal names were obtained by exhibiting specimens to several Indians, including some of the older men of the tribe. Where specimens in hand were not available, care was taken to make sure of the identity of the animals named; this was easy, of course, in case of such readily described animals as the porcupine. In a few cases it was considered safe to use good colored plates figuring easily identified species; but wherever possible specimens in hand were exhibited and also the same species alive in their natural habitat. Where there is a question as to identity the name is either omitted or the doubt is expressed. It is always best to show informants also specimens of all species in the region which closely resemble one another and discover whether they really definitely distinguish them, and, if so, how. Care should always be taken not to suggest to them the answer to inquiries." (Henderson and Harrington 1914:7)

Henderson and Harrington's work also contains a number of instructive warnings:

- **Don't automatically assume that your informants will have a distinct word for every distinction that seems semantically salient to you.** As Henderson and Harrington observe for Tewa, "Though several species of jackrabbits and several cottontails inhabit the region over which these Indians have roamed, they seem to recognize but one species of each." (p. 7) Conversely, don't assume that speakers will *not* make lexical distinctions that do not seem semantically salient to you.

- **Don't assume that speakers will make the same distinctions in each language they use.** Henderson and Harrington for example found their informants "using the English word 'rat' for several species of squirrels and chipmunks, yet in their own language they have usually distinct names for each." (p. 8)

- **Don't assume that speakers will categorize objects and entities in the same ways as you.** "Such cases as the bear, to which the Mohave in their own language apply a name meaning 'great badger', should be followed up to ascertain whether it indicates a supposed relationship. It may well be doubted whether the use by the Hopi of the same name for such distinct species as the Harris ground-squirrel and Say's ground-squirrel, and with slightly different pronunciation for two small chipmunks, indicates a failure to distinguish them. Our San Ildefonso informants, while applying the same name to such different species as Say's ground-squirrel and the little chipmunk, showed clearly by their comments that they did not consider them the same species." (p. 8)

Henderson and Harrington offer the following examples of classificatory differences between Tewa and English that can potentially cause problems for European fieldworkers:

1. Tewa has no word meaning 'animal' (though they sometimes borrow Spanish *animal*).
2. Tewa has no word for 'mammal'.
3. Bats are considered birds; one insect is also grouped in the bird category.
4. Tewa has no general word for reptiles or lizards or insects or crustaceans.

- **Be careful not to force your conceptions on your informants, and avoid fitting their responses into the Procrustean bed of your own conceptual world.** "In discussing such matters [as species], one's words, whether one speaks in his own language or attempts to apply a primitive language, represent definite mental concepts, but may convey to primitive people, who have not such concepts, ideas quite foreign to those intended. So also we are in constant danger of unconsciously injecting our own concepts into the words used by our informants in expressing their ideas. It is exceedingly difficult to question them about abstract ideas without framing the queries so as to suggest one's own views and thus color the replies." (p. 9)

- **Don't assume that the intuitions of your informant hold for the entire community.** "Indians differ as much individually as do other races in their capacity, experience, and opportunity for observation and in their interest in the mysteries of Nature. One person may have had abundant opportunity for the observation of the various species of deer, but paying slight attention to the little chipmunks and hence not distinguishing the different kinds of the latter, while with another person the reverse may be the case. Hence the information obtained from a single informant may not at all represent the knowledge or ideas of his people. This makes it advisable whenever possible to check the information obtained by enlisting the services of several informants." (p. 8)

• **Avoid mistaking descriptive or comparative terms for actual names.** "When an Indian informant is shown a foreign species with which he is not familiar, he may, as is the case with a representative of any other race, designate it by what appears to be a name but which on analysis proves to be a descriptive or comparative word or phrase and not a native name for the species, as when a small white marine shell is exhibited and a word is applied which means that it looks like a bone." (p. 9)

• **Beware of apparent synonymy.** Henderson and Harrington state that "there are not many instances where more than one name is applied to an animal species. The additional name is regularly descriptive. Thus owls may be called [in Tewa] mɑhuŋ or tsiso'jo. 'big eyes'." (p. 11) I would add that informants sometimes have no clear sense of the distinction between two particular forms, such as *bucket* vs. *pail* in English, and may randomly interchange the two while still feeling there is a difference between them that they are unable to express. Many speakers take this confusion one step further and create slightly different meanings for two terms that were originally synonymous; one can find many English speakers for example who differentiate *bucket* vs. *pail* in terms of one being metal and the other wood, one being larger than the other, one only being used at the beach, and so on.

To the points raised by Henderson and Harrington we would add the following warnings:

- **Beware of subtle semantic nuances.** Words are often distinguished from one another by only the subtlest shades of meaning; consider for example *dog* vs. *hound, cad* vs. *lout*, or *irritate* vs. *annoy*. Ambiguities resulting from these subtle differences can lead informants to misinterpret you, and vice versa. I once elicited a phrase for "sunshower" that literally meant "bird's rain" according to my informant. I happened to know that the cognate of the "bird" word in a related language meant "sparrow", so I asked the informant if what he had rendered as 'bird' actually meant a specific type of small bird. At this point the investigation broke down, because I could not be sure that the two of us were using the same set of distinctions between "bird", "small bird", and "sparrow". In cases like this, you can often clarify matters by using visual and lexical aids, as we suggested earlier.

  Informants who are not native speakers of your language also tend to use tenses, moods, and numbers incorrectly, since the precise domains of usage for these categories are normally very complex, and differ from language to language. Therefore, if an informant says that a particular verb form means "she ate", you should consider the possibility that it might actually mean "she was eating", "she had eaten", "she had been eating", "she used to eat", and so on. (In chapter 9 we describe difficulties of this sort encountered with our Gujarati informant.) One of our informants once produced the form hak^{h}il when asked the word for "get dressed". Since this is a perfectly plausible form for the word in his language, we noted it down without question. The next day, though, he produced hak^{h}nil for the same verb; we then realized that hak^{h}nil was in fact the infinitive form of the

verb, and hak^hil was the past participle. The informant had
initially said hak^hil because, as it turned out, at the time he could
only remember a specific idiom that included the verb, and this
idiom happened to use the past participle. Since the past
participle is sometimes identical to the infinitive in this language,
it did not occur to him that the form might be different.

Semantic nuances of this sort are often difficult to tease apart
with informants, but seeing how the forms are used in context
can be helpful.

- **Beware of polysemy**. If an informant tells you that a given
  word means 'squid', this does not entail that the word *only*
  means 'squid'; it might also mean 'octopus', for instance. An
  Armenian asked the word for 'meal' would probably provide
  tʃaʃ, but this word also happens to mean 'lunch', 'food', and
  'noon'. More amusingly, according to Pillai (1983:202), the
  Malayalam word kʌkṣʌ means not only 'girth rope of an
  elephant', but also 'waistband of a woman, a courtyard, a
  surrounding wall, inner room or harem of a palace, objection or
  reply in an argument, the orbit of a planet, a boil in the armpit,
  armpit, flank, river side, forest, dry grass, bull or buffalo, a
  hiding place, harem, scale of a balance, sin, a tortoise, a treasure
  of Kubera, a narrow undercloth covering the privities [sic], a
  dog, a harem supervisor, a poet, a painter, a debauchee'!

  You should also be aware that if your informant produces a
  word for a given meaning, this is not necessarily the only word
  that can have that meaning (contrary to what Henderson and
  Harrington stated above). Try whenever you can to ask your
  informant if there are any other words with the same meaning.

- **Beware of homophony and near homophony**. Armenian, for example, has two words np [voɾ] and nn [vor], the first of which is a relative pronoun, and the second of which means 'ass (anatomical)'. However, many Armenian speakers pronounce these two in an almost or totally indistinguishable manner. You would not want, due to an unfortunate mishearing of these two words, to offend your informant with an untimely reference to his posterior when you were simply trying to make a relative clause! Listen carefully to the pronunciation of each item you elicit, and make sure to check your transcription of each item that contains one or more tricky sounds.

- **Beware of misparsing**. People do not hear each other perfectly at all times; I can't begin to count the number of times that I've been told "fine" in response to the question "what are you doing?". Make sure, therefore, that your informants hear each of your questions correctly. Also make sure that they interpret each question correctly. Since informants typically are not native speakers of your language, they will often have mistaken ideas about the meanings of words in your language. For example, they may have learned incorrectly at some point that *skunk* is the word for 'hedgehog'. If you then ask them the word for 'skunk', they could give you their word for 'hedgehog', and you would be none the wiser. (As we discuss in later chapters, our Gujarati informant had a problem like this with the word *almost*, which he uses in the sense of 'all' or 'always'.) Problems of this sort can be avoided to a certain extent by using visual aids such as pictures of objects, animals, and so on, as described earlier by Henderson and Harrington, or by mentioning the forms that the words take in another language with which the informants are more familiar.

- **Beware of productive loans from other languages**.   Many languages have a superstrate language that they freely borrow from, because all speakers of the substrate language are bilingual. As a result, you need to take extra steps in such cases to insure that the lexical items you collect are actually the "native" words.   A colleague once asked a Spanish speaker residing in the United States how to say "raccoon"; she responded *el racun, la racuna*. In fact, these are borrowed from English *raccoon* (which itself is originally an American Indian word); the "native" Spanish word is *mapache* (which is also ultimately of Amerindian origin). When you speak the language from which the informant is borrowing words, these importations can be easy to spot. If you are not familiar with the superstrate language, though, you should keep an eye open for this phenomenon.

  The inverse also often happens: a bilingual informant says that a given form isn't actually part of their minority language, but rather is a borrowing from their majority language. Sometimes this is true, and a word from the majority language has slipped into the informant's production of the minority language on a one-shot basis, but many times the borrowed word has actually become part of the lexicon of the minority language. For instance, my wife's father, a native speaker of Farsi, often says that a given word he has produced isn't Farsi but Arabic, when in fact the Arabic word was borrowed into Farsi hundreds of years ago and is now their only word for that concept.

- **Beware of folk etymologies**. Informants often like to present their theories of how words came to be the way they are; you should take all such theories with a grain of salt. My Abkhaz informant, for example, once proclaimed that their word for "land dragon", a-gʷəlʃap, was formed from the words a-gʷə 'heart' and ɑ-ʃɑpˀə 'hand', because the hands of dragons are located close to their chests. In fact, the word is originally a loan from an Iranian form guʃab 'dragon'. When informants wax etymological, you should make sure to note down what they say, but if you are going to be making claims about the history of the language, be sure to check in reliable etymological publications first.

- **Make sure you know exactly what form you're eliciting**. Recall the famous story of the kangaroo, which according to some people is an aboriginal word meaning "I don't know", which is what a native guide uttered to an early British explorer inquiring as to the name of a passing kangaroo. (See Dixon and Ramson 1992 for discussion of the correct etymology of kangaroo and other aboriginal words in Australian English.) This, in brief, is the famous "gavagai" problem: if your informant points at a passing animal and says *gavagai*, he could mean "look!", "rabbit", "animal", "look! There's a rabbit over there!", "boy, that makes me hungry!", and so on (cf. Pinker 1994:153-157 for further discussion). You should be sure that you are clear on the exact meaning of what your informant tells you, lest you become the butt of a kangaroo anecdote five hundred years from now. Be especially careful with taboo items, since people will often use circumlocutions to avoid having to say the real words (consider all of the English expressions used for "lavatory"[10], for example).

- **Finally, make sure to double check everything you collect, if possible.** I learned the need for this the hard way, when I

---

[10] My favorite is *Gary*, a Cockney rhyming slang from derived from 70s singer Gary Glitter, which rhymes with the slang term for toilet, *shitter*.

unwittingly asked one of my informants the same ten words two sessions in a row. When I returned home and discovered my crime, I also discovered that most of the ten words had different forms on the two days! All sorts of factors conspire to produce anomalies like this, so it is imperative that you double and triple check all of the data that you elicit.

5. What to collect

We conclude this chapter by suggesting (following the exercises) some vocabulary to collect from your informants. As we have already mentioned, it is generally best to stick to basic items, but you should try to tailor these to the individuals you are working with— city dwellers obviously will not be familiar with most farm implements, and farmers will probably not know words for different types of bicycle locks. A colleague once took a Field Methods course with a speaker of Igbo, and was told to collect words from the word list in Samarin 1967. One of the words on the list was 'ice', which, he realized too late, probably didn't exist in Nigeria! As it turned out, the informant happened to know the word, because refrigerators had recently been introduced into his area of Nigeria. When this happened, they had to make up a word for ice, which they decided to call "hard water". (Note, while we are on the topic, that it may not be wise to ask informants what they call "hard water" and "soft water", since this distinction does not exist in reality or in the lexicon of most countries!)

Suggesed Readings

Beekman, John. 1968. Eliciting vocabulary, meaning, and collocations. Notes on Translation 29:1-11.

Healey, Alan. 1970. List of words suitable for monolingual eliciting. In Alan Healey, ed., Translator's field guide, 395-404. Ukarumpa: Summer Institute of Linguistics.

Johnston, Raymond. 1980. Grammar and basic vocabulary in Oceanic Austronesian languages: A standard elicitation schedule. Ukarumpa: Summer Institute of Linguistics.

Matteson, Esther. 1976. Developing the lexicon of an unwritten language. Notes on Translation 59:18-27.

Exercises

1. You have heard rumors that men and women use different vocabularies in the language you are working on. You have only one informant, who is male. How do you verify the rumors, and if they are true, how do you study the female vocabulary?

2. Discuss two ways to collect slang terms for sexual acts without offending your informant.

3. Draw up a list of 25 words that all residents of a large city would know, but rural folk would be unlikely to know.

4. Draw up a list of 25 words that all rural folk would know, but residents of a large city would be unlikely to know.

5. Identify ten words from one of the vocabulary lists provided that you suspect might be difficult to elicit successfully.
    *   State why you might have trouble eliciting these words.
    *   Discuss some ways in which you might overcome these difficulties.

6. Discuss how you might go about collecting the exact range of meanings for a given word, including idiomatic meanings, situations in which it can *not* be used, and so on.

7. Collect from your informants the expression in their language for the words in the Swadesh list that follows. Discuss any interesting challenges or insights that emerged during the collection process.

List 1: The Swadesh list

all	dull (knife)	guts
and	dust	hair
animal	ear	hand
ashes	earth (soil)	he
at	eat	head
back	egg	hear
bad	eye	heart
bark (tree)	fall (drop v)	heavy
because	far	here
belly	fat (substance)	hit (v)
big	father	hold (in hand)
bird	fear (v)	how
bite (v)	feather (large)	hunt (v game)
black	few	husband
blood	fight (v)	I
blow (wind)	fire	ice
bone	fish	if
burn (intr)	five	in
child (young)	float (v)	kill (v)
cloud	flow (v)	know (facts)
cold (weather)	flower	lake
come	fly (v)	laugh (v)
count (v)	fog	leaf
cut (with a knife)	foot	left (hand)
day (not night)	four	leg
die (v)	freeze (v)	lie (on side)
dig	fruit	live (v)
dirty	give	liver
dog	good	long
drink (v)	grass	louse
dry (substance)	green	man (male)

many	say (v)	swell (v)
meat (flesh)	scratch (itch)	swim (v)
mother	sea (ocean)	tail
mountain	see (v)	that
mouth	seed	there
name	sew (v)	they
narrow	sharp (knife)	thick
near	short	thin
neck	sing (v)	think (v)
new	sit (v)	this
night	skin (of person)	three
nose	sky	throw (v)
not	sleep (v)	tie (v)
old	small	tongue
one	smell (perceive	tooth (front)
other	odor)	tree
person	smoke	turn (veer)
play (v)	smooth	two
pull (v)	snake	vomit (v)
push (v)	snow	walk (v)
rain (v)	some	warm (weather)
red	spit (v)	wash (v)
right (correct)	split (v)	water
right (hand)	squeeze (v)	we
river	stab (or stick v)	wet
road	stand (v)	what?
root	star	when?
rope	stick (of wood)	where?
rotten (logs)	stone	white
rub	straight	who?
salt	suck (v)	wide
sand	sun	wife

wind (breeze)	woman	yellow
wing	woods	you (sg. and pl.)
wipe	worm	
with (a person)	year	

List 2: A frequency list (based on Armenian)

[informant's	appear, seem	bear (animal)
language]	appearance	beautiful
[informant's	approach, draw	because, since
nationality]	near	before
a	around	begin
a few	art	beginning
able	as much	behind
about	as, like	believe
according to	ask	beloved, dear
after	attention	between
again	baby	big, great
air	bad	bill, account
airplane	battle	birth pang
alive	be: 1. exist	black
all	2. be	blood
allow, let	3. copula	blue
almost	be able	book
alone	be born	border, limit
already	busy	boy
also	ready	branch
although	silent, quiet	bread
always	strong	breath
and	agree	bride
animal	surprise	bring
announce	be tired of	brother
answer	be used to	building

burn	cut	eat
but	dance	embrace
by means of	dark	end
call	daughter	enemy
carry, bear	day	enough
case	dear	enter
cause	death	entirely
century	deceive	equal
certain, definite	decide	et cetera,
chair	deep	and so on
change	demand	evening
chief(ly)	die	ever
child	difference	every
city	different	evil
class, lesson	difficult	example
clean	divide	except
climb	division	existence
close	do	explain
cloud	doctor	eye
cold	dog	face
collect	door	fact
color	dream	factory
come	drill, make a	fall (down)
condition	hole in	fall, autumn
contest, struggle	drink	familiar
continue	drive	family
corner	during	far (away)
correct	each	fate
cow	each other	father
create	early	father's brother
creation	earth	fear
culture	easy	feel

field	goal	homeland
fill	god	hope
finally	gold	horse
find	good	hot
finger	government	hour
finish	grab	house, home
fire	grass	how
firm, strong	green	how much
first	ground	I
flee	guest	idea
flesh	hair	if
floor (of a building)	half	illness
	hand	important
flower	hang	in
follow	happen	in front of, before
foot	happy	
for	hardly, scarcely	increase, grow
force, strength	have	influence
forehead	he	inner
foreign(er)	head	inside
forest	heart	instead of
forget	heaven	is not
forgive	heavy	it
form	height	keep
friend	help	king
future	here	kiss
game	here, behold, voila	know (facts)
general		know (people)
girl	hero	knowledge
give	high	lake
glass, cup	his, her	large
go	history, story	last (final)

late	meet	nothing
law	member, limb	notice
leader, ruler	method	now
learn	middle	number, figure
leave, depart	milk	numerous, many
less, few	mind	obvious
letter	month	of course
level, position	more	often
lie down	mortal	old
life	mother	on
light	mother's	one
like (v)	sister/brother	only
like, similar	mountain	open
likewise,	mouth	opinion
similarly	movement	or
lion	much	order (command)
listen, hear	name	other
literature	nation, race	otherwise
little (amount)	national	outer
live	nature	outside
long	near	pain
look (at)	need	palm (of hand)
love	never	paper (sheet of)
low, quiet	new	part
luck, success	nice	pass
machine, car	no	path
mistake	no one	peace
man	none	people
matter, problem	normal, usual	perhaps
mean	nose	person, spirit
meaning	not	picture, painting
meat	not only	piece

place	reveal	silent
play	ridicule	simultaneous
play music	right (correct)	sing
poem	rise	sister
poet	river	sit
point, peak	role	small
political	room	smile
popular	root	smoke
population	row (line)	snow
possible	run	so that,
present	sad	in order to
pretty	same	soldier
push	say	solve
put, place	school	sometimes
quantity	sea	son
question	season	song
quick, fast	see	source, fountain,
rain	self	spring
raise	sentence	speak
reach	serious	speech
read	sharp	speed, quickness
reality, fact	she	spill
receive	sheep	spirit
red	sheet	spouse
regarding,	ship	spread
toward	shoe	spring
relationship	shore	star
remember	show	state, condition
repeat	sick	stay, remain
rest	side	step
result, effect	sign, mark	still
return	silence	stone

straight	type, kind	wide
student	under(neath)	wife
subject, topic	understand	win, conquer
sun	until	wind
system	valley	window
take	value	wine
take place, occur	various	wing
teacher	verb	winter
tell, relate	very	with
than	village, town	without
that	villager, peasant	woman
that is, i.e.	vineyard	word
theater	voice	work (n and v)
then	wait (for), expect	world, land
therefore	walk	write
thin	wall	writer
thing	want	year
think	war	yes
this, that	wash	you
throw	water	young person
time	way, manner	
today	wear	
together	weather	
tongue, language	what	
too much	whatever	
toward	when	
train	where	
trait	which	
tree	whichever	
trip, journey	white	
try, attempt	whole, entire	
turn	why	

4   Collecting Texts

One evening in October 1961, Tevfik Esenç and myself were the guests of Zülküf Has, who had wanted to introduce me to his parents. His father narrated this story in Turkish, but the next day Zülküf refused to dictate it to me in Abkhaz, finding it indecent and suitable to waken the animosity of the Man tribe, who were numerous in the Abkhaz villages of the Hendek region, if they were to catch wind of it. Tevfik had no such scruples, and narrated the story to me in Ubykh a few days later. Zülküf then agreed to translate the Ubykh version into Abkhaz, under the aegis of Tevfik, so that he would not be held responsible as author.

Georges Dumézil, describing how he
collected the story of *Zakaria Dagwa*

We have paid only cursory attention to text collection thus far, and yet this is one of the most important parts of fieldwork. In this chapter, we discuss the benefits of collecting texts, and provide suggestions for successful text collection.

1. Introduction

Text collection is the process of recording—preferably electronically—connected speech from an informant, and then transcribing, translating, and analyzing the recorded material. The recorded passage might be a personal narrative, or a folk tale, or even a dialog, if you are lucky enough to have more than one informant. The key is that the informant speak, uninterrupted, for long enough to produce the kind of natural speech that does not come out in sentence-by-sentence elicitations.

The collection, transcription, translation and analysis of texts serves several purposes. First, it gives the linguist a body of data which is relatively pure and uncorrupted. No matter what subfield you are working in (phonology, syntax, etc.), there is always the danger of obtaining corrupted data through elicitations and grammaticality judgements. With text collection, many of these risks are avoided. Also, the informant is likely to focus on the story itself, rather than worrying excessively about pronunciation or choice of words. (On the other hand, there are certain dangers inherent in recording connected speech, such as the possibility of genuine speech errors, which are more common than one might think.) Second, words and constructions which would otherwise go undiscovered often pop up in recorded texts. It is simply not possible to think up elicitations for every type of construction that might occur in a language, and so the collection of texts often fills in some of the gaps that the linguist would otherwise have left unfilled. One might forget, for example, to check for a passive imperfect subjunctive verb form during elicitation sessions, but this form could then turn up spontaneously in the collection of a text. Third, text collection sometimes provides investigators with data that are interesting to humanity at large, as well as to linguists. Fascinating folk tales, many of which have never been written down, can come out when one asks an informant something as simple as, "Tell me a story". This helps put the language being studied into a larger social context. Fourth, your informants may only be able to provide you with information of the sort you are looking for via a very specific sort of narrative. When working with one of the last speakers of the Armenian dialect of Van, for example, we found that she was only able to speak in the dialect when singing songs that her mother had taught her; when speaking regularly, her grammar and pronunciation were those of standard Armenian with a Boston accent. Finally, texts are useful when it comes time to write up the results of your studies. A transcription of a story told by the informant makes an excellent appendix to your book or paper, something that anyone can read and understand.

2. Materials and methods

Many linguists are technophobes, and there is nothing wrong with that. One can go a long way in linguistics with a pen and a pad of paper. Still, a microphone and a tape recorder are so useful for text collection as to make them a virtual necessity. It is not only a question of convenience, but also of the quality of the data collected. If you try to transcribe a whole passage on the fly, you will end up having to ask for certain things to be repeated, and this breaks up the natural flow of speech that is so important to good text collection.

There are two schools of thought on the methodology of text collection. One camp says that text collection should be done in a tightly-controlled laboratory setting. This generally means sitting down with informants and asking them directly to recite stories. The advantage of this approach is that the informant has a chance to think about what to say. As a result, you are likely to get a lot of complete, well-formed sentences, which may be especially useful for syntacticians. The disadvantages of this approach, however, are numerous. The first is that you are collecting somewhat artificial speech, in the sense that the speaker is highly conscious of the process of speaking. A story collected in this fashion represents a more careful, elevated register than the informant is likely to use on a day-to-day basis. The other major problem with this approach is that your informant may be intimidated by the laboratory setting you have created. The best stories tend to come out in the course of spontaneous conversation, not when an informant is put on the hot seat. For example, we once had an informant who was very talkative and entertaining in everyday conversation, but became very guarded and taciturn when we recorded him at his house with a large, fancy microphone. (This is a variant of the Observer's Paradox, discussed in chapter 10.) The next time, we addressed this problem by conducting the interview while strolling along a river, using an unobtrusive microcassette recorder. This had the desired effect, as the informant returned to his outgoing ways. (Don't try this exact technique if you're studying pronunciation, though—the tape was difficult to decipher, because of all the background noises that are inevitable when one is outdoors.)

The other way to approach text collection is by trying to integrate it into your regular sessions. People who work this way attempt to minimize the distinction between text collection and other parts of fieldwork (including the friendship that you have hopefully built with your informants). The hope is that stories will flow naturally out of the conversations that arise during an elicitation session. Incidentally, this is closer to the way one would treat a friend in a normal social setting. We recommend this approach, because we have found that our best stories have been collected in this manner. The key to this approach is to have your tape recorder running at all times, so that you will be ready when a story comes along. Adopting this approach does not mean that you cannot steer the informant toward telling a story. On the contrary, this is a skill that every field linguist should have. Your goal should be to coax your informant into telling a story without making it obvious that this is your aim. This way, you can record data which reflects the way your informant speaks in unguarded moments. You can also try recording some stories told spontaneously and others told in planned situations, and then compare the informant's speech in both situations, looking for any interesting differences. The planned narrative may well omit discourse particles and similar items, such as the Abkhaz gʲə discussed in chapter 10. One final possibility recommended by Peter Ladefoged is to ask your informants to recount a story that someone else told to them.

Regardless of one's philosophical approach, text collection should begin with a tape recorder and a microphone, preferably good ones. (Check chapter 6 for some tips on what sort of equipment to use.) The next step is to get the informant talking, through either direct elicitation or indirect persuasion. Once the informant begins talking, your top priority should be to pay attention to the story and interact with the informant as you would with any friend recounting a tale. You may wish to make notes to yourself as the informant speaks, but there is no need to transcribe everything. Most importantly, do not interrupt your informant with unnecessary questions or comments; this can be taken care of later. Such interruptions merely distract the informant, and may cause him or her to switch to a more careful speech register, or stop the story altogether.

After the informant has finished speaking, it is often useful to play the tape over right away, to check for any acoustic problems, or to ask the informant for explanations of words or phrases that might cause problems later on. In fact, if you are collecting a folk tale or a personal narrative, you may wish to collect a translation of the passage at this point, while it is still fresh in the informant's mind. In this case, it may be necessary to do a quick transcription of the text while working through it, just so that you know how to match up the words with their English glosses. The key is to make this a quick, functional transcription, rather than a terribly accurate one. There is no need to waste the informant's time with narrow transcription at this point; you can always review the tape later.

As always, an informant's glosses are not to be trusted without some testing and corroboration, so it often takes considerably more time to iron out the proper translation of the passage than to record it. All of the strategies and tricks mentioned in the previous chapters will come in handy here, as you try to figure out not only the literal meanings of individual words, but also the meaning of the story as a whole. The final step in the text collection process is narrow transcription, which can be accomplished, for the most part, without the informant's help, provided that the sound quality on the tape is reasonably good.

3. Types of texts

One may collect any of a number of types of texts: folk tales, fables, legends, riddles, superstitions, sayings, songs, ritualized blessings and curses, ditties, poems, jokes, and so on. In this section we describe three common varieties of folkloric texts that you might enjoy collecting. Remember that not all types will work equally well on any given occasion; different individuals will prefer different topics and different sorts of narratives, and a given individual will not always be in the right mood to tell a specific kind of story.

3.1. *Personal narratives*

A personal narrative is simply a story told by an informant about his or her life. This might be a description of some episode in the informant's life, or it might be a description of life in his or her home town, or it could be the story of what the informant had for breakfast that morning. In fact, the term 'personal narrative' is little more than a general heading. The idea is simply to get the informant to tell some sort of story, regardless of what it is about. Your informant may tell you all about how his sister was abducted by space aliens, and that is fine, as long as you get it on tape. Our Vank[h] informant provided us with a nice narrative, one which actually took place in the future. He told us all about an upcoming trip to Armenia that he had planned. The purpose of the trip was to obtain medical care for his ailing father, and he described to us every detail of the trip, including how and when he would find doctors to help his father, and what he would say to them.

A major advantage of personal narratives is that they generally represent natural speech, of the sort that a speaker produces spontaneously. It is also easy to obtain a translation of a personal narrative, since the story is usually familiar to the informant. In the case of the narrative collected from our Vank[h] informant, for example, we had little trouble coming up with a good translation of the whole passage, although the glosses of individual words caused some problems, as is to be expected. By contrast, a speaker may have more difficulty translating a folk tale, since folk tales often revolve around strange things happening to strange characters, and are told in archaic words, phrases, and idioms. (Imagine trying to explain to someone, in a language you have not mastered, how Cinderella's carriage turned into a pumpkin at the stroke of midnight.)

On the downside, personal narratives can be difficult to collect, because informants are sometimes reluctant to talk about their own lives. Even if they are not actually shy or secretive, they may not understand what you want from them, and may not see why you would be interested in hearing about the mundane minutiae of their lives. Fortunately, there are friendly, honest ways to coax someone into talking. The most important thing is to establish some sort of trust with the informant. You may wish to tell a little story about yourself. This serves two purposes: it shows the informant that you are willing to share information, as well as collect it; and it demonstrates to the informant what you are looking for. If you are still having trouble collecting a personal narrative at this point, try asking some general, non-threatening questions about your informant's hometown, or about his or her daily routine. These questions often lead to stories before you know it. Once again, your informant may be reluctant to share even this sort of personal information with you, but it is generally worth trying. Most people actually enjoy talking about themselves, particularly about things which are important to them.

Another disadvantage of personal narratives is that one must rely totally on the informant's ability to put together a coherent story. Unlike with a folk tale or a story provided by the investigator, the informant has no framework to limit him or her. As a result, the story may end up being far too long or too short, or it may be completely incoherent. This is particularly a problem for students in field methods classes, who are constrained by the length of the paper or project that they are supposed to produce.

3.2. Folk tales

We all have some idea of what constitutes a folk tale. In eliciting and collecting a folk tale, one is essentially asking the informant to tell a traditional story taken from his or her culture. The great advantage of folk tales is that they are often of considerable general interest. They also tell us something about the informant's culture which we might otherwise not have learned. Furthermore, informants are sometimes more willing to recite a folk tale, if they know one, than they are to talk about their own lives.

There are exceptions to this rule, however. In some cultures, folklore is considered the property of the community, and therefore is not meant to be shared with outsiders (Samarin 1967:143). In this case, it can be all but impossible to collect a folk tale. Fortunately, this is a problem faced primarily by linguists who go into the field to study small, isolated communities. Most informants who are willing to come and talk to a classroom full of students are also fairly willing to share their folklore. In some cases, informants will claim that they do not know any folk tales, but this is invariably wrong. With a little encouragement and the right context, they generally remember at least a handful of stories.

Unfortunately, folk tales do not always provide the best linguistic data, because they are often told—performed, really—in a specific linguistic register. In reciting a folk tale, an informant is likely to use words and constructions that he or she might not otherwise use, simply because they belong to the story. How often do you hear English speakers say *once upon a time*, other than when they are reciting fairy tales? It is difficult to know, as an investigator, which constructions found in a folk tale might be marked, or even disallowed, in regular speech. Related to this problem is the question of register: people often use a more formal, sometimes even archaic, register when telling a traditional tale. (Of course, an archaic register can be interesting from a historical perspective; see chapter 12.) This is another way in which folk tales do not represent natural speech. Finally, one is less likely to get a wide sampling of grammatical constructions with a folk tale than with certain other types of texts. The action frequently takes place entirely in the past, so the variety of tenses that one encounters is limited. In fact, some languages, such as German, have a special narrative past tense which is reserved for precisely these sorts of stories, and rarely if ever surfaces in spontaneous speech.

3.3. Invented texts

Linguists sometimes find it useful to make up a text for an informant to translate and recite in his or her own language. This can be an extremely productive method of text collection. It is particularly useful in cases where one has a limited amount of time with the informant. In collecting a prepared text, one has control over what words and constructions the informant uses, and this allows one to cover a wide selection of data points very efficiently. Imagine, for example, that you only have time for one, two-hour session with an informant, and you want to learn everything you can about his or her language during that time. If you only record a folk tale, you may not end up learning anything about the tense system, for example, simply because it is underrepresented in the tale you collect. In fact, you have no way of knowing what you might miss. By asking the informant to translate and recite a prepared story, however, you can survey a wide variety of phenomena, or you can even target phenomena that are of particular interest to you.

Of course, it is always possible that the informant will nullify your efforts by mistranslating your passage in some way.

This is one of the main disadvantages of the invented text approach, and it is why you need an informant with fairly good skills in English—or whatever language the prepared text is in—and some facility for translation. If not, all of your fancy constructions may come out as a series of simple sentences in the informant's native language. You might start with a sentence like *Having eaten lunch, the man left the house and was attacked by a dog*, only to have it translated as *The man ate lunch; the man left the house; the dog bit the man.* In fact, it sometimes happens that an informant does not understand part of the passage at all, and ends up translating it completely incorrectly. This can be especially dangerous, because you do not have the same sort of control over a text recording that you do over an elicitation session. It is tough to know when your informant has mistranslated something, because you do not have the luxury of asking questions, at least until the story is over.

Another problem with this approach is that the data you collect will not represent entirely natural speech. One danger is that the informant's speech will be broken up by the process of translation itself, and will not flow naturally. This is especially true if the informant is asked to translate the story line by line. We therefore encourage you to have the informant translate the whole passage before you record it. In fact, you may wish to do a couple of "dry runs" before getting the final version. This way, the informant has a chance to become acquainted with the story and to practice telling it, ensuring that the version you record will contain connected, somewhat natural speech. A final disadvantage to this approach is that stories collected in this manner have even less ethnographic value than personal narratives. Once cannot expect a translation of a prepared text to reveal much about an informant's culture.

In spite of all these problems, the invented text approach can be worth pursuing. There is often no better way to collect a large body of reliable data about a language in a short period of time. Furthermore, it provides the linguist with a controlled sample for comparison between languages, dialects, or individual speakers.

3.4. Invented texts—samples

As stated above, the purpose of an invented text is to collect a variety of important or interesting words and grammatical constructions. The question, then, is what to collect.

3.4.1. Sample word list

The Swadesh List provided in chapter 3 gives good samples of common, useful lexical items. If you decide to write up your own text, look over these lists and try to include as many of these key terms as is possible, reasonable, and appropriate.

3.4.2. Sample topic list

When coming up with a text for the informant to translate, you should tailor the text to fit your own interests as an investigator. If you are particularly interested in case systems, for example, then your text should include a lot of noun phrases in different grammatical environments—as subjects, as direct objects, as objects of prepositions, etc. The list of phenomena one could test for is almost endless, and it is impossible to cram all of these into a single passage. Still, there are certain canonical topics that it is good to refer to when drawing up a text of this sort. We include here a list of some of these.[11]

---

[11] For a more complete list of important topics to cover when writing up a grammar, we recommend looking at the outline for the Croom Helm Descriptive Grammar Series, originally published in *Lingua* 42.1, 1977.

Noun Inflection
    definiteness
    number
    gender
    case
Pronouns
    strong: *may stand in isolation*
    weak: *cannot stand alone; phonologically independent*
    clitics: *cannot stand alone; phonologically dependent*
    reflexives
Verb Inflection
    person
    number
    gender
    tense
    aspect
    mood
    voice
Adjective Inflection
    definiteness
    gender
    number
    case
    comparatives/superlatives
Adverbs
    comparatives/superlatives
Noun-Verb Agreement
Noun-Adjective Agreement
Noun-Noun Agreement (possessives)
Verb-Adverb Agreement

Copulas
> Existentials
> Identification
> Characterization

Numerals
> numeral inflection/agreement
> cardinals/ordinals

Quantifiers
> objects of quantifiers
>> case
>> number
> quantifier scope

Phrase Structure
> noun phrases
> verb phrases
> prepositional/postpositional phrases
> adjective phrases
> coordination of phrases

Main Clauses
> intransitives
> transitives
> di-transitives
> declaratives
> interrogatives—yes/no questions
> imperatives
> performatives
> coordination of clauses

Subordinate Clauses
> indirect questions
> indirect statements
> relative clauses
> result clause

equatives

comparatives

ECM—infinitive sentential complements

Extraction

wh-questions

extracted subjects—focus, emphasis, topicalization

extracted objects—focus, emphasis, topicalization

heavy-NP shift

Negation

sentential negation

negation of specific elements

negative polarity items

3.4.3. Sample texts

Making up a text can be difficult, so we have provided two samples. Neither of them contains all of the grammatical constructions one could hope to test for, but each has certain advantages. Additionally, they are both short and fairly light-hearted, as well as being applicable to most cultures. Incidentally, the first passage is a modified version of a story which actually happened to one of my friends (or so this friend claims) who was working in the United States Peace Corps.

There is a woman who lives in a small village. She is afraid that she may be sick, so she decides to go to a doctor. The best doctors all live in the big city, so she will have to travel five or six hours to see one. She tells the other people in the village that she will be leaving to see the doctor, and they ask her "What sort of illness do you have? Could we be sick, too?" She explains about her illness, and says that she will have to take a sample of her stool (excrement) for the doctor to examine. Several other people have also felt sick, and they ask her to take samples of their stool, and show these to the doctor. She agrees, and the next day, she leaves for the city with two whole bags full of stool samples, one from each of the villagers.

When she arrives in the city, she gets off the bus and starts walking toward the doctor's office. Suddenly, she is attacked by a man who runs up behind her, grabs her bag, and runs off. "Stop! Thief!" she yells, but he doesn't stop. Then she has to laugh, because she realizes that he has just stolen a whole bag of shit.

This passage contains a number of the phenomena listed in section 3.4.2. There are quantifiers, as in *The best doctors all live in the city*, and there is an indirect statement: *She tells the other people...that she will be leaving...* There is also an imperative, *Stop!*, and a direct quotation. There are subordinate clauses, such as *when she arrives in the city*, and a potentially dual form, *two bags*. Additionally, one could easily modify the story to suit specific interests or needs. Imagine, for example, that you were interested in the comparative and superlative forms of adjectives. You could go through this passage and find several places in which to add comparatives and superlatives. After making the appropriate alterations, you would have a text that would give you data for your personal research interests and cover an array of other topics.

The second passage is also a retelling of something that happened to one of my friends.

A young man, who lived on a farm in the country, had begun drinking heavily. He was only 15 years old, but he drank every day, and so his parents were worried about him. His mother and father talked about this problem. They had to do something, but they couldn't think of anything.

Finally, they decided that his father should discipline him in the old-fashioned way: by getting him so drunk that he would never want to drink again.

The young man and his father drove into the nearest town, which was about 30 miles away, and they went into a bar. The young man's father told the bartender, "Give us two vodkas, and don't stop serving them". They each drank about 10 drinks, but the young man did not pass out. He sat and drank them all, and did not get sick. At midnight, his father gave up and decided to go home, so they got in the car and left. After driving for about 5 minutes, the young man's father drove slowly off the side of the road, and passed out over the steering wheel. The young man picked his father up, moved him out of the way, and drove the car home by himself. When he got home, his mother was awake. He carried his father into the house and said "Hi, Mom. Here's your husband", and went to his room to sleep.

It is no mistake that both of these stories have a somewhat racy tone. We chose stories about bags full of excrement and drunken teenagers because, in many cases, these sorts of stories help to loosen an informant up and get him or her in the mood to talk. This is important because the "invented text" approach to text collection is so clinical that it often causes informants to freeze up. They do not see the point of translating an unfamiliar story, and so they have a hard time doing it. If you give an informant a story with some flair, however, and with some sort of punchline, then he or she can see that the process can be fun. Unless you have an unusually prudish and businesslike informant, any efforts you make to show that you are fun-loving are likely to be appreciated.

4. Potential problems

As with any other area of fieldwork, there are certain problems that come up frequently in the collection of texts. Below are descriptions of some of these problems, along with our tips for avoiding or combating them.

- **Speech errors.** Your informant may make speech errors during the telling of a story, which you as a non-native speaker are not likely to pick up. These can be corrected by going over your transcriptions with the informant. But beware that your informant may also try to "correct" the text after the fact by putting it into a more elevated register.

- **Appearing nosy.** Asking someone to recount a personal story, or even a folk tale, can appear highly invasive, if the request is not presented properly. One of the keys is to ask questions in a general, non-prying way, so as to allow the conversation to flow comfortably. For example, rather than saying "Tell me a story about your mother", you could simply ask your informants what life was like for them as a child. You might want to ask some questions about the town your informant lived in, or about other more neutral topics. We have noticed that it is best not to ask too many personal questions in a row; one or two is usually fine, but three or more is pushing it. We therefore try to ask a variety of neutral questions in between any personal ones that we might have. It is generally possible to get the information you want in this way, without the informant feeling that you are being too nosy.

- **Cultural misunderstandings (hypersensitivity).** Most linguists are well-educated, somewhat worldly individuals. As a result, we are aware that many of us have led lives of privilege compared to those of our informants, and so we are careful not to highlight this fact.   In some cases, however, sensitivity to cultural differences can be overdone, at which point it becomes transparent and insulting.

When creating a text for an informant to translate and recite, for example, linguists are generally careful to make sure that the story is culturally neutral. In other words, it should not be about going to a football game and eating cheese fries. On the other hand, it is important to realize that most of the informants we work with have had extensive contact with western society and with the so-called marvels of modern technology. If you give your informants a story about a man in a loincloth going down to the river to catch fish with a spear and a straw basket, they may be insulted, and rightly so.

One way to get around this problem is by bringing up traditional terms in the context of discussing a neighboring group of people, rather than your informants' own village, ethnicity, or country.   This way the informants can speak freely without impugning their own culture. Our Homshetsi informants, for example, were reluctant to talk about traditional items of clothing such as peasant shoes, aprons, caps, and so on, because they considered these to be outdated and beneath their current level of culture. We ended up collecting the words for these items successfully by producing cartoons of Armenians wearing exactly the clothes in question: our informants were then more than happy to reveal the names for these objects, as it was Armenians rather than Homshetsis who were wearing them. (They then went on to say that they remembered older folk in their own village wearing items of this sort.)

- **Mechanical failures.**   There is nothing worse than going through a whole story, and then finding out that your tape recorder was not working, either because of operator trouble or a real mechanical problem. During an elicitation session, you always have your notes to look back on, and so it is not so bad if you do not catch everything on tape. With text collection, however, it is imperative that the tape recorder function properly. It is therefore a good idea to check your equipment before meeting with your informant, and then to do a dry run before you begin in earnest. Also, try to have a spare machine handy.

- **Informant clamming up.** Sometimes informants simply clam up, which can make collecting a text be like pulling teeth. More often than not, an informant's reluctance to talk is due to the setting. People become very self-conscious when they feel that they are being put on the spot and asked to perform, and this effect is only exaggerated when they know they are being recorded. (Think of being asked to tell a joke; it can be almost impossible to come up with one on demand.) When put in this situation, informants may find that they are suddenly unable to think of a single story to tell.

    There are some tricks you can use in this situation to loosen up your informants. One is to ask them to tell you about a close call with death. Most people have had such experiences—or they imagine that they have, even if they were never in any real danger—and they are usually willing to talk about them. Another is to ask about some other important events in your informants' lives, such as getting married or getting in a fight with someone. The key here is to stir up vivid memories and get your informants talking.

- **The informant as editor.** It is often necessary to have your informant help you review a story that you have collected, so as to come up with the best possible transcription and translation.

You may be surprised to find, however, that when you play the tape back to your informant for the first time, he or she will not be happy with it. People are often unaware of their own linguistic habits, and are shocked to find that they are not as eloquent and articulate as they had imagined. In some cases, informants have been known to demand that they be allowed to revise the tape and correct the "errors" they made.

Vaux once recorded an excellent story from his Abkhaz informant, one which lasted half an hour and contained numerous interesting historical and folkloric references. He decided to transcribe the whole story, but found this to be an almost impossible task. After hours of work, he had transcribed only a small portion of the tape, and was not very confident about the accuracy of his work. He arranged to meet with the informant again, so that they could go over the tape together. The informant knew the Abkhaz writing system, so he actually transcribed the whole tape himself. In the process, however, he edited out all the discourse particles, and made structural changes to numerous sentences. He even insisted on re-recording the story! When asked, he was reluctant to transcribe what was actually on the original tape, because he felt that it did not do justice to his skills as a story-teller.

In this sort of situation, it is best to try to reach a compromise which will make everyone happy. For example, you might allow your informant to make the desired revisions, and keep a copy of this version of the transcription. It could actually prove useful, particularly if you are interested in syntax, since it gives you some information about the informant's native-speaker intuitions. Also, the revised version is generally similar enough to the original one that it can be useful when you sit down to analyze the original. Once you have collected a revised version, ask your informant if he or she would be willing to go over the tape again and transcribe the original version of the story. You can explain that you are interested in both the ideal version of the story *and* the original version. With any luck, your informant will humor you and agree to help you out.

Suggested Readings

Bryant, Margaret. 1945. Proverbs and How to Collect Them. American Dialect Society 4.

Finnegan, Ruth. 1992. Oral Traditions and the Verbal Arts: Guide to Research Methods. London: Routledge.

Leaders, Marlin. 1991. Eliciting figures of speech. Notes on Translation 5.4:31-45.

Pittman, Richard. 1970. A method for eliciting paradigmatic data from text. In Alan Healey, ed., Translator's field guide, 377-78. Ukarumpa: Summer Institute of Linguistics.

Rupp, James. 1974. On eliciting metaphors. Notes on Translation 53:17-22.

Exercises

1. Make up your own story for your informant to translate and recite. Try to include as many of the grammatical phenomena listed in section 3.4.2 as possible. Discuss some of the problems that arise in trying to incorporate so many different features into a single story.

2. Have your informant translate and recite one of the stories provided in section 3.4.3. (You may wish to modify the text ahead of time, to fit your research interests.) Record this translation of the story, and see how it compares to the English version. Which grammatical phenomena came through in the translation, and which did not? For example, were passives translated as passives, or were they re-worded in the active voice?

3. Collect the same story twice. Compare the two versions, and see what is different. The exercise works best if you use a story that the informant produced spontaneously the first time, and you then ask him or her to repeat it. The key is to see what effect the difference in elicitation methods has on the register the informant uses, and on the content of the story.

4. Collect, transcribe, translate and analyze a story on a topic of your informant's choice. Ask him or her to tell you a favorite story of some kind. Discuss the difficulties you encounter.

5. Imagine that your informant has suddenly become very tight-lipped. Discuss some ways in which you might get him or her to produce a story.

6. Run a short English text through a Web translator, such as the Google translation tool (http://www.google.com/language_tools) or Babelfish (http://world.altavista.com/), rendering the text into a language of your choice that is available in the service. After you have obtained your translation, translate this new text back into English using the same program. Look for differences between the original and the final version, and discuss how you think these differences crept into the text.

5   Identifying nuances of meaning: Semantics

This chapter is not about theoretical semantics. We do not cover truth tables, predicate calculus, or any such matters. The focus of this chapter is on basic semantic issues that arise during fieldwork. Specifically, we discuss ways of figuring out the meaning of informants' words, phrases, and sentences. Attention is also paid to a related issue: getting informants to understand what *you* mean. Whether or not you are interested in semantics as its own field of study, these issues are bound to come up in working with informants, particularly if they are not fluent speakers of your native language.

1. Sample interview 1
In order to demonstrate some common semantic problems that arise when working with informants, we make frequent reference throughout this chapter to two elicitation sessions that we conducted with a Gujarati informant. The first of these focused on kinship terms. This session was particularly instructive for a number of reasons. First, Gujarati has a much richer system of kinship terms than does present-day English, so that a major focus of our efforts was determining the precise meaning of the terms our informant gave us. Second, the relative poverty of the English system of kinship terms meant that we had to come up with elaborate, often extralinguistic ways to describe the filial relationships we were interested in. For example, English does not have a word for 'the mother and father of your child's spouse', and so we had to come up with ways to convey this meaning to our informant, who does not speak English terribly well, in order to find out if Gujarati has a word like this (it does). Third, the fact that we were studying kinship terms virtually ensured that the session would prove productive,

because there are only so many possible filial relations, and they are identical across all cultures (except those that practice inbreeding, perhaps). In other words, while we often had trouble determining the meaning of a Gujarati kinship term at first, we knew that there were a finite number of meanings it could have, and that we would arrive at the correct one sooner or later. Likewise, we knew that it would ultimately be possible to describe to our informant even the most improbable filial relationship (father's cousin's daughter's husband's...), given enough time and effort. Your father's younger sister is always your father's younger sister, no matter what language you speak. This is not the case when you are working on other types of words or phrases. Prepositions, for example, present many difficulties, because there is no guarantee of semantic equivalence across languages.

As you read this section, we hope you will get a sense not only of the difficulties we encountered, but also of the methods we used to overcome these difficulties. We try to point out places where we attempted strategies that left us empty-handed, as well as highlighting points at which we came up with solutions to our problems. As you will see, one of the greatest assets to have when working with an informant is the ability to sense when you are being understood, and when you are not. We often thought that we had figured out the meaning of a word, and then moved on to something else, only to find out later that the informant had simply agreed with our inaccurate definition of the word because he did not really understand us.

1.1. Warming up

It is sometimes best to start off a session with a few warm-up questions, just to get things going. In this particular interview, we started off by asking our informant, whose name is Sabbir, how to say "My name is Sabbir". We chose to elicit this sentence even though we had already collected it during a previous session. What does this accomplish? To begin with, it sets the tone for the session: the linguist will ask questions, the informant will answer them, and everything will go smoothly. It is important that both the linguist and the informant have some idea of how things should go. Of course, you have to avoid being too repetitive, because this tends to annoy informants; as always, common sense should be your guide. Secondly, starting off with a simple elicitation or two gets the informant back into the swing of things. Keep in mind when you start a session that some time has probably passed since your last meeting with your informant, and that while you have remained a linguist during that time, your informant has not remained an informant. He or she has likely been off leading a normal life away from linguistics, and so it may take a few minutes to warm back up to the task of translating sentences like "Which man did who say killed what?" Finally, in the case of this particular session, asking a few simple questions served to tactfully divert our informant's attention from his own interests, so that we could then begin asking him the questions we were interested in asking. This particular informant loves to be helpful, and on this day he had actually come armed with two Gujarati-English textbooks—books for Gujarati speakers learning English, not the other way around—and appeared ready to give us a lecture from these textbooks. Although learning Gujarati for purposes of communication would be nice, this was not actually our objective on this particular day, and so we needed to persuade him, tactfully, to work with us on our terms.

(Incidentally, this is not an uncommon problem. Vaux and several colleagues once arranged a meeting with a visiting scholar who was a native speaker of Uyghur, hoping to collect some data on Uyghur phonology and syntax. The scholar/informant showed up at the meeting with an incomprehensible handout that he had made up, and proceeded to give a lecture on Uyghur as if he were teaching a first-grade grammar class.)

1.2. What is our informant saying?

It is often not immediately clear what one of your informant's utterances means. Of course, you may simply ask, "What does this mean?" but there is no guarantee that the informant's reply will be satisfying. Native speakers are often unable to express the precise meaning of individual words and morphemes, particularly function words such as prepositions or conjunctions. Furthermore, your informant may not speak English well enough to explain to you what a given word means. For example, we asked our Gujarati informant if he knew of a word meaning 'paternal uncle'. In fact, we did not say 'paternal uncle', but rather asked him "What do you call your father's brother?" He replied with the word kɑkɑ. He then quickly added that this person could also be called tʃɑtʃɑ. When I asked him what tʃɑtʃɑ meant, he replied "tʃɑtʃɑ means kɑkɑ". Because he did not know the technical term 'paternal uncle', and because he had just given us the word kɑkɑ, this seemed like a perfectly reasonable way to define tʃɑtʃɑ.

In this situation, we had a small problem to solve. We needed to know what the exact definition of tʃɑtʃɑ was, and how it was different from kɑkɑ, but our informant did not see that we were interested in such fine semantic distinctions. This is actually a very common problem: how does one distinguish between apparent synonyms? It is a fact about human language that there are very few absolute synonyms, if any, and yet most non-linguists believe that their languages are full of them. For this reason, one often has a hard time convincing an informant to make a distinction between two words, even if such a distinction clearly exists. We decided to start with the direct approach, and this time it worked. I asked our informant what the difference was between these two words, and he explained that they refer to the same things, but that kɑkɑ is used by Hindu people, and tʃɑtʃɑ by Muslims. (tʃɑtʃɑ is in fact the Urdu word for 'father's brother'; another Gujarati friend of ours, a Hindu, felt that kɑkɑ was the only Gujarati word for this concept.)

In other cases, things may not go nearly so smoothly. We had an awful time, for example, trying to figure out what the Gujarati words βeβɑi, kuʈumb, and pijʌɾ meant, and what the semantic differences between them might be. The trouble began when Vaux asked our informant if he knew of a word used to refer to one's father and all other male members of the family on the father's side—apparently this concept is honored with its own word in some cultures. Our informant immediately responded with the word βeβɑi.[12] As mentioned above, nothing is more useful to a field linguist than a sense of when communication is breaking down, and at this point in the session, both Vaux and I had a gut feeling that our informant had not really understood what Vaux was referring to. It just seemed improbable that he should grasp the notion of 'father plus all male relatives' and give us the appropriate term in less than a second. We asked him to define βeβɑi, and he then said that he would call all of his wife's relatives his βeβɑi, including her mother and sisters. So, we were right: he had not understood us initially.

Unfortunately, things did not get any easier at this point, because we still did not feel confident that we knew exactly what βeβɑi meant. In an attempt to clarify matters, we asked our informant what his wife would call all of *his* relatives, and he responded with the word pijʌɾ. Once again, we felt that something was amiss, and so we asked him to define pijʌɾ. He then said that all of *his wife's* relatives would be called pijʌɾ. Our informant picked up on our frustration, and tried to help out by saying "βeβɑi

---

[12] This word is written <vevai> in the official Gujarati orthography, but our informant generally pronounces what is written <v> as a voiced bilabial fricative, [β].

is a local word. All the people use the βeβai". This demonstrates how important it is to keep your emotions under wraps, because otherwise you are sure to end up corrupting your data. Informants are generally eager to please, and so if they see that you are becoming frustrated, they will do whatever it takes to make you feel better, including making things up. This is by no means malicious; on the contrary, when informants invent or embellish data, they are generally aiming to help.

One of us ended up getting a handle on the situation by drawing a family tree and asking our informant to circle all the members that each word referred to. This did not take care of the problem altogether, because for most of these kinship terms there is also the question of who is speaking, not only who is being referred to, but it did allow us to make some progress. With the drawing and a good deal of patience, we were able to conclude that pijʌɾ is the word that a woman uses to refer to her own family, once she is married.[13]   Before she is married, she calls her family her kuʈum(b).[14] Her marital status is important, we found, because once she is married, she becomes part of her husband's family. She then calls them her kuʈumb, and her original family becomes her pijʌɾ. A man's family is always his kuʈumb, whether he is married or not, since he is not considered to change families when he marries. Unfortunately, we were not as thorough as we should have been, and we did not find out whether a man calls his wife's family pijʌɾ, or if only she uses this word. It is always best to test for as many variables as possible, and in this case, we failed to do so. We did finally come up with a definition for βeβai, however, although we did not feel entirely certain about its accuracy. It seems that βeβai

---

[13] Gala (n.d.) glosses pijʌɾ as 'the paternal house of a married woman'.
[14] kuʈumb is glossed by Gala (n.d.) simply as 'family'. Our informant did not pronounce the *b*, but a second informant and Gala (n.d.) did.

is the term used to refer to the family of one's son-in-law or daughter-in-law.[15]

Another type of problem arises when the English language is simply not up to the task of translating a given word or phrase from the informant's language. Our Gujarati informant provided us with an illustration of this problem, as he attempted to define the word b[h]ab[h]i. In this case, his difficulties with English were not responsible for the communication breakdown; rather, the word simply did not lend itself to translation into English. Actually, his initial definition of b[h]ab[h]i as 'wife of one's older brother' was perfectly easily understood. Later on in the session, however, it came out that there was more to the story of this word. Our informant explained that in his culture a special relationship holds between a man and his b[h]ab[h]i, in which it is expected that they will flirt with each other, talk dirty to each other and, as our informant put it, "do every thing except boom-boom". (The same relationship holds between a man and his wife's younger sister, who is called *sari*.) Up to this point, we understood our informant perfectly, although the concept of a b[h]ab[h]i is somewhat foreign to our culture.

The confusion began when our informant explained he did not have an older brother, but that he called his cousin's wife b[h]ab[h]i, and that he engaged in all these games with her. He explained to us that a man may call his cousin's wife b[h]ab[h]i, but only under certain circumstances. He first explained that his cousin needed to be on the male side: his uncle's son. He then said that his uncle's son's wife needed to be older than him in order to be a b[h]ab[h]i, but then he decided that this was not the right definition. Next, he said that his uncle had to be older than him, but he was not satisfied with that

---

[15] This is according to our informant. A second Gujarati friend and Gala (n.d.) agree that βeβai refers only to the *parents* of one's son-in-law or daughter-in-law, and Gala specifies even further that it refers only to 'the father-in-law of one's son or daughter'.

definition either. It turned out that the problem was in getting the adjective *older* to modify the word *son* in the phrase *uncle's son's wife*. *Son* is embedded between two other nouns in this phrase, and so the only way to modify it with *older* is to say *uncle's older son's wife*, but this does not produce the desired meaning. *Uncle's older son's wife* means that the uncle's son is older than the uncle's son's other siblings, but what our informant meant was that the uncle's son had to be older than our informant. There is simply no good way to express this concept in English, especially when you are put on the spot in the middle of an elicitation session. The best definition we could come up with was "wife of an older male cousin on the father's side". Still, by being thorough and patient, we managed to figure out what our informant was saying, and we learned something interesting about both his language and his culture in the process.

1.3. What are we saying?

More often than not, confusion arises during fieldwork because the informant does not understand what you are saying, not the other way around. Sometimes this is not a semantic problem, *per se*. If your informant is not a native English speaker and does not recognize the word 'shoe', for example, then your troubles are not really of a semantic nature. Your informant may speak English well, however, perhaps even fluently, and yet communication problems still arise. Sometimes this is because the meanings of words do not match up across languages as nicely as we would like them to. Take the English word *eat*. We all know what it means, and it seems logical that its counterparts in other languages should mean the same thing. In general, they do, but at the margins they may differ. The German word *essen*, for example, is used for the consumption not only of food, but also of pills and other medications. This meaning is not part of the English word *eat*. *Essen* cannot be applied to animals, however, while our *eat* can. These seemingly minor differences between the meanings of words are the sort of thing that can prevent an informant from understanding the subtleties of an investigator's questions. We have had many problems of this sort with our Gujarati informant.

Early on in our session on kinship terms, we tried to find out the name of our informant's father. (This is not always the best idea, since personal names are a taboo subject in some cultures.) We hoped that knowing the real names of some of his family members would help us avoid confusion later on, since we would be able to use terms like 'Ali's daughter' as shorthand for 'your mother's sister's son's daughter'. The conversation that developed out of this attempt at elicitation shows how an investigator's questions can be confusing, as seen below.

Cooper:	How do you say *My father's name is* ... How do you say *father*?
Informant:	Father? bɑpu-dʒi.[16] [pause] pita-dʒi.
Cooper:	bɑpu-dʒi or...
Informant:	pita-dʒi. Father.
Cooper:	OK, so how do you say ... What's your father's name? [Note that no part of this sentence was intended as an elicitation.]
Informant:	tʌmɑrɑ pita-nū nɑm sū[17] tʃʰe ?
	[your.pl. father-gen. name what is
	'What is your father's name?']
Cooper:	Wait, no. How do you say ... OK ... I'm asking you. What is your father's name?
Informant:	mɑrɑ pita-dʒi-nū nɑm mohʌmːʌd tʃʰe.
	'My father's name is Mohammad'.

---

[16] -dʒi is a suffix of affection meaning roughly 'dear'.

[17] The official form is ʃū; as we mention elsewhere, our informant (and many other speakers of South Indian languages) freely interchange s and ʃ.

Because most of our exchanges during a session come in the form of elicitations, the informant had no way to know that, on this occasion, we were requesting real-world information from him, and not a translation of the sentence *What is your father's name?* What cannot be seen from the above transcription is that we had to use gestures and body language to show him that we actually wanted to know his father's name, which is what made the second attempt more successful than the first.

When a session is going particularly well, you may get so deeply into talking about the informant's language that the use of English for elicitation becomes a hindrance. This tends to happen when, as mentioned above, the correspondence of meaning between English words and words in the informant's language is not one-to-one. In such cases, you may find that the informant does not understand your elicitation because the phrasing you use in English is too cumbersome and imprecise. If you know a word in the informant's language that will make your meaning clear, it may be worth trying it out. We have ended up using Gujarati words frequently when working with our informant. For example, at one point our informant gave us the words derɑni and dʒetʰɑni, which mean 'husband's younger brother's wife' and 'husband's older brother's wife', respectively. We were interested in seeing just how extensive the system of kinship terms is in Gujarati, so we decided to ask how you would say 'husband's older brother's wife's mother'. This phrase is almost unparsable in English, however, so we simplified things by asking "What do you call the dʒetʰɑni's mother?" (It turned out that there is no word for this specific concept, and that this person is simply called 'mother'.)

Be sure, however, not to underestimate the potential semantic complexity of your informant's language. At another point in this session, we decided again to test the limits of Gujarati kinship terminology by asking how a man would refer to his brother's son's daughter. An English-speaking fieldworker might not normally think to ask about forms like this, since it seems to an English speaker like a non-concept, or at least a concept for which there would be no special word. However, our informant hesitated for a moment, then came up with the word: bʰʌtɾidʒo tʃʰokɾi.[18]

The elicitation method has many limitations, one of which stems from the fact that the question "How do you say X?" is not always as precise as we would like it to be. Particularly when one is talking about people, it can be unclear whether this question asks what you call someone to his or her face, or what you call him or her when speaking in the 3rd person. We are not talking about the evil names that one makes up for people when they are not around, but rather about the very common practice of addressing people with terms that we do not use when they are not present. For example, many people refer to their mothers as "my mother", but address them as "Mom". It is easy for informants to misunderstand an investigator's questions because we are rarely aware of this distinction when we ask things like "What do you call the man who cuts your hair?" This came up frequently with Gujarati kinship terms. On one occasion, we asked our informant what he called his wife's father, expecting to find out how he referred to him in the 3rd person, and he said that he called him bɑpu-dʒi, meaning 'father'. He also said that he called his wife's mother mɑ or mɑtɑ-dʒi, meaning 'mother'. Objectively, we had no reason to believe that this was not true. It is certainly conceivable that he would refer to these people as his father and mother, even in the 3rd person. We later asked him what he called another relative, however, and he responded with a personal name. At this point, we realized that he had misunderstood our question all along (with good reason). We clarified what we meant by "What do you call X?" and then went

---

[18] bʰʌtɾidʒo means 'nephew', and tʃʰokri means 'girl'.

back to check on 'wife's father' and 'wife's mother'. Sure enough, there was a specific word used to refer to each of these people: sʌsʌɾo and sɑsu, respectively. (It turns out that these words actually mean 'father-in-law' and 'mother-in-law' respectively; in other words, they can apply to the parents of either the wife or the husband.)

As you become more experienced at fieldwork, you learn to recognize situations in which your informant is likely to misunderstand you. You also develop a repertoire of strategies you can use to make yourself understood. When you are presented with such a problem, and you find that you come up with a good solution to it, be sure to jot it down in your notes, as you may wish to use this trick again.

2. Sample interview 2

Moving from a relatively simple issue—kinship terms—to a couple of real killers, we tackled quantifiers and prepositions in our next interview with our Gujarati informant. The differences between these two sessions, in terms of both productivity and atmosphere, were unmistakable. Our session on kinship terms went much more smoothly and was much more entertaining for all the parties involved.

2.1. Quantifiers and prepositions: an overview

Before moving into a discussion of the interview itself, we should put in a few words about the topics covered in this session—quantifiers and prepositions—and explain why we chose them. We decided to cover these topics with our informant because, in addition to illustrating certain important points about semantic confusion in fieldwork, they are of interest within the field of theoretical semantics. As a result, our task was doubly difficult, when compared to the session on kinship terms. We had to structure the session in such a way as to tackle relevant theoretical questions—not so much an issue with kinship terms—while also confronting the usual practical issues related to communicating with our informant.

Our first topic was quantification and quantifier scope. Quantifiers are words like *all*, *some*, *none*, *many*, and so forth. Languages vary in terms of what quantifiers they have, and how they are interpreted. The general question that one wishes to answer, however, is "What interpretations can a quantifier have, and what factors determine their interpretation?" The sentence in (1) has two quantified NPs (noun phrases governed by a quantifier) *every man* and *some woman*.

(1)   Every man kisses some woman

The interesting thing about this sentence is its ambiguity. It could have either of the interpretations shown in (2). In (2a), the interpretation is that there is some specific woman whom every man kisses. In (2b), the interpretation is that there are several (perhaps many) different women, and that every man kisses at least one of them.

(2)   a.   for some woman y, every man x, x kisses y
        b.   for every man x, for some woman y, x kisses y

                        (Data adapted from Larson and Segal 1995)

The difference between these interpretations is assumed to be one of "scope". In the former interpretation, *some woman* has the broadest scope, and is therefore interpreted independently of *every man*, while in the latter interpretation, *every man* has the broadest scope, and is consequently able to dictate the interpretation of *some woman*. As we discuss below, we gave our informant sentences like this one to translate into Gujarati, and then tried to figure out the meaning of his responses, sometimes with only limited success.

Our other main topic was prepositions. Specifically, we were interested in the interpretations of prepositions, as opposed to the syntactic behavior of prepositional phrases. This was another interesting but difficult topic. We wanted to see what sorts of spatial relations, or motions, are indicated by individual Gujarati prepositions, but we were faced with the difficulties inherent in defining a preposition verbally. As discussed below, our informant was also stumped by this problem, and sometimes resorted to "acting out" prepositions rather than defining them in English. (This is perfectly acceptable, of course.)

2.2. Boredom

The biggest problem we had during this session was our informant's boredom. Coming on the heels of a whole session on kinship terms, this interview was something of a let-down for him. Instead of asking him questions about his family and Gujarati culture, we were suddenly asking him about the different possible interpretations of the word "all". This sort of topic can be uninteresting to informants for a number of reasons. One is that they consider it irrelevant and pointless; they may see no reason why one would want to know about the possible interpretations of a sentence containing a quantifier. Another reason is that informants may feel powerless, or even left out, when the session turns toward theoretical topics like quantifier scope. It is easy to see why. When the topic is something like kinship terms, the informant can see what the investigator is looking for. He or she may begin throwing out terms and definitions spontaneously, usually to the delight of the investigator, and may even begin to direct the course of the session, within limits. The informant may legitimately feel and act like the star of the interview. By contrast, an informant has little chance of becoming actively engaged in a session on a theoretical topic such as quantification. In the session documented here, our informant simply answered our questions, but did not contribute as spontaneously as he had in previous sessions. Fortunately, he is an upbeat and cheerful person, and so he remained in good spirits for most of the interview, and even appeared genuinely interested in some of our questions.

One of the strategies we used to keep our informant's attention was to dream up scenarios that could be somewhat humorous. For example, we began by attempting to determine what meanings the quantifier bʌd-, meaning 'all', could have in the sentence in (3).

(3) bʌda manoso bʌdi   tʃʰokɾi-o-ne   tʃumbʌn kʌɾe tʃʰe
     all men   all   women-pl.-dat. kiss   do   is
     'All the men kiss all the women'

At first, our informant was not terribly interested in determining what possible meanings a sentence like this could have. We described a scene, however, in which there were three married couples, and each man kissed his own wife. We then asked whether the sentence in (3) could be applied to this scenario. He explained that this sentence could not have this interpretation, and then added jokingly "Why you kiss my wife?!" Once we had presented him with this imaginary scenario, he was more interested in our questions.

We also made an effort to break up the monotony of this session with occasional digressions into joking, gossip, or whatever else came up. For example, after our discussion of all the men kissing all the women, our informant told us his wife's name, and asked about Vaux's girlfriend's name. Rather than immediately try to steer the talk back to quantifiers, we chatted for a few minutes about where all of our wives and girlfriends were from, what their names were, and so on. When we got back to elicitations, everyone was more relaxed and ready to dive back into the material. Later on, we somehow came upon a topic from the previous session, namely the sexual teasing that goes on between a man and his older brother's wife (b^{h}ab^{h}i). I jokingly asked our informant whether a man would ever kiss his b^{h}ab^{h}i, and he said "No, no...sometimes, maybe, but wife doesn't know!" This sort of joking around generally helps boost morale, and makes the more tedious work go smoothly. The point here is that it is a good thing to be friendly with your informant, and that you should feel free to let this friendship spill over into a work session. There is no reason that working with an informant has to be all business, all the time.

2.3. Uncertainty

We also had less confidence in the data we collected, and in our analysis of it, during this session than we did during the interview on kinship terms. Even with all our drawings and other props, we never felt entirely confident that our informant had understood our questions, or that we had accurately interpreted his responses. In the interview on kinship terms, we generally knew when we had a "right answer", and could then move on with little reservation. In this session, however, we had to work to find the correct interpretations of our sentences, and at times we did not feel entirely confident in the conclusions we drew.

For example, we were interested in the relationship between quantifiers and negation, so we wanted to find out how to say 'no man kisses all the women'. As always, our first task was to convey the meaning of this sentence to our informant. Using the direct approach first, we prompted him with this sentence, and he responded, te bʌdi tʃokɾione tʃumbʌn kʌɾta nʌtʰi.[19] Based on our experience from past sessions, we knew what all of these words meant, except for the verb, and so we knew that this sentence actually means something more like 'he does not kiss all the women'. In order to explain to our informant exactly what we meant by 'no man kisses all the women', we had to do a fair amount of drawing, as well as re-phrasing our questions several times. Finally, he responded with the sentence in (4).

(4) bʌd-a   manaso bʌd-i   tʃokɾi-o-ne   tʃumbʌn kʌɾi
     all-masc. men   all-fem. woman-pl.-dat. kiss   do

     sʌke[20]   nʌhi
     able   is.not

We felt fairly confident that this sentence conveyed the meaning we were looking for, but we wanted to be sure. The problem was that this sentence looks like it could mean 'all men kiss no women', or something to that effect. We suspected that the word or morpheme sʌke might be the key to getting at the true meaning of the sentence, since it was the one word we were not familiar with. The conversation that followed was a classic case of a linguist (or two) and an informant talking past each other, and getting virtually nowhere.

Vaux: So, what did you say sʌke means?
Informant: 'not'…sʌke nʌhi.
Vaux: It's all one word, or two?
Informant: nʌhi means 'not'…sʌke means 'do it'.

---

[19] [nʌtʰi] is a spelling pronunciation of the negative form of the copula, which is written <natʰiː> but pronounced [nʌhi] in standard Gujarati.
[20] Given the official orthography, we would expect [ʃake].

Cooper: What's kʌɾi?

Informant: kʌɾi sʌke one word...kʌɾi sʌke nʌhi. kʌɾu means
                 'do'...'do it'.

Cooper: So, kʌɾtʰanʌtʰi, what's that? [kʌɾtʰanʌtʰi was the
                 verb used in the previous sentence, also glossed as
                 the negation of 'do' or 'do it'.]

Informant: bʌda manaso bʌdi tʃokɾione tʃumbʌn
                 kʌɾtʰanʌtʰi means 'all man doesn't kiss to all girl'.

Cooper: Right.   And what does kʌɾi sʌke nʌhi mean?
                 What's the difference between kʌɾtʰanʌtʰi and
                 kʌɾi sʌke nʌhi?

Informant: kʌɾtʰanʌtʰi means 'too many ... not only one ... a
                 lot'. This one, only one.

It is difficult to know, in this situation, whether the sentence
you have collected actually has precisely the meaning you were
hoping to capture. If you find yourself in this situation, try not to
drag out your questioning and fine-tuning indefinitely. It is better to
simply put an asterisk next to this sentence and come back to it on
another day, when you have a new angle from which to attack it.

Our luck improved somewhat once the talk turned to
prepositions, although we still could not feel entirely certain about
our data. We were hoping to find out how Gujarati prepositions
(which are actually postpositions) reflect the difference between
motion and stasis. In English, for example, the word *under* can refer
either to something which is resting under something else, or to
something which is moving, or being moved, from some other space
into the space beneath something else. By asking our informant to
translate the sentence *The cat walks under the table*, we quickly
found that the word nanitʃe means something like 'under'. The
question remained, however, as to precisely what sense this word
had. Part of the answer to this came when our informant used

nɑnitʃe in saying "the book is under the table". We got the rest of
the story when he stood up and began spinning around, imitating a
cat running around underneath a table, and said that this, too, was
nɑnitʃe. We were able to conclude that this particular postposition
refers to an object either resting or moving round and round
underneath another object, but crucially not to motion from
somewhere else to the space underneath the other object.
(Unfortunately, our hypothesis became a bit more convoluted when
another Gujarati friend told us that nɑnitʃe is only used for 'under'
in the sense of being under a certain age; nitʃe is used for the state of
being located under something, as in bilɑdi tebʌlni nitʃe tʃʰe 'the
cat is under the table'. It is not clear to us at this point whether or
not our first informant simply speaks a different variety of Gujarati;
Gala (n.d.) concurs with the second informant's usage.)

2.4. Definitions

Over the course of this particular session, we noted repeatedly that
our informant was unsure, at certain points, about the distinction
between Gujarati and English. As bizarre as it sounds, he often
forgets which words belong to which language. This is actually not
as uncommon a phenomenon as one might think, and so it is
worthwhile to be aware of it. For example, we asked our informant
how to say 'kiss' in Gujarati, and he responded *kiss*. Only after we
pressed him a bit did he come up with the word tʃumbʌn. Later, we
asked him how to say 'book', and again he replied *book*. Since
English is widely spoken in India, we thought that he might simply
make a habit of using English words like *kiss* and *book* when
speaking Gujarati. This explanation was invalidated, however, when
we asked him how to say 'through' in Gujarati, and he said "almost
[i.e. 'always'] all people use *through*". Borrowing of closed-
category words, such as prepositions, is very uncommon, and so we
found it highly unlikely that the word *through* had actually crept into

the Gujarati lexicon. Shortly thereafter, this confusing phenomenon surfaced again, in a different form. Our informant gave us a sentence containing the word pʌsaɾ, and then said "pʌsaɾ means aɾpaɾ". This was the only definition that he gave us of this word, until we pointed out that we did not know what aɾpaɾ meant. He seemed surprised, but then told us that it meant 'through'. (It turns out that pʌsaɾ is the Hindi word for 'through', and aɾpaɾ is the Gujarati word.)

Suggested Readings

Forsberg, Vivian. 1984. On checking meaning. Notes on Translation 102:9-21.

Hofmann, Thomas. 1993. Realms of Meaning: An Introduction to Semantics. London: Longman.

Larson, Richard and Gabriel Segal. 1995. Knowledge of Meaning: An Introduction to Semantic Theory. Cambridge: MIT Press.

Exercises

1. Make up a list of antonyms. Try to think of pairs of nouns, verbs, adjectives and adverbs. Try some canonical cases, such as *hot* vs. *cold*, and then some marginal cases, where it is not clear if true antonyms exist. For example, is there an antonym of *eat*? Go through these with your informant, and see whether the same words and semantic relations hold in his or her language. Does the informant's language have two antonyms for *old*, for example, the way English does (*young* and *new*)?

2. Re-read the dialog printed in section 1.3, in which it was unclear to the informant whether Cooper was making an elicitation or a simple question or statement. Think of ways to eliminate this sort of confusion during an elicitation session. What could you say to the informant, either ahead of time or at the moment of confusion, to make your instructions clearer?

3. Try to define in words a handful of English prepositions, such as *in*, *during*, and *around*. Give examples of the various nuances of meaning that each can have. Try doing the same with adverbs like *ago* and *anymore*. Think of how you might test these different semantic domains when working with an informant.

4. Come up with a way to elicit color terms, particularly how to know exactly what range of colors a given term covers.

6 Describing acoustic and articulatory patterns: Phonetics

Edward W. Scripture, a famous phonetician who also had training as a physician, ironically quotes the current description of a particular laryngeal articulation which would, had this description been accurate, have inevitably resulted in the fatal strangulation of the speaker!

Roman Jakobson
Six Lectures on Sound and Meaning

1. Articulatory phonetics

1.1 Introduction

As you begin to develop a feel for the language you are working on by collecting basic vocabulary items, you should begin to pay more attention to the nature of the individual sounds produced by the informant, with an eye (or ear) towards determining exactly how each allophone sounds and how it is produced. At this point we confront essentially the same challenge faced by infants learning their first language: how does one figure out what gymnastics the native speakers are performing in their vocal tracts in order to produce a given sound? Some sounds are easy to figure out, of course, since the articulators used to produce them are readily visible. With most sounds, though, one typically can't see what's going on inside the vocal tract when they are produced. It is not always wise or even possible to go by your informants' descriptions of how they produce sounds. Trying to mimic the sounds yourself and then analyze your own production is also fraught with difficulties. The best solution is often to use instrumental techniques of various sorts, but these too are frequently impractical or unfeasible.

In the first part of this chapter we discuss the types of articulatory information that you should try to collect when working with an informant, and present the pros and cons of the most popular strategies for collecting this information.

1.2. What to describe

Before we launch into our discussion of how to collect articulatory information, it will be useful to have an idea of what sort of information one should collect. Basically, it is sufficient (for our purposes) when describing the phonetic structures of a language to elicit and describe each of the allophones in the language, in comparable contexts. This involves examining the complete set of vowel and consonant contrasts, as well as the principal prosodic patterns such as stress and intonation.

When you are examining the sounds produced by your informant, you must be wary of a few potential pitfalls. Some informants may have speech "defects"; for this reason, you should try to compare the pronunciation of your informants to that of one or more other speakers of the language, in order to determine where their pronunciation stands relative to that of the larger speech community. You should also be aware that individual sounds are not always produced in exactly the same way. As a result, it sometimes is difficult to tell whether two pronunciations are manifestations of the same phoneme or not. In these situations, it is best to check with your informant.

The production of a speech sound can be described in terms of three components: a phonatory source, an active articulator, and a passive articulator. (For further discussion of these points, see Ladefoged 1993.)

1.2.1. Phonatory source

The phonatory source is typically one of three airstream mechanisms, which produces a stream of air that the vocal tract can modify to create the variety of sounds used in human languages. The three airstream mechanisms are:

- **Pulmonic** (lung) airflow. This is the regular phonatory source for speech, which you can easily demonstrate by trying to talk while you are breathing in or when the wind has been knocked out of you. Since both of these events preclude airflow up from the lungs and through the vocal tract, it is almost impossible to speak under these conditions.

- **Glottalic** airflow is produced by closing the glottis and then raising or lowering the larynx, thereby pushing air either upwards or downwards in the vocal tract. Ejective sounds (such as we find in many languages of the Caucasus, North America, and Africa) are produced by raising the glottis in this way, and implosives (such as we find in many languages of Africa and southeast Asia) are produced by lowering it.

- **Velaric** airflow, which is responsible for the distinctive sound of clicks, is produced by touching the tongue to the velum, making another closure further forward in the vocal tract, and then rarifying the air between the two constrictions, releasing the forward constriction, and then releasing the velar constriction, producing a loud ingressive flow of air.

1.2.2. Active articulators

The **active articulators**, which are parts of the vocal tract that actively manipulate the airstream produced by the phonatory mechanisms just described, are six in number: the lips, tongue, velum, uvula, pharynx, and larynx. (1) The **lips** are used to produce labial, labiodental, and labiovelar sounds. (2) The **tongue** has three principal subcomponents: the *tongue front* (or *coronal* area), which has two main subparts, the *tip* and the *blade*; the tongue *dorsum*, which is involved in the production of dorsal (also called velar) consonants, and the features high, low, and back in vowels (and some consonants); and the *tongue root*, used in the production of vowel tenseness, pharyngeal and uvular consonants, and obstruent voicing. (3) The **velum**, or **soft palate**, can be lowered to allow airflow through the nasal passage (producing nasality), or raised to shut off this airflow (producing non-nasality). (4) The **uvula** is generally used only in conjunction with the tongue dorsum, in order to produce uvular sounds such as q, χ, and ʁ. (5) The **pharynx** contains three subcomponents: the tongue root; the epiglottis (apparently used distinctively only in a few Caucasian languages); and the pharyngeal wall, which is used in the production of pharyngeal consonants. (6) The **larynx** is responsible for several modes of phonation—voice, murmur, and creak—and is also used in the production of the glottal stop (ʔ), h, and glottalic airflow.

1.2.3. Passive articulators

There are three main passive articulators, which the active articulators exploit to produce various **manners of articulation**: (1) the teeth; (2) the alveolar ridge[21], and (3) the palate, which contains two subparts, the hard palate and the soft palate or velum. There are four important manners of articulation: stop, fricative, approximant, and nasal. **Stops** (p, t, k, b, d, g, etc.) involve complete closure at

---

[21] Be careful not to confuse dental and alveolar articulations. English t and d are alveolar; in other words, they are produced by touching the tip of the tongue to the alveolar ridge, immediately behind the upper teeth. In most other languages, on the other hand, t and d are dental, produced by touching the tip of the tongue to the back side of the teeth.

some point in the vocal tract. **Fricatives** (s, z, ʃ, ʒ, etc.) involve a closure somewhere in the vocal tract that is not complete, but is sufficient to produce turbulent, noisy airflow. (**Affricates** are sequences of a stop plus a fricative that behave as a single phoneme.) **Approximants** (j, w, etc.) involve a low degree of constriction in the vocal tract relative to stops and fricatives. **Nasals**, as mentioned earlier, involve airflow through the nasal passage.

Each of the manners of articulation just described, except for nasal, can be produced by the collaboration of an active articulator in conjunction with any one of the three passive articulators. In order to get a better idea of the different types of sounds that are produced by the various permutations of active and passive articulators, you should consult the IPA chart in the appendix at the end of this book. Languages typically draw from the set of sounds illustrated there, though as we mentioned in chapter 2, your language may well contain one or more sounds that are not covered by the IPA scheme. Nevertheless, it should be possible to model all of the sounds in the language of your informant in terms of the three components of speech production outlined in this section.

1.3. Observing articulations

Now that we know the basic tools for describing speech sounds, we need to know how to go about observing the production of these sounds. With some sounds this is very easy, since the mechanisms involved in their production are readily visible. With sounds of this sort, you can typically make satisfactory descriptions simply by observing your informants as they speak. For posterity's sake, though, and also in order to double check your own real-time observations, you should make video recordings of your informants speaking. Since a single unaided video camera can only capture an individual's vocal tract from one perspective at a time, it is a good idea to use a mirror if you can, positioned so as to reveal the prospect of the individual's head that is perpendicular to that of the camera.

Simple external observation of this type can be very effective for sounds involving activity of the lips, jaw, and to a lesser extent the teeth and the front part of the tongue. Raising and lowering of the larynx can also be observed in this manner. Unfortunately, this simple and unobtrusive technique does not work for most articulatory activities, which take place deeper within the vocal tract. In order to get at these articulations, more intricate and problematic techniques are required.

1.4. Describing articulations

One strategy that is easy to implement, though not always reliable, involves eliciting directly from your informants a description of how they produce a given sound. The advantages of this technique are that it is relatively painless for your informants (especially compared to some of the instrumental techniques to be discussed in section 1.6), and it can give you an idea of how speakers view their own production of the sounds in their language.

Unfortunately, this approach is riddled with difficulties. For example, some sounds involve articulators that people generally cannot feel, such as the tongue root and the pharyngeal wall. Even when the articulators involved are ones for which humans have a large degree of proprioception, one typically should not accept at face value the informants' descriptions of the activities of these articulators. Individuals who have not received training in phonetics, phonology, speech pathology, or anatomy normally do not know what to look for in their pronunciation, and lack the descriptive tools to label in a useful way what they do observe. As a result, people asked to describe properties of their own speech (as well as the speech of others) generally produce useless responses such as "you just feel it", "it's kind of harsh", "it's very whiny and nasal", "it's sing-songy", and so on.

You can begin to overcome this problem by giving your informants some training in articulatory phonetics, but even this measure is not necessarily enough. Almost all people, linguistically trained or otherwise, have a tendency to force the sounds they hear and produce into predetermined categories, corresponding in most instances to abstract notions of what the sounds should sound like (based on their spelling, for example). To take one example, in my experience teaching students in introductory linguistics courses, ninety-eight out of every hundred students describe American /e:, o:, i:, u:/ as [e, o, i, u]. Many of these, especially those who are bilingual or non-native speakers of English, pick up on the fact that these vowels often have an offglide in American English ([ɛɪ] for /e:/, etc.). Very few, though, accept that the back vowels are typically unrounded and centralized (/u:/ is pronounced as something like [ɨw], and /o:/ as [əw]). The students' reluctance is presumably related to the fact that these transcriptions do not correspond very closely to our ideas of what sounds "should" sound like.

Let us say, though, that by *force majeure* you have managed to conquer all of the problems just discussed. Can you now rely on your informants' descriptions? There is no way of being sure without independent evidence. I was once interested in studying the production of an Abkhaz consonant, which was described in the literature as a palatalized glottalized (ejective) voiceless uvular stop, [qʔʲ]. What was at issue at the time was the position(s) occupied by the tongue dorsum during the articulation of this particular consonant. The informant to whom I had recourse had already received several years of excellent linguistic training, and was quite competent at producing linguistically salient descriptions of his pronunciation. When I asked him to describe his production of the [qʔʲ], he responded that his tongue dorsum made contact with the soft palate just in front of the uvula, and air swirled around just behind the constriction as this went on. This impressively specific description conformed fairly closely to what we know about the way in which glottalized uvular consonants are produced in other languages. Nevertheless, my informant's admirable effort was ultimately of limited utility, for two reasons: he was unable to distinguish consistently between the tongue positions involved in plain versus palatalized consonants (which was very important in this case), and it was unclear what to make of his observation that air was swirling around behind the constriction formed by the tongue, because this statement could be construed in several different ways.

Our conclusion thus far, therefore, is that direct elicitation of articulatory information from one's informants can be useful if one has no other options available, but it is preferable to employ other more precise techniques if possible.

1.5. Reproducing articulations

It is often said, especially by phoneticians who are talented mimics, that the best way to figure out how a sound is articulated is to try to reproduce the sound yourself until your informant accepts your pronunciation as accurate, and then to describe what your vocal tract is doing to execute the sound. This technique is in fact a variant of what children do when learning their first language, according to some noted linguists. However, we do not recommend it for adult fieldworkers, for a number of reasons. Most individuals, linguistically trained or otherwise, are not good mimics, and it is therefore quite possible that you will never be able to pronounce a given sound to your informants' satisfaction. Even if you do manage to win the informants' approval, this could be for the wrong reasons: for example, they may have tired of your wildly inaccurate essays at pronouncing what to them is a marginal and meaningless component of their language, and they may therefore have decided to terminate your line of questioning by ratifying your pronunciation, even though it is still skewed and deviant.

It is also quite possible that your informants, in spite of their eagerness to assist you in your scheme, will lack the auditory and perceptual wherewithal to determine reliably whether or not your pronunciation is accurate. I once had a colleague, for example, who was unable to discriminate between l and r, even though he was able (on the basis of articulatory information) to pronounce them distinctly!

Should you actually manage to recreate something approaching the proper pronunciation, this still does not mean that you have discovered the articulatory strategies employed by your informants, because there is more than one way to produce each acoustic target.[22] Say, for example, that you are trying to reproduce a voiced obstruent of some sort. There are many articulatory activities that can be used to facilitate the production of voicing in obstruents, such as advancing the tongue root, lowering the larynx, and prenasalization. You may have managed to mimic the acoustic effects of obstruent voicing by lowering your larynx, but this does not imply that your informants lower their larynxes as well, rather than using one of the other voicing strategies.

One final danger of the mimicry technique is that your own ear may betray you. In other words, you may think that you have managed to get a sound exactly right, but actually be (in the words of one of my old teachers) "exactly wrong". Many times I have witnessed students in Field Methods classes insist that they have nailed the pronunciation of a foreign sound, only to be told by the informants that they haven't gotten it right.

---

[22] We assume that technically there is only one way of producing a specific acoustic signal, but this is not relevant for our purposes, since the sounds used by human languages are not unique acoustic signals, but rather abstract bundles of articulatory information that have general auditory cues.

1.6. Instrumental study of articulations

This exhausts the set of simple, unobtrusive methods for investigating unknown articulations. What we are left with is an array of instrumental techniques, which have the advantage of being highly reliable, but suffer from the disadvantage of being inconvenient and intrusive. (The discussion in this section is largely based on Stone 1997, which the interested reader should consult for further details on instrumental study of speech articulations.)

Measuring the activities of the vocal tract is very difficult, because the articulators differ greatly in speed and range of movement, structure, and location. Because of the diversity of articulators, there is no single instrument that can document the activities of all of the articulators satisfactorily. There are three basic kinds of instrumental techniques that can be used in different situations: imaging, point tracking, and measures of complex behaviors. In this section we review only the techniques that are relatively practical for a field linguist; this excludes costly and inconvenient options such as magnetic resonance imaging (MRI) and computed tomography (CT), for example. The serious reader should consult Stone 1997 for detailed discussion of these more complicated techniques.

We will mention here only two techniques that are used to examine articulations directly: palatography and electroglottography.

1.6.1. Palatography

Palatography involves the study of the palate and the articulators that come into contact with it. There are two types of palatograph, or devices for studying the deeds of the palate; one is relatively simple, and the other is less so.

The best way to determine what parts of the palate have been contacted by the tongue in a given word is to coat the tongue with a mixture of equal parts of olive oil and powdered charcoal

(Ladefoged 1997:160). You should then ask your informant to produce a word containing the consonant in which you are interested, and no other sound that requires touching the tongue to the palate. After the informant has done this, you should examine the palate using a mirror, preferably of the type employed by dentists, which you can insert easily into the informant's mouth. The parts of the palate touched by the tongue will now have a blackish color. These blackened areas reflect the sum of the articulatory contacts between the tongue and the palate in the pronunciation of the words investigated; they do not show the position of the tongue at any single moment.

When doing palatography, you should allow your informants to practice the task extensively. It is important for them to be able to relax after you have coated their tongues with the mixture, so that they speak naturally. When you are done with the technique, you should try to capture the results of your efforts on film, preferably with both a regular camera and a video recorder.

The advantages of using this type of palatography are that it is relatively easy to execute, it uses simple materials, and it is cheap. The disadvantages are that it is intrusive and awkward; it provides information about only one component of a speech event; it only provides information when the tongue touches the palate; and it only depicts the total sum of linguo-palatal contact during a given string of speech. Nevertheless, it can and has been used to good effect in the field by some phoneticians.

If you need more detailed information about the activity of different areas of the tongue and palate over a period of time, it is also possible to use a plastic pseudo-palate (Stone 1997:11). Pseudo-palates typically consist of a thin plastic mouthguard molded to the shape of the informant's palate and upper teeth; into this are affixed varying numbers of electrical contacts that send out an electrical signal when touched by the tongue. The advantages of pseudo-palates are that they document sequences of linguo-palatal contacts over time, rather than just a single sum of tongue activities; they can be used by laypeople with a relatively inexpensive computer system; and they do not flood informants with radiation. The drawbacks of pseudo-palates again are that they reflect only one component of a speech event and only provide information when the tongue touches the palate; furthermore, they tend (much like a sports mouthguard) to interfere with normal speech production, and the large numbers of electrical contacts and wires can unnerve your informants.

1.6.2. Electroglottography

If it is the larynx you're interested in, relatively direct observations of laryngeal activity can be made using an electroglottograph, a set of two electrodes placed on the surface of the neck, one on either side of the larynx. These electrodes provide an electrical signal proportional to the degree of contact between the vocal folds and to the movements of the larynx beneath the skin. In this way, it is possible to get a fairly accurate idea of the activities of the vocal folds during the production of speech (Ladefoged 1997:157, q.v. for further details concerning electroglottography).

1.6.3. Positive and negative aspects of instrumental techniques

The instrumental techniques outlined in this section have a number of positive qualities in their favor. They are very accurate relative to the more informal schemes sketched earlier in this chapter, and they are relatively devoid of human error. In addition, they provide results on a computer or on film that are easy for others to interpret. However, instrumental techniques for studying articulation also suffer from a plethora of problems. Many of the most scientifically useful devices employ X-rays, which may have been allowed when working with Siberian villagers in Soviet Russia, but are too dangerous to use in significant doses in this day and age (for this reason we have not mentioned any of the X-ray techniques here). In addition, all instrumental techniques except for pellet tracking systems and imaging techniques interfere with speech production, and even if they don't, they are typically too intrusive, involving electrodes in the mouth, tubes down the nose, and so on. Finally, the instruments themselves are generally prohibitively expensive, immobile and therefore impractical for field situations, they require an expert user, and they are too specialized to be able to capture all aspects of a speech event.

In sum, there is no perfect way of elucidating articulatory activities in regular field situations. The best compromise between usefulness and reliability of information on one hand and minimality of discomfort on the other is to use acoustic information. As Stone (1997:12) summarizes, "devising instruments that are non-invasive, unobtrusive,…and still measure one or more components of the speech event is so difficult that most researchers prefer to study the speech wave and infer physiological events from it." We therefore turn our attention to the study of the speech wave, or acoustic phonetics.

2. Acoustic phonetics

Sounds, accents, and all sorts of modulations…are the main source of energy for a language, and…make a given phrase, otherwise quite ordinary, uniquely appropriate.

Jean-Jacques Rousseau
On the Origin of Language

There are several reasons why it is advantageous for fieldworkers to develop an understanding of acoustic phonetics. Perhaps the most important of these reasons is that our intuitions are sometimes misleading. For example, people (whether linguistically trained or not) tend to fit unfamiliar sounds into the phonetic or phonological categories of their native language. The Nahuatl word for a popular taste treat, [ʃokolatɬ], was misheard by early European invaders as what eventually became our word *chocolate*. A bridge in Madras, India, was initially named after the engineer who built it, a man named Hamilton. This name contained several sounds and sequences not present in Tamil, the local language, and consequently was interpeted by the local residents as a more familiar sequence [ambuton]. (Interestingly, this pronunciation was later identified with the Tamil word *ambattan* 'barber', and the bridge subsequently came to be known as *Barber's Bridge*!)

The problem of unreliable hearing even infiltrates one's native language. English speakers, for example, tend to hear the plural morpheme in words such as *bees* as [-z], though normally it is in fact voiceless [-z̥], which in its voicelessness is closer to [s] than to [z]. This seems to be because the [-s] in this case is an allophone (variant pronunciation) of the English phoneme /z/, and speakers' perception of what they are saying is heavily influenced by its phonemic (mental) representation.[23] In studies of other near mergers, such as that between the medial vowels in *ferry* and *furry* in a dialect of Philadelphia, speakers who themselves produce an acoustically measurable distinction fail to distinguish the two

---

[23] This problem is so deeply ingrained in the case of the English plural that two professors of linguistics who read the first edition of this book wrote to "correct" us, saying that the plural in *bees* is definitely voiced. Both careful listening and acoustic study confirm that it is normally [z̥] in this situation; this has been corroborated in many phonetic studies (Pierrehumbert 1993, Pierrehumbert and Talkin 1992). Pierrehumbert and Talkin (1992) further note that "phrase-final voiced consonants are also typically devoiced" in English (109). Haggard (1978) reports that voiced fricatives in general are rarely voiced throughout in English and are particularly likely to be voiceless in word-final position. In his sample, 92% - 100% of the duration of final fricatives was voiceless.

phonemes reliably even when listening to recordings of their own speech (Pierrehumbert 2003).

Knowledge of acoustic phonetics is also important insofar as it enables you to interpret recordings, which are often the only document of a speech event. Even when you do have access to native speakers of the language in question, it is not always possible to parse what they say in real time, either because they are speaking too quickly, a noise in a nearby room distracted you, you dropped your pen, you momentarily lost consciousness, or you simply couldn't understand what they were saying. In these situations, as well as when you need to double check your field notes, the recordings you have made are often the only means by which you can figure out what is going on in the informants' speech.

Acoustic analysis also enables us to make very subtle observations that simply are not possible for the unaided ear. No matter how good your ears are, for example, it is impossible to measure the duration in milliseconds of voicing in stops in different contexts. Furthermore, it is not possible without quantitative measurements of this type to prove that there is a statistically significant difference between one group of stops and another, or between the sounds in two different languages.

For these reasons, we present in this chapter a brief overview of acoustic phonetics, focusing on the sorts of equipment you can use, how to use it, and how to analyze the data you obtain with it. Since the basic techniques and concepts of acoustic phonetics are well discussed elsewhere (see the suggested readings at the end of this chapter), the discussion we present here is relatively brief, being limited to the facts that are most relevant for beginning students and fieldworkers. We intentionally avoid discussing aerodynamic techniques, since these are too complicated and intrusive for introductory-level fieldwork; interested advanced readers should consult Ladefoged 1997.

2.1. Equipment[24]

In order to begin your study of acoustic phonetics, you need the right equipment.   For introductory fieldwork there are three essential pieces of equipment: a recording device, a microphone, and a computer speech analysis program.

2.1.1. The recording device

There are basically two ways of recording your informants—analog and digital.   Conventional tape recorders use analog technology, whereas digital audio tape (DAT) recorders, compact disc recorders, mini-disc recorders, digital video disc (DVD) recorders, and computers use digital technology. Digital recording devices are far superior to analog ones for our purposes, but we consider both below, since it is not possible for everyone to afford digital equipment or bring it into dangerous field situations.

Analog tape recorders have the advantage of being very affordable, easy to find in stores, and easy to purchase tapes for. However, they fall short in sound quality, durability, and speed control. The main shortcoming is that analog systems often do not have a large enough signal to noise ratio, which is the difference in intensity (loudness) between (1) the maximum signal that can be recorded without overloading the tape and (2) the background noise level. The signal to noise ratio should be at least 45 decibels (dB), but many analog recorders fail to reach this level of fidelity, which can hinder your attempts at acoustic analysis.

The second problem with analog recorders is that they store their information as a series of magnetized particles on a tiny strip of audio tape. This magnetic medium is very fragile, and in fact loses some of its magnetic charge (and hence some information in the original recording) every time you play the tape. Tapes like this of

---

[24] The discussion in this section is largely based on Ladefoged 1997, which the interested reader should peruse for further details.

course are also susceptible to demagnetization, which can destroy all of your data. Conversely, it often happens that magnetic images of sounds previously recorded on the tape fail to be removed by your newest recording, with the unpleasant result that you may hear old music or speech in the background when you play back your new recordings. You can avoid this problem by using only new blank tapes for your field recordings, or (if you must use old tapes) by demagnetizing the tapes before you record over them.

Another weakness of analog systems is that the recording heads become dirty over time, which compromises their ability to record new signals faithfully. This can be alleviated to a certain extent by cleaning the heads with a head-cleaning cassette, which may improve the frequency response in your system by as much as five kHz.

Finally, analog recordings made on tape recorders are notoriously prone to variations in tape speed, due to the wearing down of batteries, power surges, the difficulty of moving the tape at the beginning of the reel versus the end of the reel, and so on. These fluctuations in tape speed can be a significant nuisance when it comes time to analyze your recordings. You should therefore try, when using an analog device, to record a signal with a known frequency such as a tuning fork at the beginning and end of each session, so that you can check the speed of the recording during subsequent playbacks.

Should you decide to use an analog tape recorder, make sure to begin each session by recording the date, the place, the names of the speakers, fieldworkers, and whoever else is present, and the materials you will be using (if you are eliciting words from a specific dictionary, for example). It is important to mark your tapes in this way in case you lose the case in which the tape is normally kept.

We strongly recommend that you make your recordings in some digital medium, rather than with an analog tape recorder. The main reason for this is that any digital recording device is going to have a degree of sound fidelity far superior to that of any analog recorder. For example, the average DAT recorder has a signal to noise ratio of about 96 dB, more than twice the level you need to make high-quality recordings of speech. The frequency response, which is a measure of the ability of the recording device to reproduce the complete range of frequencies and their respective intensities in the original sound source, is also far superior in digital recording devices. If you are recording speech, a frequency response range of about 60 Hz to 12 kHz is quite sufficient, since human languages do not systematically manipulate frequencies above or below this zone. Any DAT machine can record frequencies in this range, but only a few analog systems have this capacity.

In addition to these advantages in the realm of acoustic fidelity, digital media also tend to be easier to manipulate, less susceptible to fluctuations in recording speed, and more durable. The catch is that DAT recorders currently cost about $500-1000, and other digital systems (especially computers) can cost even more. We recommend that you use a mini-disc recorder, which is both affordable (a good machine can be obtained for under $200) and easy to use.

No matter which type of recording scheme you choose, make sure that you check your recordings both during the session and as soon afterwards as possible, in order to make sure that you recorded everything successfully. Beware: it is not enough to see the recording level meter flashing up and down! I learned this lesson the hard way, when in the middle of recording a twenty-minute story from one of the last speakers of Zok (a language once spoken in Nakhichevan), I realized that I had forgotten to release the Pause button. (To make matters worse, the informant died before I could meet with him again...)

2.1.2. The microphone

The recording device that you select is only as good as the microphone that you use. For this reason, it is important to procure the best microphone that you can. You should of course make sure that it can register all of the frequencies that are produced in human speech, but you should also make sure that it does not add too much background noise to your system. Faulty cords and dirty connections often add excessive amounts of hiss, so be sure when assembling your recording system that your microphone and its cord do not suffer from these problems.

We recommend that you use a lip microphone, such as one often sees worn on the heads of pop singers who do a lot of dancing in their performances and therefore cannot use a conventional microphone. (These lip microphones now come with most voice recognition software programs.) Lip microphone systems actually contain two microphones, one pointed directly towards the speaker's mouth, and one pointed in the opposite direction. Any sound that is registered by both microphones is removed, with the desirable consequence that most background noise is excised from the signal. This is particularly important for field recordings, because extraneous noises that you may be able to weed out of your consciousness at the time will become surprisingly disruptive when you listen to your tapes later.

When you actually begin recording, make sure that the loudness of the signal is as great as possible without overloading the system. Loudness varies with the square of the distance between the sound source and the microphone, so for example a screaming baby ten feet away is four times quieter than a baby five feet away, and a hundred times quieter than a baby one foot away. Therefore it is important in situations with lots of background noise that you place your informant as close to the microphone as possible (without distorting the signal, of course). For the same reason, you should be sure to keep your informant a constant distance away from the microphone. Lip microphones produce both of these results simply and effectively, whereas it can be much more difficult with a conventional hand-held microphone.

Most computers now come with a microphone, so you can digitize your speech directly into the computer. A setup of this sort has the advantage of avoiding all the intermediate wiring required in the systems described above. We strongly recommend that you use a high-quality lip microphone rather than the microphone that comes with the computer, though, because the latter type tends to be of relatively low quality, and typically does not attach to the speaker's head, thereby sacrificing stability. Recording directly into a computer is also impractical in field situations, unless you have a portable computer. If possible, you should try to record your informants on computer and on tape simultaneously. If you must choose one or the other, though, record directly into the computer, because this system is more flexible, allowing for immediate playback of any portion of the recording that you select. This is extremely convenient when you need to contrast two sounds or listen to an individual sound many times, whereas the same tasks are very difficult with tape systems.

2.1.3. Computer software for speech analysis

Once you have made your recordings, you need to enter them into your computer in a form that can be interpreted by a speech analysis program. Most newer computers can digitize recordings directly from a sound source plugged into one of their input ports, so we will not discuss specific digital converters here. However, you will need to know a few things about how the recordings are converted into digital form in order to make the best use of your materials.

Sound waves are digitized by sampling various characteristics of the waveform at specific time intervals. The frequency of these intervals, which is called the sampling rate, must be at least two times the frequency of the highest frequency component in the waveform; to be safe, you should use a sampling rate of 2.5 times the highest frequency used in speech. Since, as we mentioned earlier, human speech manipulates frequencies of up to 12 kHz, the sampling rate you use to digitize your recordings should be at least 30 kHz. Many newer computers allow the user to sample at 44 kHz, so this requirement should not pose a problem.

When the computer samples the waveform, it can measure features such as frequency and amplitude within a certain range of values. A 16-bit sampling system, for example, can distinguish between 32,000 different levels of amplitude (or whatever component of the wave is being considered), which provides a signal to noise ratio of 96 dB. An 8-bit system can distinguish 256 levels of amplitude, with a signal to noise ratio of 48 dB, which is still better than that of most tape recorders. Obviously, you want to configure your system to the highest possible bit setting, so that the maximum number of levels of amplitude, etc. can be distinguished.

Once you have digitized your recordings, you can begin manipulating them with speech analysis software. Some useful commerical programs for both beginning and advanced users include KayPENTAX's *Multi-Speech* and *Computerized Speech Lab (CSL)* (http://www.kayelemetrics.com/), Agora Language Marketplace's *Signalyze* (http://www.signalyze.com/; available for Macintosh only), and instruNet's *Soundscope* (http://www.instrunet.com/; available for Macintosh only). Freely-available software packages are frequently as sophisticated and as easy to use as commerical products. WaveSurfer from the Royal Institute of Technology in Stockholm (http://www.speech.kth.se/wavesurfer/) and Praat (http://www.fon.hum.uva.nl/praat/) run on Windows, Macintosh, and Linux. SFS/WASP from University College London (http://www.phon.ucl.ac.uk/resource/sfs/wasp.htm), the CSLU

Toolkit (http://cslu.cse.ogi.edu/toolkit/index.html), and SIL's Speech
Analyzer (http://www.sil.org/computing/speechtools/download.htm)
are currently available for Windows only.

2.2. Analyzing acoustic data

You can use any of the software just mentioned, together with the
digitized versions of your informants' speech, to elucidate a wide
range of phonetic questions. With just a few techniques of acoustic
analysis, you can clarify what vowels you are hearing; whether
consonants are aspirated or voiced; whether vowels are nasalized;
whether a given segment is a singleton (short) or a geminate (long);
and so on. It is also possible to study more complex issues such as
the effects that neighboring consonants and vowels have on each
other.

2.2.1. Analytic techniques

The main technique that you will need to master in order to study the
acoustic properties of speech is **spectrographic analysis**.
Spectrographic analysis makes use of spectrograms, which graph
three variables: frequency on the vertical axis, time on the horizontal
axis, and intensity in terms of the relative darkness of the individual
points on the graph. Spectrograms are of two basic types: **narrow-
band** spectrograms are more accurate with frequencies than with
time distinctions, and **wide-band** spectrograms are more accurate
with time divisions than with frequencies.

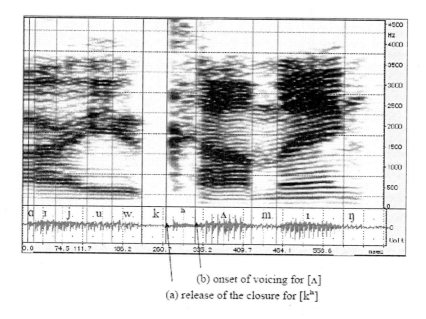

(b) onset of voicing for [ʌ]

(a) release of the closure for [kʰ]

Figure 1. Narrow-band spectrogram of the question "are you coming?"

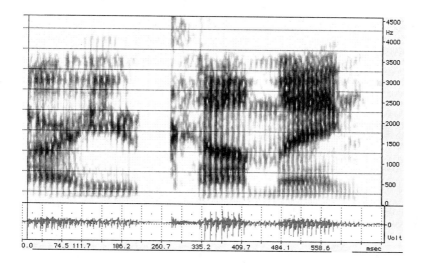

Figure 2. Wide-band spectrogram of the question "are you coming?"

Narrow-band spectrograms have the advantage of allowing you to study closely individual harmonics (multiples of the fundamental frequency, the rate at which the vocal folds come together), but they also make it difficult to discern the formant structure of an utterance. Wide-band spectrograms are good for identifying formants, but bad for identifying individual harmonics. Since it is generally more useful to know about formants than about harmonics, we recommend that you concentrate on producing wide-band spectrograms.

The formants we just alluded to are frequencies which a given configuration of the vocal tract allows to emerge with the greatest intensity. The reason that formants are so important for acoustic analysis is that they are one of the primary acoustic correlates of different sounds; in other words, sounds are most readily discriminated by their different formant structures. We return to this topic in the next section.

Spectrograms can also be used to study pitch, voice onset time, aspiration, and segment length. Pitch (roughly equivalent to fundamental frequency) values can be inferred from the values of the harmonics in narrow-band spectrograms, since, as we mentioned earlier, the harmonics are simply multiples of the fundamental frequency. Voice onset time can be read directly off of either type of spectrogram (though it is perhaps easier with wide-band spectrograms), by noting the time span between the release of a consonantal closure and the point at which voicing begins. For example, we have marked the release of the closure of the [kʰ] in figure 1 with an (a), and we have marked with a (b) the beginning of voicing in the vowel following the [kʰ]. The difference between these two points indicates that the VOT for this particular [kʰ] is about 50 milliseconds.

Aspiration can be measured in the same way, since it typically occurs in the period between closure release and voicing onset. Segmental length can be measured simply by determining the space on the horizontal axis occupied by the segment in question. For example, we can use this method to determine that the [ʌ] in figure 1 is approximately 80 milliseconds long.

Other analytic techniques that can be useful for beginning fieldworkers include pitch tracking, linear predictive coding (LPC), and FFT plotting. FFT (Fast Fourier Transform) plots the amplitude of individual spectral components, and therefore enables you to determine the formant frequencies at a given point in an utterance. It is important to maximize the number of FFT points plotted by your software, for the same reason that we mentioned earlier when discussing the sampling of amplitude. In figure 3 we provide in the upper right hand corner a wide-band FFT plot for the Italian word [pia], together with an LPC plot of the spectrum of a slice of the [i] in the lower right corner. Both the FFT and LPC graphs indicate spectral peaks at about 350 and 2400 Hz, corresponding to the expected first and second formants respectively for [i].

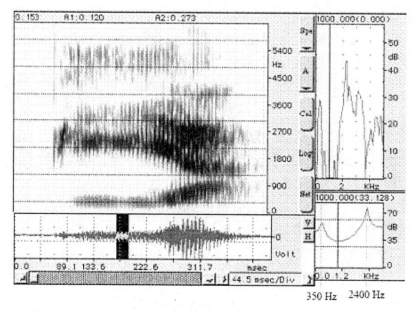

Figure 3. Italian [pia]

2.2.2. Acoustic correlates

As we mentioned in the previous section, formants play a central role in distinguishing the acoustic signatures of different speech sounds. However, certain other components of the acoustic signal are important as well. In this section, we survey the primary acoustic correlates of the main categories of sounds.

Vowels can be distinguished in terms of the values for the first and second formants, and to a lesser extent the third formant. As you can see in figure 4, the first formant (F_1) correlates with vowel height: the higher the tongue position during the production of a vowel, the lower the value of its first formant. The second formant (F_2) correlates with backness: the further back the tongue is during the production of a vowel, the lower the value of its second formant will be.

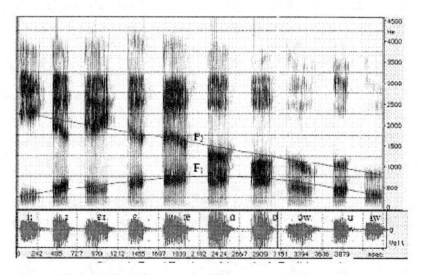

Figure 4. F_1 and F_2 values of the author's English vowels

You can keep track of these acoustic correlates by memorizing the general shape of the chart below:

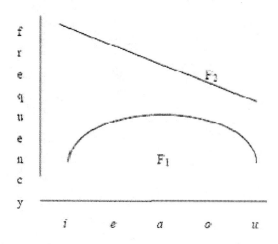

Note that the distinctions reflected in this chart are relative; one can say that [i] has a lower F_1 than [a], but one cannot identify a specific frequency value for the first formant of [i], [a], or any other vowel (cf. Peterson and Barney 1952).

The acoustic correlates of consonant types are slightly more complicated. Fricatives, especially sibilants (i.e. *s*-type sounds) are characterized by loud random noise in the frequency range between 2 and 8 kHz. This is exemplified in the spectrogram below for the English voiceless fricatives [f], [θ], [s], and [ʃ]. (Note that in my speech the fricative noise extends beyond 12 kHz.)

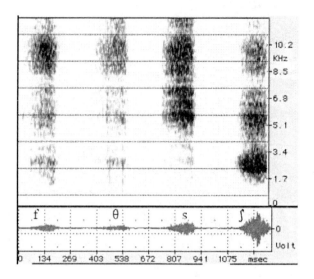

Figure 5. English voiceless fricatives

Nasals typically have broad resonance peaks (which you can see as dark horizontal lines on a spectrogram) at about 250 Hz, 2500 Hz, and 3250 Hz (though the latter two are often harder to see). If you look carefully at the portion of the spectrogram corresponding to the labial nasal [m] and the velar nasal [ŋ] in figure 2, you should be able to identify all three of these resonance peaks.

Stops are readily identified as periods of silence on a spectrogram, reflecting the fact that no noise comes out of the vocal tract when it is completely closed at some point along its length. This can be seen, for example, in the spectrographic representation of the [kʰ] in figure 1. Voiced stops, however, may have a small horizontal line at the bottom of the spectrogram, reflecting the frequency of the vibration of the vocal folds.

Differences in place of articulation can also sometimes be inferred from spectrograms. Often the best clue is the formant transitions between the consonant in question and a neighboring vowel. Labial consonants (as well as round vowels, unsurprisingly) can be identified by the fact that they begin with relatively low formants, which then typically rise when the consonantal closure is released. Coronal consonants typically have relatively high second and third formants. Dorsal consonants can often be identified by the so-called "velar pinch", which refers to a convergence of the second and third formants during the periods immediately before and after the consonantal closure. For example, if you look closely at the portion of the spectrogram in figure 1 that corresponds to the sequence [ɪŋ], you should see that the second and third formants of the [ɪ] draw closer together as the tongue moves into a position to produce the velar [ŋ].

Suggested Readings
Interested readers should consult Ladefoged 1993, chapter 1, 5, 7, and 8, and Ladefoged 1997 for further elaboration on all of the points raised here, as well as other topics that are more appropriate for more advanced students. Much more advanced and detailed discussion can be found in Stevens 1998, chapters 1-10.

Hollingsworth, Kenneth. 1999. The MiniDisc: a better way to do field recordings. Notes on Anthropology 3.4:56-63.

Hunt, Geoffrey. 1992. The indispensable tape recorder. Notes on Linguistics 56:5-9.

Ladefoged, Peter. 1993. A Course in Phonetics, Third Edition. Fort Worth: Harcourt Brace Jovanovich Publishers.

Ladefoged, Peter. 1997. Instrumental Techniques for Linguistic Phonetic Fieldwork. In William Hardcastle and John Laver, eds., The Handbook of Phonetic Sciences. Oxford: Blackwell.

Ladefoged, Peter. 2003. Phonetic Data Analysis: An introduction to phonetic fieldwork and instrumental techniques. Oxford: Blackwell.

Stevens, Ken. 1998. Acoustic Phonetics. Cambridge: MIT Press.

Stone, Maureen. 1997. Laboratory Techniques for Investigating Speech Articulation. In William Hardcastle and John Laver, eds., The Handbook of Phonetic Sciences. Oxford: Blackwell.

Exercises

1. Your informant speaks Tigrinya, which has an interesting set of ejective fricatives. Describe a way in which you might get her to produce an accurate and reliable description of these sounds.

2. You only have access to your informant over the phone, because he has moved permanently to Daghestan. How might you construct a reasonable description of the articulatory phonetics of his language?

3. Describe the articulatory activities involved in your own production of the sound *t* in *ten*, *stop*, *hat*, and *tree*.

4. Describe the articulatory activities involved in your own production of a bilabial click (the sound you make when pretending to kiss someone from afar).

5. Describe the articulatory activities involved in your own production of the sound *r* in *car* and *bird*.

6. Pick four sounds in the language spoken by your informants, two "easy" (i.e. similar to ones in English) and two "hard" (i.e. unlike any of the sounds in the languages you speak). Ask your informants to describe how they produce these sounds, and note down what they respond. Discuss any difficulties that arise, including stumbling blocks you encountered in getting them to produce relatively scientific rather than impressionistic descriptions. For the sounds you were more familiar with, discuss how the informants' descriptions compared to your knowledge of the articulatory gestures involved.

7. Provide a description of the phonetic system of the language you are studying, following the model of the "Illustrations" in the Journal of the International Phonetic Association, such as the treatment of Irish by Ní Chasaide 1995.

8. The following spectrogram represents the sentence *I don't want to sew it up*, pronounced by a male speaker of American English. (i) Transcribe the sentence as you think the man would have pronounced it. (ii) Match your transcription with the spectrogram, indicating for each symbol in the transcription the portion of the spectrogram to which it corresponds. Try to follow the model provided in figure 1 in this chapter.

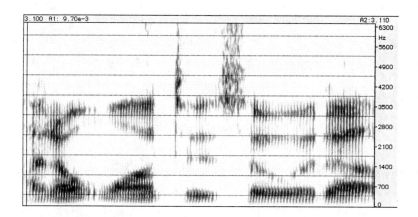

7   Identifying sound patterns: Phonology

Phonology frees us from a kind of nightmare which had weighed upon us.

Antoine Meillet, quoted by Jakobson
Six Lectures on Sound and Meaning

1. Introduction

In this chapter we present the basic phonological components that one finds in human languages, and we discuss various ways in which the structure of these components can be elucidated in the language spoken by your informants.   We first consider phonological processes that apply to individual sound segments, and then we turn to phenomena that affect larger phonological domains such as syllables and words.

In order to carry out the basic phonological research that is described in this chapter, it is necessary to be familiar with a few fundamental concepts of phonological theory. For our purposes, the most basic of these concepts is that words have two different forms: the one that we store in our memory, and the one that we pronounce. Take, for example, the English negative morpheme[25] that we find in words such as *inept, indecent,* and *incapable*. Let us assume that we store this negative morpheme in our brains as /ɪn-/. How then do we account for the fact that this morpheme is actually pronounced in several different ways? In *impossible*, for example, it is pronounced as [ɪm-], in *incapable* it is pronounced as [ɪŋ-], and in *inept* it is pronounced as [ɪn-]. The answer to this question is that the forms that we store in our brains, or *underlying representations*, can be

---

[25] Loosely speaking, a morpheme is the minimal unit of meaning in a language. In English, for example, *dogs* contains two morphemes: *dog*, which means 'a domesticated carnivorous animal, *canis familiaris*', and *-s*, which means 'plural'. For more details, see chapters 8.

affected by various types of *rules*, which cause the actual pronunciations of individual words—*surface representations*—to differ from their underlying representations.

In the case of *impossible*, for example, the underlying form is /ɪn-pɑsɪbl̩/. This undergoes a rule that requires /n/ to have the same place of articulation as a following consonant. The result of this rule is that the *n* assimilates to the labial place of articulation of the following *p*, thereby becoming *m*. The surface representation that ends up being pronounced therefore is [ɪmpʰɑsɪbəl] (we discuss in the next paragraph the rule that aspirates the p). The derivation of the word *impossible* can be schematized as follows:

underlying representation	/ɪn-pɑsɪbl̩/
	↓
ə-insertion	ɪnpɑsɪbəl
	↓
nasal place assimilation	ɪmpɑsɪbəl
	↓
aspiration	ɪmpʰɑsɪbəl
	↓
surface representation	[ɪmpʰɑsɪbəl]

Rules that apply to individual segments, which are the sort we will focus on in this chapter, have the effect of producing different surface pronunciations of single underlying segments. The underlying forms of these segments are called *phonemes*; the different surface forms in which a given phoneme appears are called *allophones*. The English phoneme /t/, for example, has several different allophones:

- voiceless unaspirated [t] in *stop, mistake*, etc.
- aspirated [tʰ] in *top, pretend*, etc.

- flapped [ɾ] in *later, party*, etc.
- glottalized and unreleased [ˀt̚] in (the American pronunciation of) *hat, Atlantic*, etc.
- palatal affricate [tʃ] in *tree, betray*, etc.[26]

In this chapter we will be interested in the questions of how one identifies the allophones that are used in a given language, and how we can figure out the rules and constraints that produce these allophones from the inventory of phonemes in the language. These ultimately reduce to the same question, since identifying allophones goes hand in hand with identifying rules and constraints, and vice versa. In what follows, we break our consideration of this question into two parts, the first dealing with rules, and the second with constraints.

2. How to identify phonological rules

In order to identify rules in the language you are studying, you will first need to find alternations between different segments. These alternations can be either within a paradigm (as in the case of the vowel in Spanish *tengo* 'I have' vs. *tienes* 'you have'), within a single morpheme (as with English *in-*), or within a single segment in different environments (as with the allophones of English /t/ mentioned earlier). Identifying these alternations is essentially the same task as identifying the allophones in the language you are studying.

There are various ways of going about this task. The easiest way is to draw your information from existing grammars or dictionaries; if tools of this type are available for your language, you should make sure to consult them. However, these rarely contain all

---

[26] This allophone of /t/ is actually produced with a tongue position intermediate between that of [t] and of [tʃ], but we have used [tʃ] here for typographical convenience.

of the information you will need to construct a reasonable model of the phonological component of your informant's grammar: published descriptions tend to be incomplete, your informant's dialect may well differ from the one described in the dictionary or grammar, and so on. You therefore must check all published descriptions of the language against your own field notes. Sometimes, simply asking your informants directly whether or not their dialect contains a phonological rule that you have read about can be very effective.

But what should you do when there are no relevant materials written about your language? In this case, there are two ways to investigate the phonological system. If you have the right kind of informants, you can of course ask them if they have noticed any alternations in their own language. This can produce surprisingly useful results, but often does not. It is important to remember that speakers typically are not aware of fast speech and allophonic rules (that is, rules that produce sounds that are not part of the phonemic inventory of the language). For example, if you were to ask speakers of English if their language contains any alternations between different sounds, they might well think of [k] ~ [s] in *electric* : *electricity*, [i:] ~ [ɛ] in *serene* : *serenity*, and so on. On the other hand, they would almost certainly be unaware of rules such as *s*-retroflexion (*street* → [ʃtʃɹiːˀtˀ]), aspiration (*pin* → [pʰɪn]), devoicing (*bun* → [b̥ʌn] or [pʌn]), and palatalization (*keep* → [cʰip]). In fact, most individuals would probably also fail to notice more obvious phenomena such as the *t*-insertion that many speakers have in words like *else* [ɛlts] and *false* [fɑlts].

You should also be aware of the fact that literate speakers are often influenced heavily by spelling. Surprisingly often, speakers will try to alter their pronunciation to match what they know to be the spelling of a given word, particularly when they are speaking carefully. Even when they do not alter their pronunciation, informants are generally reluctant to acknowledge that their pronunciation differs from the sequence of letters in the official orthography. For example, speakers of English will typically insist that the *p*'s in *pit* and *spit* are the same, even though the former is aspirated and the latter is not. Moreover, speakers of dialects which possess sounds not found in the literary dialect will deny that they pronounce these sounds differently from the standard. For example, one of my informants who speaks a nonstandard dialect of Armenian initially insisted to me that the palatalized consonants he was producing were *not* palatalized. The reason for this was that these particular palatalized sounds correspond to non-palatalized sounds in standard Armenian. Ironically, once I had demonstrated to his satisfaction that his sounds were in fact different from their standard Armenian equivalents (in this case, by pointing out the parallel to his other native language, Russian, which also contains both plain and palatalized consonants), he promptly began to scold me every time I had difficulty discerning whether a consonant he had just produced was palatalized or not!

To sum up, you cannot always count on your informants to produce reliable insights into the workings of their phonological systems. When this comes to pass, you are limited to making your own observations based on the lexicographical and other data you have collected. There are two keys to carrying out this procedure successfully: (1) look at individual sounds to see if they alternate in different phonological contexts or in different members of a paradigm; (2) look for common phonological processes, because some of these are bound to occur in your language. We consider the second strategy in more detail in section 5, and focus here on the first strategy.

When you are basing your analysis solely on data you have collected from your informants, you need to beware of productive phonological processes. Oftentimes, segments optionally undergo either a productive rule or a more restricted rule, and you want to avoid missing the latter type, which you are much less likely to hear employed by your informants. For example, the English word *hat* can be pronounced either as [hæ$^{?}$t˥] or as [hæt^h]; the former pronunciation results from the application of an optional rule of glottalization, and the latter results from the productive rule of aspiration that applies to stops when no other rules have applied. If you are having American informants produce words in isolation, you are likely to hear only [hæt^h], whereas if you are eliciting only casual connected speech, you are likely to hear only [hæ$^{?}$t˥] (or [hæɾ] before a vowel, as in *that hat is ugly*), and never [hæt^h]. How can one go about finding rules that are restricted in their occurrence, and are often superseded by productive rules? As in similar situations discussed earlier, you can always try to read grammars of the language in advance, to see what sorts of rules are already known to exist. You can also ask your informants if they know of any other ways of producing a given form: asking this of an American a propos of [hæt^h] might elicit the alternate pronunciation [hæ$^{?}$t˥], for example. Rules that are more restricted in their application and distribution are also more likely to appear in connected speech than in careful speech, so it is a good idea to collect texts, conversations, and so on.

One last tip: resist the common temptation to fall into despair about finding alternations and rules in the language you are studying. One of the most common reactions in students examining a language for the first time is "this language is completely straightforward! It has no rules!" Your informants will generally be all too happy to contribute to this notion, for various reasons that will become clear to you when you start working with them. Rest assured, though, that *all* languages have rules, and lots of them. Stick to your guns, follow the guidelines we set out in this chapter, and you will soon have more rules than you bargained for.

3. How to identify phonological constraints

Constraints can be a bit more difficult to identify than rules. The reason for this is that constraints are often static: they do not appear as alternations within a paradigm or changes to a segment in a specific environment, but rather they manifest themselves as generalizations over the entire vocabulary. In order to find constraints, you therefore need to identify possibilities that *could* exist, but do not. For example, students are taught in English-speaking schools that we form comparatives by adding *-er*, and superlatives by adding *-est*: *fast, faster, fastest*. What they are not taught is that there is a constraint which holds over these two morphemes. This constraint disallows the addition of *-er* and *-est* to words containing two or more syllables: **expensiver, *expensivest; *intelligenter, *intelligentest; *decayeder, *decayedest, *oftener.* (Some bisyllabic words that end in an unstressable syllable are also allowed, such as adjectives in *-y* and *-ow*: *happier, narrower*, etc.) English has many other constraints, including one that disallows verbs formed by adding *-ize* to adjectives with final stress (**corruptize*, etc.), one that disallows syllables beginning with ŋ-, one that disallows the short lax vowels {ɪ ɛ ʊ} from occurring in word-final position, and so on.

If you are going to identify phonological constraints in the language you are studying, you will have to do a lot of work on your own time. It will help to pore over the data you have collected, looking for environments where a specific phoneme should be able to occur but doesn't, cases where you expect a certain morpheme to appear but it doesn't, and so on. We will not discuss these techniques in detail here, because by and large they do not require working with an informant, and the tricks involved are more properly the domain of an introductory textbook on phonology and morphology (we recommend Swadesh 1934, for example).

However, there are two constraint-related activities you can engage in with your informants. (1) You can directly ask them if they know of any constraints on the distribution of segments or morphemes in their language. This can be facilitated by giving examples of constraints in English or another language with which both you and they are familiar. The direct interrogation method normally does not work, but it can't hurt to try, and you may obtain some useful results. (2) You can use your informants to verify or disprove constraints that you think may exist in their language. This is an extremely rewarding technique, as it does not require informants to conduct any conscious analysis of their language. If you present your informants with a list of forms violating the constraint you have postulated, they will normally be able to say immediately whether these forms are acceptable or not. They may also be able to produce counterexamples immediately if you present them with a generalization you have come up with, such as "there are no words that begin with [ŋ]". We highly recommend this strategy, because it can save you dozens of hours looking for counterexamples yourself in dictionaries and grammars.

4. Constructing a phonological analysis

When you are constructing your phonological analysis by identifying rules and constraints, two major concerns will inevitably arise. The first involves the point at which you should begin constructing a phonological analysis relative to the point where you start collecting data. The second involves the intellectual and mechanical challenge of selecting underlying forms.

4.1. When to conduct a phonological analysis

There are two schools of thought on the question of when to begin constructing a phonological analysis. One camp, of which the phonetician Peter Ladefoged is a notable proponent, maintains that you should begin phonological analysis immediately when conducting fieldwork (cf. Ladefoged 1997). In a certain sense, it is impossible to do otherwise, because one cannot transcribe without having conducted some amount of phonological analysis—one needs to have decided what sounds are different and what sounds are not, what to write down and what not to write down, how much detail to write down, and so on. Each of these decisions involves a fundamental sort of phonological analysis, without which fieldwork would not be possible. Let us put aside this technical point, though, and assume instead that by phonological analysis we actually mean *conscious*, *intentional* phonological analysis. There are at least two advantages to beginning this sort of analysis as soon as you start collecting field data. (1) When you analyze your data immediately, it is much easier to know what questions to ask next, or at least in the next session. Explicit formulation of an analysis has a way of revealing flaws in your thought processes that would otherwise have remained blissfully and dangerously unnoticed. These flaws can then be tested and corrected through further questioning of your informants. (2) If you go over your data immediately, you can check your transcriptions for consistency. Especially in the first few sessions, you are likely to mishear many forms, unless you check all data rigorously with your informants as soon as you collect them. By looking over your field notes, you may be able to catch some of your transcription errors when you compare related forms. The problem with this strategy, though, is that you may go too far in your corrections, and remove variations that result from the application of phonological rules, and are not actually mistakes in transcription.

This problem is the *pou sto* of the other school of thought, which maintains that it is not a good idea to begin phonological analysis right away. It is better, the reasoning goes, to let the data take you where they will, unhindered by your biases and expectations. This strategy can work very well for fieldworkers with excellent ears, but needs to be tempered somewhat for individuals who have difficulties with transcription. Linguists who can only work with a particular set of informants for a limited period of time should also steer clear of the late analysis philosophy, in order to avoid discovering after their time has elapsed that they missed or mistranscribed key information.

4.2. How to pick an underlying form

When you finally get down to the business of analyzing the data you have collected, one of the most fundamental questions you will have to grapple with is how to pick an underlying form for a given segment, morpheme, or word. (In case you are wondering why it is necessary to bother coming up with underlying forms when doing fieldwork: having a phonemic analysis in your head that can generate appropriate underlying forms for the data that your informants produce can add consistency to your transcriptions, clarify what information you need to collect from your informants, help you create a phonemic writing system for the language, and so on.) Let us take a concrete example, the allophones of English /t/. Recall from our earlier discussion that there are five types of *t*-sounds: [t], [tʰ], [ɾ], [ˀt˺], and [tʃ]. Assuming that these are all allophones of a single phoneme, how do we decide what the form of this phoneme is? In almost all cases, you want to select one of the surface allophones, rather than some other segment that never actually appears. With the five allophones above, for example, it does not make sense to postulate the voiceless uvular stop /q/ as the underlying phoneme from which they all are derived, unless you have extremely strong evidence in favor of such an abstract analysis. The particular allophone that you choose as the underlying form should be the one from which it is easiest to derive the other allophones, via simple, well-motivated rules. By this reasoning it would not make sense to derive our five allophones from [tʃ], because we would then have to postulate a large set of problematic rules, such as one changing /tʃ/ to [tʰ] at the beginning of stressed syllables, in order to account for words such as *tap* [tʰæp]. This rule is not only implausible phonetically, but also predicts that words such as *choose* should be pronounced *[tʰuːz], and so on. It turns out in this particular case that the best candidate for the underlying form is /t/, because we can derive the other allophones from this via relatively straightforward rules. By "straightforward rules" we mean the type of rules that are common cross-linguistically, and plausible phonetically. We enumerate some rules of this type in section 5.

Beware that with some sets of allophones, it may not be easy to identify the underlying form. Turkish has a high vowel, for example, which surfaces as [i], [y], [ɨ], or [u], depending on the phonological context in which it occurs. Each of these allophones can be derived with equal ease from each of the other allophones, so it is extremely difficult to pick any one of them over the others as the underlying form. In cases like this, it is normally acceptable to shelve the task of picking a phonemic representation.

5. Common phonological processes

If you are having trouble identifying phonological rules and constraints in spite of the advice we have given so far, it can be very helpful to look out for common phonological phenomena. We provide below a list of phonological phenomena which are so common cross-linguistically that we guarantee you will find at least a few of them in whatever language you choose to study.

- Consonant-vowel interactions, such as **palatalization** (e.g. /k/ and /g/ become [c] and [ɟ] respectively before front vowels in English), **nasalization** (e.g. vowels become nasalized before nasal consonants in English), and **rounding** (e.g. English consonants are often pronounced with lip rounding before round vowels in the careful speech of older speakers).

- **Aspiration**, typically of voiceless consonants at the beginning of syllables, and sometimes of consonants at the end of words.
- **Unrelease** of consonants at the end of a syllable (i.e. before other consonants or at the end of a word).
- **Voicing** of consonants after nasals, between vowels, or adjacent to voiced consonants.
- **Devoicing** of consonants in word-initial position, in word-final position, or adjacent to voiceless consonants.
- **Simplification** of consonant clusters and affricates (e.g. the common American pronunciation of [lɪfs] for *lifts*, etc.).
- **Epenthesis** (insertion) of vowels in unpronounceable consonant clusters (e.g. English [ɹɪðəm] for *rhythm*), epenthesis of consonants either between two vowels, at the beginning of a vowel-initial word, or in certain kinds of consonant clusters (typically a nasal followed by a sonorant or a fricative, e.g. [sʌmpθɪŋ] for *something*).
- **Glide insertion** between two vowels.
- **Deletion** of vowels next to other vowels, and of consonants next to other consonants or at the end of a word.
- **Assimilation** to the place of articulation of a following segment, particularly by nasals (cf. the *in-* morpheme discussed earlier).

6. Stress

What's the difference between a rheumatic man and a healthy man who lives with his parents? One is well at some times and has a rheumatism others, and the other is well at all times and has a room at his mother's.

Leonard Bloomfield
The Study of Language[27]

Linguists use the term 'stress' to refer to portions of a word or utterance (normally vowels or syllables) that are relatively prominent ('accent' is sometimes used to refer to the same phenomenon). This prominence normally appears as greater volume or intensity, but can also involve relatively high or low pitch (q.v. section 8). All languages have stress systems of some sort, but unfortunately it is not always easy to figure out how the stress system in a given language works, either because the system itself is very complicated, or simply because it is difficult to discern where the stresses are.

6.1. Identifying stress

There are a few tricks that you can use to help you identify stresses if you are having trouble hearing them. One option, of course, is to ask your informants where they feel the stresses occur in a given word or phrase. Sadly, this method is not always reliable, because native speakers often are not aware that they assign stresses to words, and even if they are aware of this fact, they tend to be unsure of where the stresses fall, and may consequently give you inaccurate judgements. Furthermore, people are typically unable to identify secondary stresses in their language consistently, so you will have to rely on your own judgement to discern these.

You can also make your life easier when identifying stresses by bearing in mind that languages use only a limited number of

---

[27] If you don't get the point of this quote, try pronouncing it aloud.

different stress systems.   These systems fall into three basic categories: alternating, non-alternating, and lexical. We will not consider lexical systems here, because in these each word has an idiosyncratic stress, and it is therefore difficult or impossible to predict where the stress will fall in a given word. We will consider alternating stress systems in section 6.3. In non-alternating systems there is only one stress per word, which always falls on the same syllable or vowel, regardless of the length of the word.   (But beware—most such languages have isolated exceptions!)   The particular syllable or vowel that languages of this type choose is always either the first, second, last, or second-to-last (= penultimate) syllable.   In French and Armenian, for example, stress always falls on the last full vowel of a word, whereas Icelandic, Czech, and Hungarian stress the initial syllable, and the Armenian dialects spoken in Karabagh and Nakhichevan stress the penultimate full vowel.

Each of these stress types can be sensitive to prosodic weight; in other words, it can treat heavy syllables differently than light syllables. (Some languages treat only syllables containing long vowels as heavy; others add all syllables ending in one or more consonants to this category. All syllables not considered heavy are light.) Mongolian, for example, stresses the first heavy vowel in each word. This is analogous to the initial-stress systems such as we find in Icelandic, except that only heavy syllables, rather than all syllables, are considered when identifying the first syllable in a word. (When a Mongolian word contains no heavy syllables, the initial syllable is stressed.) As a result, if the stress system in the language you are working on is sensitive to prosodic weight, you can generally get an idea of where the stress will fall in a given word on the basis of its segmental structure.

6.2. Secondary stress

Many languages distinguish various levels of secondary stress, in addition to the primary stresses just discussed. These are naturally even more difficult to identify than primary stresses, but yet again there are a few tricks you can use to identify their presence. One technique involves looking for interactions between secondary stresses and other phonological rules that are more readily observed.

Stress Clash, for example, typically demotes or deletes the primary stress and promotes a secondary stress to its place. Consider the word *Illinois*, which is pronounced with primary stress on the final syllable and secondary stress on the initial syllable. If we add to this *River*, which has initial stress, we create a Stress Clash, i.e. a situation where two stresses are adjacent: *Illinóis River*. English, like most languages, dislikes adjacent stresses, and in this case demotes the first of them. When the stress on *-nois* is demoted, the secondary stress on *Ill-* becomes the primary stress, yielding the form we actually pronounce, *Íllinois River*. Once we know that stress clash in English leads to the promotion of secondary stresses, we can use this knowledge to infer for example that the *New* in *New York* must have a secondary stress rather than being stressless, because of the related form *Nèw York Cíty*.

Secondary stresses also block the application of some phonological rules, such as vowel reduction and flapping in English. The first *a* in *Alabama*, for example, fails to undergo the rule that reduces the second and fourth *a*'s to [ə], because it bears a secondary stress (àlabáma). Similarly, the first *t* in *rotate* fails to become a flap (ɾ]) because it precedes a secondary stress (cf. *rotor* [ˈɹəwɾɹ]).

As with primary stresses, you can also facilitate your identification of secondary stresses by being aware of the typology of stress systems. For example, it is useful to be aware that the non-alternating systems mentioned earlier can also have a single secondary stress on a specific syllable. Armenian, to take one example, invariably assigns secondary stress to the initial syllable.

This brings us to the last variety of stress system, which involves alternating stress. Systems of this type differ from non-alternating systems only in terms of the secondary stresses, which are assigned to alternating syllables rather than to a single specific syllable. These systems come in four varieties:

1. Primary stress on the first syllable, secondary stress on alternate following syllables (x́xx̀xx̀x..., as in English *Ténnessèè Titans, Míssissìppi River*, etc.; also in languages such as Maranungku).
2. Primary stress on the last syllable, secondary stress on alternate preceding syllables (...xx̀xx̀xx́, e.g. in Weri).
3. Primary stress on the penultimate syllable, secondary stress on alternate preceding syllables (...xx̀xx̀x́x, e.g. in Warao).
4. Primary stress on the second syllable, secondary stress on alternate following syllables (xx́xx̀xx̀x..., e.g. in Araucanian).

If the language you are studying belongs to one of these varieties, it should be relatively easy to identify secondary stresses. Nonetheless, you should always listen carefully to the forms produced by your informants, because you never know when they might produce a form that violates your expectations.

One final trick that you can use to identify primary and secondary stresses involves poetic meter. Many languages employ in their poetry various types of meter, which typically refer to word stresses. English limericks, for example, employ the following metrical scheme:

(1) [x](x)x|x́xx|x́xx|x́(x)[x]   There was an Old Man of the Coast
    [x](x)x|x́xx|x́xx|x́(x)[x]   Who placidly sat on a post;
    [x](x)x|x́xx|x́(x),   But when it was cold,
    x|x́xx|x́(x)   He relinquished his hold,
    x|x́xx|x́xx|x́(x)[x|x[xx]]   And called for some hot buttered toast.[28]

(Square brackets enclose beats of silence; parentheses enclose beats that can optionally be silent or not.)

If you know the metrical scheme employed in a given poem, you can use it to identify stresses. In the limerick above, for example, we can deduce that the *a* in *placidly* is stressed, because it occurs in the first stressed position of the second line.

6.3. Stress traps

We conclude this section by mentioning a few phenomena that can lead you astray in your stress studies if you are not careful. One common problem is that speakers do not always have clear intuitions about stress placement in individual words. My beginning students often claim that they cannot hear any distinction in prominence between the syllables in a compound word like *cream cheese*, for example. As a result, they often make mistakes in their assessment of where the primary and secondary stresses fall on individual words. You should beware of this same problem occurring with your informants.

Another problem involves compound and phrasal stress, which do not always coincide with word stresses. We already saw, for instance, that the compound *New York City* is pronounced *Nèw York Cíty*, not **New Yórk Cíty*, as we would expect if its components *New Yórk* and *Cíty* were combined mechanically. This problem can

---

[28] Edward Lear, *Book of Nonsense*, 1846.

also be seen in the limerick that we looked at earlier, where the word *buttered* occurs in two unstressed positions in the meter, corresponding to the fact that in the phrase *hot buttered toast* it is unstressed. This of course fails to match the stress pattern of the word in isolation, *bútter*. What you need to do to avoid confusing word, compound, and phrasal stresses is to begin your investigation by collecting words in isolation. Once you have figured out how stresses are assigned to individual words, you can then move on to compounds and phrases, and see how stress works with those constituents.

You should also be aware that some words in some languages can have more than one stress pattern. Many English speakers, for example, can stress the compound word *cream cheese* on either the first or the second syllable. For this reason, it is important to make sure that you have collected all possible stress patterns for the words in which you are interested. (This is not always easy, because most informants will become *very* bored if you ask too many stress-related questions at one time! In many situations, you will be limited to observing stress variations in recordings of connected speech.)

Another phenomenon that can throw a wrench in your work is contrastive stress. Many languages can assign stress to a syllable that otherwise would be unstressed, if that syllable is being contrasted with another syllable. Consider, for example, "I said *GoldSTEIN*, not *GoldBERG*', where contrastive stress is assigned to the second syllable in each word, rather than the expected initially-stressed *Góldstein, Góldberg*.

Finally, you should beware of clitics, which attach to stressed words but do not bear stress themselves. These words, such as the English negative *-n't*, can interfere with your analysis of stress systems if you are not careful. Let us say that in the language you are studying, 500 of the words you have collected show final stress, but the remaining 10 show penultimate stress, because they contain a monosyllabic final clitic. If you were not aware that these 10 words contained a clitic, you might end up saying that the 10 words were exceptions to the general pattern, or you might spend hours trying to figure out some more satisfying generalization, resulting in either frustration or an incorrect solution. This sort of situation is not easy to avoid, because your informants will normally not be able to tell you if a given word is a clitic or not, and you therefore will have to figure this sort of thing out yourself.

7. Syllables

Many phonological rules and constraints make reference to syllable structure, so it is a safe bet that the language you are studying will too. To get at these phenomena, you should begin by constructing an inventory of syllable types in your informants' language. You can start by ascertaining what consonant sequences can occur at the beginning of a word, and what consonant sequences can occur at the end of a word. You can develop a good idea of what is allowed and what isn't fairly quickly, simply by observing the data you have already collected, and by asking your informants straightforward questions such as "Do you have any words that begin with *pr-*?", "Can a word begin with *pr-*?", and so on. Be sure to ask your informants about sequences that are *not* possible, in addition to sequences that *are* possible. It is a good idea to identify the set of possible monosyllabic words as well; you may well find that certain types of monosyllables do not occur or are not allowed. (Many languages, such as Osaka Japanese, require that words contain at least one heavy syllable, or two syllables.)

Moving on to vowels, you should ascertain what sorts of vowel sequences can occur within an individual syllable. Many languages restrict the range of vowels that can occur in certain types of syllables; for example, closed syllables may allow only lax or short vowels, stressed syllables may allow only long vowels or diphthongs, unstressed syllables may allow only a reduced subset of the vowel inventory, and so on. Also check on vowel-initial words, because many languages do not allow vowels (or some subset thereof) to occur in word-initial position. Some languages extend this constraint to word-internal syllables, and thereby disallow vowel sequences. You should pay extra attention to the pronunciation of words that appear to begin with a vowel, because these often actually begin with a glottal stop ([ʔ]).

Once you have identified the set of possible word-initial and word-final consonant sequences, and the set of possible vowel sequences, you are well on your way to figuring out the inventories of possible onsets, nuclei, codas in the language. The set of onsets typically (but not always) corresponds to the set of possible word-initial consonant sequences; the set of codas typically corresponds to the set of possible word-final consonant sequences. The nucleus of a syllable consists of whatever lies between its onset and its coda. To give you a quick example, the English word *picture* has the following syllable structure (O = Onset, N = Nucleus, C = Coda, R = Rime, σ = syllable):

(2)

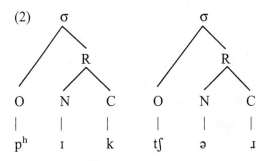

Not all languages syllabify words in the same way; for example, some languages syllabify a sequence like *apra* as *ap-ra*, whereas others syllabify it as *a-pra*. (This can vary even within dialects of a single language; some varieties of African English syllabify window as [wɪ.ndo], for example.) In most cases you will be able to use a number of diagnostics to determine how your language divides up syllables. It is generally a good idea to start by seeing if your informants have intuitions about syllable divisions in their language. This can be done by having them pronounce words very slowly, and taking note of where they insert pauses within the words. You can also ask your informants how many syllables a word contains. If they are not familiar with the concept of syllables, you can give them some examples from your own language, or another language with which they are familiar; this is normally enough to give a person an idea of what you are looking for. Once you have gotten your informants to state the number of syllables in a word, ask them what the individual syllables are. In most cases they will have clear intuitions about where the boundaries between syllables occur, and will be able to answer your question immediately. If they do not, it could either be because you have not explained the task lucidly enough, or because something tricky is involved in syllabification in their language. In English, for example, many people in rhotic areas (i.e. outside of England and the northeastern United States) have difficulty identifying the syllable boundaries in words like *Mary*, because the *r* is actually ambisyllabic (attached to both syllables).

When examining syllable structure, it can also be instructive to see how poetic rhyme works in the language you are studying. Poetic rhyme typically involves (logically enough) the rime component of syllables, so by determining what rhymes in the language you can also infer what segments in a given word belong to the syllable rime, as opposed to the nucleus.

Finally, you should try to ascertain which syllables types in your language count as heavy and which do not. As we mentioned earlier, languages almost always treat one of the following two sets of syllables as heavy: (1) syllables containing long vowels; (2) syllables containing long vowels or ending in one or more consonants. There are various ways of determining what counts as heavy. Poetic meters often distinguish between heavy and light syllables, and if your language has meters of this type, you can get very far by surveying the metrical positions in which different words can occur. Stress systems are often sensitive to syllable weight as well; the Latin stress system, for example, assigns stress to the penultimate syllable if it is heavy, but otherwise to the antepenultimate syllable. If the language you are studying turns out to be of this type, you can figure out a great deal about its prosodic structure simply by determining which kinds of syllables can be stressed and which cannot. There are many further tests for syllable weight, which can be found in most textbooks of theoretical phonology, such as Kenstowicz 1994.

Remember that some languages do not distinguish between heavy and light syllables, so you should not be dismayed if repeated attempts to adumbrate the prosodic structure of your language prove fruitless.

8. Tone and intonation

There are three principal categories of tone systems:

1.   Those which use tones phonemically to distinguish between meanings of individual words (e.g. Chinese, Venda).
2.   Those which assign consistent tone contours to individual words, but the tones are predictable from the stress patterns of the words (e.g. Japanese).
3.   Those which use tones only for pragmatic intonational purposes (e.g. English).

If you will be working with a language of type 1 or 2, we strongly recommend that you practice discriminating between different tones before you begin your fieldwork. If tapes or computer recordings are available for the language you are studying, practice with these as much as possible. If no materials exist for your language, obtain recordings for another tone language; some good possibilities include Chinese, Japanese, Thai, and many of the Bantu languages of Africa.

No matter which type of tone system you are studying, we suggest that you be very wary of taking at face value impressionistic judgements of intonation and tone. In our experience, people's judgements of pitch contours are wrong as often as they are right. It is much better to rely on either the intuitions of native speakers, or instrumental measurements.

Tone in linguistic systems corresponds by and large to pitch (though this is not the entire story). Here is what some typical phonological tones look like in terms of their pitch contours, as reflected in a narrow-band spectrogram. The horizontal lines are *harmonics*, or multiples of the fundamental frequency (F_0). The first harmonic, which we have labelled as such in Figure 6 basically corresponds to the pitch of the (female) speaker's voice. The four syllables rendered in the spectrogram present the four phonemic tones in Mandarin Chinese, as instantiated in the words ma_{55} 'mother' (3a), ma_{35} 'hemp' (3b), ma_{214} 'horse' (3c), and ma_{51} 'scold' (3d). The numbers in the transcriptions refer to relative pitch height, 5 being the highest and 1 being the lowest.

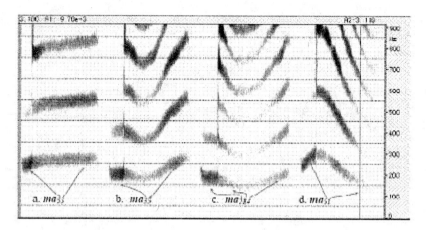

Figure 6 narrow-band spectrogram of Mandarin Chinese tones

Unfortunately, it is not always practical to rely on instrumental measurements to determine tonal contours. Since the inventory of tones in a given language is always relatively small, though, you should with some practice be able to learn to identify the tones in your language consistently. Your task will be simplified by the fact that linguistic tones are not continuous like real-world pitches, but rather are discrete and draw from a limited set of possible contours. Many tone languages of Africa, for example, only use combinations of high (H) and low (L) tones. East and Southeast Asian languages employ more tonal contrasts, but never greater than six or so.

Even after you have mastered the tones in the language you are studying, you must always stay on your toes, because tone languages tend to display all sorts of tonal alternations in different morphological and phrasal contexts. Some of the tonal phenomena that you need to be on the lookout for include:

- **floating tones** (tones which are associated with a particular morpheme, but only surface on an adjacent morpheme)

- **boundary tones** (tones associated with the edge of a phonological or syntactic domain rather than with an individual phoneme or morpheme)
- **tone spreading** (assimilation of the tone of one or more vowels to the tone of another vowel)
- **tone merger** (combination of two level tones to produce a contour tone, e.g. a high tone plus a low tone combining to give a falling tone)
- **tone fission** (splitting of a contour tone into its constituent level tones, e.g. a rising tone splitting into a low tone followed by a high tone)
- **tone deletion**

For more details on these and other tonal phenomena, interested readers can consult a recent textbook on phonological theory such as Kenstowicz 1994.

One final tip for those of you working with tonal languages is to bear in mind that tonal distinctions often go hand in hand with register distinctions (creaky voice, breathy voice, etc.). In some languages of Southeast Asia, for example, low tones are often accompanied by creaky voice. These register distinctions should not be difficult to discriminate, so we will not elaborate on them here.

9. Reduplication

A substantial percentage of the world's languages employ various sorts of reduplication processes. Reduplication involves the copying or duplication of some subpart of a word, and comes in two main varieties: full reduplication and partial reduplication. Full reduplication is fairly common, and quite straightforward. It is used for various functions, such as intensification of meaning and indication of morphological category (e.g. Malay gadʒɑ 'elephant' → gadʒɑ gadʒɑ 'elephants'). There is not much to say about full reduplication from a phonological perspective, but you should check for its appearance in your language nonetheless, because it may be morphologically interesting, and informants are often amused or intrigued by it.

Partial reduplication involves the copying of only a subpart of a word, and is of much greater phonological interest, because one wants to know the principles determining what portion of the word is copied. Ilokano, for example, forms plurals by copying part of the singular form: klase 'class' → klas-klase 'classes', kaldiŋ 'goat' → kal-kaldiŋ 'goats'. In this particular case, it appears that one builds and the prefixes the biggest possible syllable, starting from the left edge of the base form. In other cases different phonological elements such as segments and feet may be manipulated in partial reduplication. Be on the lookout for prosodic templates: \some reduplication phenomena force the reduplicated portion of the word to be of a certain shape, such as a heavy syllable.

Both full and partial reduplication can involve fixed melodic material. Schm-reduplication in English, for example, involves full reduplication combined with a fixed word-initial sequence *schm-* (e.g. *lunch schmunch*). Another common scheme is to alter the vowel of the base form, as in *flim flam*.

We highly recommend that you try to collect reduplication phenomena in the language you are working with. This is not only because of their phonological and grammatical interest, but also because they are relatively easy to collect and transcribe, and informants tend to be titillated by discussion of reduplication phenomena in their own language.

10. Truncation

Truncation involves the reduction of a word into some smaller form, typically by chopping part of it off. Many if not all languages have at least one type of truncation, which appears in the formation of hypocoristics (nicknames). English, for example, has one way of forming nicknames in which a maximal syllable is formed from the original name, and then *-ie* or *-y* is added: *Ann* → *Annie, Jennifer* → *Jenny*, etc. (Note the similarity of this process to the Ilokano plural rule discussed in the previous section.) You should find that the language you are working on has at least one nickname formation, and it should be easy and fun to collect examples of it from your informants.

11. Language games

A final fun class of prosodic phenomena involves language games, which again you should find in most or even all languages. (For some reason, though, many informants insist, when first questioned, that their language has no language games. When they do this, you should try prompting them with games from your own language, or another language that they speak. This is normally enough to trigger their memory.)

Language games manipulate the internal structure of words, either for secrecy or for sport, and the ways in which they change words are often of significant linguistic interest. They tend to involve certain specific phonological processes:

- Insertion of fixed material before or after each syllable nucleus, followed by a copy of the nucleus (English has such a game popular in the African-American community, where *-iz-* is inserted before each vowel, e.g. *lunch* → *lizunch*).
- Displacement of the initial consonant sequence in a word (as in Pig Latin, e.g. *lunch* → *unch-lay*).
- Reversing of phonemes or syllables (as in French Verlan, which normally reverses the order of syllables in each word, e.g. *l'envers* 'reverse' [lɑ̃vɛʀ] → *verlan* [vɛʀlɑ̃]).

- Replacement by fixed melodic material of each nucleus, coda, or other phonological element (as in the English song that replaces all of the vowels in the phrase "I like to eat apples and bananas" with each of the vowels {a e i o u} in turn).

Again, language games should be fairly easy to collect from your informants, and should provide hours of wholesome entertainment for all parties involved, in addition to yielding useful information about the prosodic structure of the language. For these reasons, we recommend that you try to elicit language games at some point during your fieldwork, perhaps when you sense that your informants are getting bored with whatever other task you are working on at the time.

Suggested Readings

Readers who require further information on how to identify phonemes and allophones, construct phonemic analyses, and so on can consult any of a number of seminal works in structuralist phonemics, such as Swadesh 1934, Hockett 1942, or Pike 1970. Other useful materials of more recent vintage can be found in Robinson 1970, Kelly and Local 1989, and Carr 1993, chapter 2.

Nespor, Marina, and Irene Vogel. 1986. Prosodic Phonology. Dordrecht: Foris.

Spencer, Andrew. 1996. Phonology. Oxford: Blackwell. (Chapters 3 and 7.)

Exercises

1. Take a rule or constraint that you have identified in the language you are studying, and see whether or not your informants acknowledge its existence. If they do not, think of reasons why this might be the case. If they are consciously aware of the rule, speculate as to why this might be so, given what we discussed in this chapter.

2. You have decided to create an orthography for your informant's language, which currently has none. Discuss the merits of using a system that conveys allophonic distinctions, versus a system that conveys only phonemic distinctions.

3. If you are working with informants who do not have a Roman-based writing system, try creating one for them. (If they do, create an IPA-based transcription system for them.) Present the system you have developed to your informant, and document and analyse their reactions to it.

4. Collect a language game from your informant and develop an analysis of how it works. If possible, try to follow the example of Plénat's (1995) treatment of Verlan in terms of the amount and variety of data you collect.

5. If you are working with a type 3 language (see section 8), record a short (3-4 sentence) passage from your informant and transcribe its intonational contours.

6. Discuss what a language game might reveal about the structure of the language you are studying.

You are having trouble deciding whether or not your informants are inserting an epenthetic vowel in word-initial clusters. For example, given a word written <kra> in their orthography, you cannot tell whether they are pronouncing it as [kra] or [kəra]. Discuss some ways in which you might ascertain which of these two forms they are actually saying.

8 Identifying words structures: Morphology

With this chapter, we shift our focus away from the individual sounds of the informant's language, and begin looking more closely at its grammar, which we use loosely to mean syntax, semantics, and morphology. This line of inquiry makes up an important part of fieldwork.

Grammatical investigation does not actually begin at ground zero, however. By virtue of prior inquiry into lexicography and phonology, the investigator should already have some clues about the basic grammatical structure of the informant's language. Additionally, any reading done on the language or the language family to which it belongs will provide further hints.

1. Focus of inquiry

1.1. Starting out

When beginning work on the grammar of the informant's language, it is important to start small. One cannot just dive in and start trying to figure out how wh-raising works in Bedouin Arabic without first learning a few things about the morphology of the language. We have found it useful to begin by trying to get a grasp on the system of nominal morphology in the informant's language. This has two obvious advantages. One is that nouns are some of the easiest words to collect in isolation, and so one may come up with a good stock of nouns in several different morphological forms before it becomes necessary to get into lengthier elicitations. The other advantage is that once the investigator has a good handle on the nominal morphology of the informant's language it becomes much easier to parse longer utterances accurately. Without this knowledge, an informant's utterances appear as little more than a string of words (or

worse, if you are unable to identify the word boundaries). To see
how this works, take a sentence in Latin such as (1).

(1)   *poeta   rosam   amico   dat*
         poet   rose   friend gives
         'the poet gives his friend a rose'

Even if you know the meanings of the individual words contained in
this sentence, it is impossible to decipher its whole meaning unless
you have a grasp of Latin nominal morphology. Otherwise, the
sentence could have one of six possible meanings: *the poet gives his
friend a rose, the poet gives the rose his friend, his friend gives the
poet a rose,* etc. It is the endings on the nouns—the morphology—
that tell you who is giving what to whom. *Poeta* is marked with the
nominative suffix *-a, rosam* is marked with the accusative suffix
-am, and *amico* is marked with the dative suffix *-o.*[29]

The precise goal of working on nominal morphology will
inevitably vary from linguist to linguist. For those whose primary
area of theoretical interest is morphology, the study of nominal
morphology will make up an important part of their research. They
may wish to gain as comprehensive an understanding as possible of
the whole morphological system in the informant's language. By the
same token, there are linguists whose main interests lie outside the
area of morphology, but for whom this line of investigation will still
prove important. Syntacticians, for example, are likely to be
interested in morphological phenomena such as agreement and case
marking, which are closely linked to syntax.

---

[29] This is a highly simplified account of Latin nominal morphology. In
reality, all Latin nouns belong to one of five *declensions*, or noun classes.
The case and number endings are different for each declension, so that, for
example, *-a* is the nominative singular ending for nouns of the first
declension, but not for those of any other declension.

Languages vary greatly in the degree to which they show overt marking in their nominal morphology. When starting work on a previously unstudied language, you cannot take for granted that it will have any overt nominal morphology at all. On the other hand, it is also possible that the language will have a system of nominal morphology which seems almost impossibly complex. Certain Inuit languages are famed for having words made up of a root and three or four suffixes stacked one after the other, each fulfilling a different function. A good way to begin your inquiry is by trying to determine whether the informant's language has any overt nominal morphology at all.

We often start with plurals. Most languages which have overt morphology have a plural affix of some kind, and eliciting plural forms is relatively straightforward. You simply ask the informant what his or her word is for a given object, and then ask how to refer to two or more of these objects. Of course, there may be some difficulties involved. For example, the citation form that your informant gives you may not be the form you want. In Homshetsma, for example, plurals in isolation are always given in the definite form, even though a simple form unmarked for definiteness exists. If asked how to pluralize ɑsdaʁ, 'star', for example, a Homshetsma speaker produces ɑsdaʁ-ni-e, 'the stars'. The form ɑsdaʁ-nɛɹ, which means simply 'stars', is not used in isolation, which makes the investigator's job somewhat difficult.

Another potential problem is that your informant will not understand what you are getting at. In fact, this is the central problem of working with an informant, especially where grammar is concerned. Many informants that linguists work with are not proficient in English (or whatever the linguists' native language happens to be). They may not understand what you mean when you say "How do you say 'shoes'"? Even if your informants are proficient in English, they may not be used to examining their languages on an abstract level, divorced from real communication. They may not see the point in citing numerous different forms of a given word, when no information appears to be conveyed in the process. Still, with a little work, you should be able to get your informants to produce some plurals for you, if their languages have them. The next trick is to learn all you can about the plural forms you have collected.

Keep in mind that your informant's language may mark plurals only optionally. This is the case in Korean, where the plural marker is often omitted. When asked to form the plural of 'book', a Korean informant would be likely to respond with a form identical to the singular. In this case, the linguist must do a little extra work in order to coax a plural form out of the informant. This usually involves coming up with a context which will require the informant to use the plural form. In Korean, it turns out that the overt plural is used primarily in demonstrative constructions, as in "Where did you buy those books?" So, by asking the informant to translate a sentence which included a demonstrative, the linguist could bring out the desired plural form.

Beware that the first way of producing plurals that comes into the mind of many English speakers—modifying the noun with a number greater than one—does not work in most languages. As a general rule, numbers select the singular form of the noun the modify: two dog, ten house, etc.

1.2. Irregularities

Irregular forms exist in every natural human language. They occur in phonology, morphology, and syntax, and so you are bound to encounter some before you get too far along in working on your informant's grammar. At times, morphological irregularities will serve only as a source of frustration. You may feel that you are wading through a sea of irregular forms while you are just trying to get at the basic rules of nominal morphology. Irregular forms may also be of great interest, however. Just as it is important for a linguist to discover not only what can be said in a language, but also what cannot be said, it is also valuable to know what sorts of irregular forms exist in the informant's language. One may discover all sorts of things about the history of the morphological system of the informant's language, or one may stumble upon an irregular form which explains some otherwise perplexing grammatical feature. In English, for example, the irregular alternation between singular *foot* and plural *feet* not only tells us something about the history of English, it also introduces us to a whole sub-class of irregular plurals such as *goose/geese,* and the less well-accepted *moose/meese,* which I have in my dialect.

Still, there is no denying that irregular forms can be a hassle, particularly when you are just getting started on nominal morphology. It is a maddening fact about language that morphological irregularity is often most common in very basic lexical items, precisely those words that a linguist is likely to use in initial elicitations. It is easy to see how this works if we imagine a linguist from a far-off part of the world coming to do fieldwork on English. This investigator might ask for the plurals of some basic words, such as *child, foot,* and *mouse.* The informant would respond: *children, feet,* and *mice.* With just these examples to work with, it would be impossible to come up with an accurate general rule of English pluralization. In fact, the investigator would have done much better with *thumbtack, carburetor,* and *chicken.* For this reason, it is always best to try out a variety of words when looking for a morphological rule. It is also important to be sure that the words you collect do not all fall into some obvious natural class, such as "mammals" or "long, pointy things" which might all share a specific morphological feature not associated with other lexical items.

As mentioned above, no language is entirely consistent in the way it marks morphological features. Nonetheless, whether one is looking at plural morphology, or case endings, or any other morphological markers, most languages will exhibit some regular patterns. Typically, one can determine whether a given morphological marker is the most regular or dominant by checking to see if it is the one employed with new words. Taking pluralization as an example, it is generally the case that the basic plural marker in a language is the one used most productively with new words. So, if you suspect that a certain morpheme is the standard plural marker in your informant's language, you may wish to check its productivity. You might, for example, prompt the informant with a word that would not normally occur in the plural, or with a recent loan word, such as "television" or "computer". Keep in mind, however, that some languages have special rules for loanwords, so you will have to test your results by checking some native words as well. Some languages have no dominant plural marker, though. In Polish, for example, the phonological features of the final syllable of the stem determine what plural ending will be used, even for loanwords. In general, the best strategy is simply to test as many forms as it takes until you can come up with a rule, or several rules, that seem to work.

Incidentally, although checking the productivity of a form may seem entirely logical to a linguist, an informant may not respond well to attempts to elicit unfamiliar forms. Informants are often extremely reluctant to produce utterances expressing hypothetical situations of the sort dreamed up by linguists. This problem frequently arises with words that are not normally pluralized, such as non-countable nouns (mud, water) and place names. The latter type caused problems with one of our Armenian informants, who was particularly unresponsive where imaginary or impossible scenarios were concerned. As it turned out, one of our students was particularly interested in figuring out how plurals were formed in the informant's dialect, and so she came up with the idea of asking the informant to pluralize Vank^h, the name of his hometown. This was actually an excellent idea, since Vank^h is a real word taken from the informant's language, but it is not one that is likely to be pluralized often. The chances were good that Vank^h would be pluralized using the most productive plural marker found in the language. The informant, however, refused to provide the student with a plural form. "No two Vank^h", he said, emphatically. "Only one Vank^h!"[30] The student asked him to imagine a world in which there were two Vank^{h}s, and he steadfastly refused several times, on the grounds that there was only one Vank^h, and that the existence of more than one Vank^h was inconceivable. This stalemate was finally resolved when another student asked the informant to imagine that a group of Armenians from the town of Vank^h emigrated to the United States and founded a new town, which they also called Vank^h. The informant then said, "Oh, yes, then we would say Vank^h-er".

Searching for irregular morphological forms also provides the investigator with an opportunity to embark on what can, in some cases, be a very useful endeavor: training the informant. By using a few carefully chosen words, an investigator may demonstrate to the informant the difference between regular and irregular plurals, for example. At this point, she may ask the informant to think up some other words with irregular plural forms. If the informant sees what the investigator is looking for, and is inclined to help out, he may come up with a whole list of irregular forms with little or no prodding.

---

[30] Ironically, there are in fact two towns named Vank^h in Karabagh. This fact is not surprising given that vank^h means 'monastery', and Karabagh is full of monasteries.

1.3. Key features of nominal morphology

In cases where there already exists a body of literature on the informant's language, or on some related language or languages, one may have a good idea of what to look for in terms of how the system of nominal morphology is likely to work. It is often the case in fieldwork, however, that no such literature exists. In this situation, the investigator needs to have some idea of what features to look for. Of course, the world's languages are highly varied, and so one must always be on the lookout for unexpected morphological phenomena. Still, when working on nominal morphology, you cannot go wrong by checking for feature distinctions in three major areas: case, number, and gender.

Number is perhaps the easiest feature to check for. As discussed above, it is generally not too difficult to find out if an informant's language makes a morphological distinction between singular and plural nouns. It is worth noting, however, that there are other possibilities for number distinctions. Many languages have a dual form, which is a separate morphological category used when speakers refer to two of something.

Students who have worked with a language with a rich case system such as Latin, Russian, or Finnish will have no problem understanding what is meant by "case". Still, for some students this is not a familiar concept, so a quick overview is in order. Case marking identifies the roles played by the various noun phrases in a clause. This task is carried out by word order in English, where the difference in meaning between "the man bites the dog" and "the dog bites the man" is conveyed in the different word order. Case marking accomplishes this same task in a different manner. In Polish, for example, two sentences with the same word order can mean very different things, as seen in (2).

(2)   a.   mɛ̃ʃtʃɪznɑ tsɑwujɛ kobjɛtɛ̃

                    <Mężczyzna całuje kobietę>

                    'The man kisses the woman.'

      b.   mɛ̃ʃtʃɪznɛ̃ tsɑwujɛ kobjɛtɑ

                    <Mężczyznę całuje kobieta>

                    'The woman kisses the man.'

In (2a), the nominative ending -*a* on *mężczyzna* identifies the man as the subject of the clause, and the accusative ending -*ę* on *kobietę* identifies the woman as the direct object. In (2b), the change in the endings has the effect of changing the meaning of the sentence. Languages such as Polish which have rich case systems encode many grammatical relations in their case systems. The case-marking on a Polish noun phrase tells you whether it is the subject, the direct object, the indirect object, the instrument of some action, the point of origin of some action, the object of some other noun phrase, etc. Not all languages with case systems are as complex as Polish, but on the other hand, some are much more complex.

Aside from the subject/object distinction, which is generally encoded by way of nominative and accusative case markers—or the ergative/absolutive distinction, which normally uses ergative and absolutive case markers—one should look for case forms which indicate possession, or modification of one noun phrase by another noun phrase. In English, for example, we indicate possession by adding an enclitic -*s* to the noun phrase referring to the possessor, as in *the teacher's pet*. Your informant's language may also reflect relationships of this kind between noun phrases morphologically.

Some languages also exhibit what is called *inalienable possession*. Working with our Vank[h] informant, our students stumbled upon this problem when they asked the informant how to say 'hand', and he replied with the word tserk[h]əs. At first, the students assumed that this was an atomic, monomorphemic synonym to the English word. When they tried using tserkʰəs in a few sentences, however, they discovered that it showed some surprising properties in terms of case marking (3).

(3)   a.   tserkʰəs   (NOMINATIVE/ACCUSATIVE)
       b.   tserkʰ-av-əs   (INSTRUMENTAL)
       c.   tserkʰ-əm-əs   (LOCATIVE)

Looking at the data in (3), the class first considered the possibility that the case markers had been infixed into the root morpheme. This set off some warning signals, since infixing is relatively rare cross-linguistically. They also noticed that the plural form, 'hands', was tserkʰer and that the possessive, 'his hand', was tserkʰə, without the final -s. The students eventually figured out that tserkʰəs is not itself a root, but rather a combination of a root, tserkʰ, and a possessive marker, -(ə)s. It turns out that the words for body parts are expressed with inalienable possession in Vankʰ, which is to say that they always occur with a possessive marker, even in citation form. (3a) therefore means not just 'hand', but 'my hand'. In (3b) and (3c), the case-marker is not an infix, but rather a suffix which simply attaches closer to the root than the possessive marker.

Unlike English, many languages exhibit grammatical gender. In Yiddish, for example, every noun is marked masculine, feminine or neuter: *di feder*, *dos bukh*, and *der tsimmer* mean 'the pen', 'the book' and 'the room', respectively. *Di feder* is feminine, while *dos bukh* is neuter and *der tsimmer* is masculine. The distribution of nouns among these three classes is arbitrary. If your informant's language has grammatical gender, then describing and analyzing this system will lead to a much better understanding of the overall system of nominal morphology.

Determining if there is grammatical gender requires eliciting the words for inanimate objects and other non-human nouns, as well as for human nouns. Check to see if the words for 'time' or 'street' or 'book' show gender marking, for example. Of course, many languages have gender systems which are different from the more familiar Indo-European ones. In Swahili, for example, nouns are divided into classes which would seem completely foreign even to a speaker of Russian or German, even though these languages both have grammatical gender. Swahili distinguishes grammatically between 'humans', 'thin, extended objects', 'extended body parts', 'abstract qualities', and 'miscellaneous/animals', among others. One of the great challenges of fieldwork can be discovering what sorts of nominal classes exist in the informant's language, given the fact that many informants are completely unaware (at least consciously) of such distinctions in their own languages. The Swahili informant that I worked with had no conscious knowledge of the intricacies of the Swahili noun class system; he simply made these distinctions without giving any thought to the matter. In such a situation, one cannot rely too heavily on the informant to describe his own language. The only way to get at this sort of information is through a process of careful, thorough elicitation.

A final aspect of nominal morphology which deserves some mention is numeral classifiers, which are common in many East Asian languages. It is not entirely clear whether numeral classifiers belong under the heading Morphology or Syntax, or under Number or Gender, for that matter. Fortunately, these distinctions are not crucial for our purposes. What it is important to know is that numeral classifiers are out there, and that they can be extremely confusing for an English speaker.

In languages such as Chinese, Japanese, and Korean, numeral modifiers are always accompanied by classifiers which indicate what type of object is being counted. This is somewhat similar to saying 'three glasses *of milk*' in English, except that the classification system is much more robust in these languages than in

English. In Korean, for example, books are counted using different classifiers than are dogs, so that one actually says something like 'three volumes of book' or 'four dogs of animal' to mean 'three books' or 'four dogs'. In fact, there is no grammatical way to express a specific number of anything in Korean without using a classifier.

2. Elicitation techniques for nominal morphology

The most important thing to do when preparing for an elicitation session is to plan ahead. When you are working on nominal morphology, you should try to come up with a word/phrase list—a list made up primarily of nouns, presumably—that you can intersperse throughout your session with the informant. The actual words (or phrases, if you need them) can be selected from among those shown in any of the word lists in chapter 3, or you can make up your own. What is important is that you organize the list in a way that makes sense to you, and that will allow you to proceed through the elicitation session efficiently. So, if you plan to use the word 'carrot', then you may want to put not only 'carrot' on your list, but also 'carrots'. Needless to say, 'carrot' and 'carrots' should not be at opposite ends of your list. You may also wish to designate spaces for the various cases that 'carrot' may appear in. If you find that the informant's language has four cases, then you should always elicit and transcribe the forms of a given word in the four cases in the same order. It may also be useful to leave a space for the gender of each word. In the end, organizing a word list and setting up a notebook accordingly is not unlike setting up a spreadsheet. Each English word you use will correspond roughly to an entry in your notebook; within each entry you want to have a number of distinct 'fields' into which you can put information, and you want these fields to be organized the same way for each entry.

Building upon this principle, you can do yourself a big favor by numbering each word on your list. This way, when you elicit the various forms of a word, you can transcribe the informant's responses into your notebook, and then just jot down the number corresponding to that word, rather than having to gloss each response. So, each notebook entry will contain all the various morphological forms of the word in question—organized the same way for each entry—accompanied by a number corresponding to the number assigned to that word on your original list. You can then go back later and see which word corresponds to that number. Of course, if the informant gives you any additional information about the meaning of the word, such as "this word can mean 'carrot' or 'carrots'", you will also have to include this information in your entry.

Another point which cannot be stressed enough when discussing working with informants is that one must attempt to keep the session interesting for the informant. There are, in fact, people who get a thrill out of trying to dream up as many different morphological forms of "chicken" as possible. Unfortunately, you cannot count on your informant being such a person. So, when trying to get determine whether there is a morphological difference between "chicken" in the nominative and the genitive, you might try eliciting "the chicken's husband" rather than just "the chicken's beak", just to keep your informants on their toes.

3. Pronominals

When working on nominal morphology, many linguists like to pay particular attention to the pronominal system of the informant's language, as pronouns figure heavily in the syntax and morphology of many languages. Pronominal systems are of special interest in that they often contain irregular forms, suppletive forms, fused forms, and so forth. Furthermore, pronominal systems often exhibit feature distinctions which are otherwise unattested in the language. In English, for example, overt case marking is found only on pronouns (4), (5).

(4)   a. *The hunter* shoots the bear.
        b. The bear shoots *the hunter*.

(5)   a. *He* shoots the bear.
        b. The bear shoots *him*.
        c. *The bear shoots *he*.

In (4), the full noun phrase 'the bear' is uninflected in both subject and object position.   In (5), on the other hand, only a nominative pronoun is acceptable in subject position, and only an accusative one in object position.

It is often the case when working on pronominal systems that one cannot tell if a given word is actually a pronoun or not. Fortunately, there is a way to test this, based on the fact that pronouns typically replace full noun phrases, and not just part of a noun phrase. Because they replace full NPs, pronouns cannot be modified by adjectives, determiners, or other elements which modify nouns or other sub-phrasal nominals. If you find that a word in your informant's language can be modified by an adjective or some other complement, then it is a good bet that it is not a true pronoun. Some languages, such as Korean, for example, do not have a "complete" set of true pronouns in the way that English does. So, in Korean there is no true pronoun corresponding to 'he', 'she' or 'they'. All of these are expressed with the phrase kɨ saram, which actually means 'that person' or 'those people'. One can verify that kɨ saram is not a true pronoun by observing that it can be modified with an adjective such as miguk, 'American'. By contrast, *American he* or *that American he* would be ungrammatical in English.

Keep in mind, however, that tests such as this one are by no means guaranteed to work. There will always be cases in which it is just about impossible to tell what grammatical category a word or morpheme really belongs to. I once watched a colleague's dissertation defense get taken over by a room full of linguists arguing about whether the Cape Verdean clitic *-e* is a pronoun or a copular verb.

Another problem that one may encounter in fieldwork, and particularly when working on pronominal systems, is the dissimilarity between one's own language and that of the informant. As the world's most notorious monoglots, we English speakers tend to assume that other languages work pretty much the way ours does. So, we assume that everyone divides the world up into 1st, 2nd, and 3rd person referents of either the singular or the plural variety. We also think it natural to distinguish grammatically between male and female human beings in the 3rd person singular, but not in the plural, or in the other persons. Thus, we differentiate between *he* and *she*, but not between *you* (m.) and *you* (f.). Speakers of other languages often do things differently.

In Finnish, for example, the pronominal system makes no distinction between genders. Quechua also makes no distinctions along gender lines in its pronominal system, but it does distinguish between 'inclusive' and 'exclusive' groupings in the first person plural (6).

(6) ɲuqa-ntʃʔik   (1ST.PL.INCL.)   'we, including you'
     ɲuqa-j-ku   (1ST.PL.EXCL.)   'we, not including you'
                                      (Data adapted from Lyovin 1997)

An English-speaking linguist working on Quechua might not know about the inclusive/exclusive feature distinction, and might miss it entirely. For this reason, one should constantly be on the lookout for all sorts of feature distinctions when working on pronominal systems. In particular, there are some common phenomena not found in the English pronominal system that one should watch for: (a) the existence of an impersonal 4th person, as in Hausa, (b) the marking of a dual number, as in Yup'ik Eskimo, and (c) distinctions according to levels of honor or respect, as in Japanese and Korean.

If you succeed in quickly eliciting the basic pronominal paradigms in the informant's language, there is always the option of doing more advanced work. For example, many linguists just can't get enough of reflexive pronouns, which have been and continue to be one of the hottest topics in generative linguistics. Of course, most of the excitement centers around the syntactic distribution of reflexives (which we discuss in chapter 9), but one can begin by collecting a few reflexive forms. They should not be too difficult to elicit, as they generally occur in the object position of clauses in which the subject and the object share the same referent, as in *She$_i$ injures herself$_i$.* In order to convey to the informant what a reflexive is, you should first find a construction, like the one above, which forces its use. Once you have found an example of a reflexive, you can ask the informant to give you other examples of this word in different forms and constructions. Beware, however, that the form used for reflexives may also be a regular word in the informant's language, such as 'self' or 'body'. It may also be the case that your informant's language has reflexives which are not morphologically distinct from non-reflexive pronouns, so your search may not pan out.

4. Stumbling blocks

Even the most careful investigator is sure to run across a number of problems when collecting data on nominal morphology. In addition to the usual foul-ups resulting from miscommunications, carelessness, or even recalcitrance on the part of the informant, there are certain potential traps which are specific to the sub-field of nominal morphology.

- **Beware of numbers.** If you try to elicit a plural form by pointing to a group of objects, keep in mind that your informant may specify the exact number of objects in question, rather than giving a generic plural. This may pose unwanted problems for you, since in many languages nouns accompanied by a number do not appear in the plural. This is the case in Standard Armenian, for example, where you say ʃun 'dog', ʃun-er 'dogs', and hiŋg ʃun 'five dog'. hiŋg ʃuner can also be forced, but it has a specific referent and is not the most natural form.

- **Beware of noun classes.** Working with a Swahili-speaking informant, I once asked how to say 'telephone', and was told that the word is *simu*. When I asked for the plural form, I found that it is also *simu*. On these grounds, I decided that plurals were unmarked in Swahili. Of course I was wrong, but there was no one to catch my error. As mentioned above, Swahili groups nouns into a variety of classes based on their semantic properties. The word for 'telephone' belongs to a noun class for which there is no plural marker. Had I elicited a word from another noun class, such as ʃati, 'shirt', (plural: maʃati) I would have found there are plural markers for many nouns.

- **Don't forget about phonology.** Morphological marking may be affected by phonology, so when you find a given morphological form, you should be sure to try it out with a few words with different sounds in them. In Polish, for example, the masculine singular locative case is marked differently depending on the final consonant of the root. Generally it is formed with -*e*, as in *teatrze* [tɛatʃə], which is the locative of *teatr* [tɛatr] 'theater'. After any palatalized stop, however, or after a *k* or a *g*, it is formed with *-u*. So, the locative of *kiosk* [kjosk] 'kiosk' is not **kioske* but *kiosku*. If your informant's language has a system like this one, then figuring out the nominal morphology will be impossible without paying considerable attention to phonology.

- **Beware of overlapping forms.** In the pronominal systems of many languages, certain morphemes do double or triple duty, or worse. In English, for example, the word *you* serves as both a 2nd person singular and plural pronoun. In German, *ihr* can mean 'you (pl.)', 'her (dat.)', 'her (possessive)', or 'their'. When working on the pronominal system of your informant's language, you should keep in mind that the same morpheme may show up in one or more cases, genders, or numbers. If this situation does arise, you may wish to ask the informant how speakers go about eliminating ambiguity when context does not suffice. For example, most English speakers have a strategy for distinguishing between *you* (sg.) and *you* (pl.). Some examples are (Standard Young American) *you guys*, (Southern American) *you all* or *y'all*, (Pennsylvania) *you 'uns*, and (Irish) *yous*. One should always be on the lookout for such forms.

- **Beware of suppletive forms.** Another factor to consider when working with pronominal systems is the high incidence of suppletive forms. You may find that the morphological variations between pronominal forms in the informant's language are entirely unpredictable, even if full NPs are inflected in a consistent manner. In Polish, for example, the nominative form of the 3rd person masculine singular pronoun, *on*, is morphologically unrelated to the accusative/genitive form, *jego/go*. Also note that the accusative/genitive pronoun is cited as either *jego* or *go*. *Jego* is the free form of this pronoun, whereas *go* is a bound form, a clitic. The existence of both bound and free pronouns within a pronominal system is a common cross-linguistic phenomenon, found in languages ranging from French to Malay. Be careful, though, before you decide that you have found a real instance of suppletion. It is sometimes the case that apparently suppletive forms belong to the paradigm of another word. When you encounter an apparently suppletive form, see if it has any other morphologically related forms.

- **Watch out for interference from English.** When collecting data on case and grammatical gender, the chances of interference from English are few, since English has neither of these. When eliciting singular/plural distinctions, however, we often forget that the number distinctions drawn in English are by no means universal. A word such as *scissors* is plural in English, but its synonyms in many other languages are singular, as in Armenian *mkrat* (sg.). Likewise, a word which is singular in English may be plural in another language, as with Polish *drzwi* (pl.) 'door' [dʒvi]. Note that *drzwi* and *scissors* are plural in form but singular in meaning; this is a common phenomenon.

- **Beware of free morphemes.** There are languages in which plurals are marked with a free morpheme which does not attach to the root. This means that you may mistake an independent word for an inflectional affix. Calypso (the English-based creole of St. Thomas) provides an example of such a system, in which a separate word is added to a noun to indicate plurality (7).

(7) a.   də got   b.   də got dɛm
           'the goat'   'the goats'

Under normal circumstances, we would not have known that dɛm was an independent word. Fortunately for us, our Calypso informant is also a native speaker of standard English and very knowledgeable about linguistics. He explained to us, based on his intuitions as a native speaker, that dɛm should be treated as a word. Informants of this type are rare, but if you happen to meet any, then you should make use of their abilities. Furthermore, try to avoid letting your expectations override what your informants actually produce. A fieldworker familiar with French, for example, might become very suspicious upon hearing a French Caribbean Creole speaker produce *nu* for 'you (plural)'. ([nu] in French means 'we'; 'you (plural)' is [vu].) In this case, though, the informant is correct; some French Creoles have extended *nu* to serve as both first person plural and second person plural pronouns.

- **Look out for optional/alternative forms.** In many languages, nouns which typically take an irregular affix of some kind may optionally take a regular one. In the Kesab dialect of Armenian, for example, words which normally take the irregular -udɑ plural ending can also take the regular -iɾ plural, as seen in (8).

(8)

singular	irregular plural	regular plural	gloss
uortʃ	uortʃudɑ(kʰ)	urtʃiɾ	bear (n.)
vərts	vərsədɑkʰ	vərtsiɾ	male

This reinforces the point that it is very important to check for all possible forms when looking at a grammatical phenomenon. Do not be satisfied with your informant's first response to an elicitation. It is always best to check for variants of the forms you collect.

5. Verbal morphology

Verbal morphology is investigated primarily through the collection of verbal paradigms and texts—personal narratives, folk tales, etc. Most linguists use a combination of elicitation and text collection to develop a comprehensive description of a language's verbal morphology, but they generally begin by eliciting verbal paradigms. This chapter is intended as a starting point for the study of verbal morphology, and therefore focuses primarily on techniques for collecting paradigms. Of course, some particularly industrious students may also wish to collect and analyze texts. (For an extensive look at text collection, see chapter 4)

5.1. Finding the verb

You will probably want to begin by eliciting a sentence or two in the affirmative, preferably something simple. The key task here is just to identify the main verb and any other verbal elements in the sentence. These are the elements that you will focus on later when collecting whole paradigms. The first few elicitations should not be too complex—something like 'he runs' or 'she kisses the boy' should do fine.

When doing this kind of preliminary work, it is important to be prepared with a list of sentences that you intend to use for elicitation. These sentences should all be similar in form, which means that you don't want to start with 'he walks' and follow that up with 'she is bitten by ants'. Ideally, the sentences you use for your first elicitations should contain verbs which are sure to be understood by your informant. 'Eat', 'kick', and 'see' would be better choices, for example, than 'ponder', 'become', 'suggest', or 'engage'. Keep in mind that certain verbs which seem simple, such as 'run' or 'hit', can actually be very tricky. 'Run' often surfaces as a compound made up of two or more parts, for example.

Picking out the main verb may not prove as easy as it sounds. It is a well-known fact that not all languages exhibit the 'isolating' properties of English, in which individual words appear in relatively atomic form. In English, you can usually pick out the subject, verb and object as distinct entities (especially if you are an English speaker). If your informant's language is also an isolating language, then the your task may be relatively easy. However, if your informant speaks a highly synthetic language—a language which relies heavily on morphological markings—the verbal root may be buried among a number of morphemes expressing features such as agreement, tense, and aspect, just to name a few. Under these circumstances, you may have to collect quite a few sentences and do some careful analytical work before you decide what the basic verbal elements are. It is, in fact, possible for a language to have as many as four nominal arguments represented within the morphology of the main verb, as in Kinyarwanda (9) (data from Kimanyi as cited in Whaley 1997).

(9)   j-a-kí-mú-bá-hé-er-eje
       He-PST-it-him-them-give-BEN-ASP
       'He gave it to him for them'.

Fortunately, most languages do not have a verbal system which is as complex as that of Kinyarwanda. If it does turn out that your informant's language is extremely rich in verbal morphology, then it is important to remember that your informants will probably have little conscious understanding of the various types of agreement, tense marking, and so forth that go on in their language. For this reason, you should avoid relying too heavily on your informants for glosses or explanations of individual morphemes. Working on Abkhaz, which marks agreement with subjects, objects, and various sorts of indirect objects, we found that our informant was sometimes unable to separate out and gloss individual agreement prefixes. When asked to segment a verb, he could distinguish the root from the prefixes, but would occasionally insist that all the prefixes were actually a single morpheme. If pressed further on these occasions, he would give what amounted to random glosses for the various prefixes. Still, his ability to distinguish roots from prefixes allowed us to identify the main root verb in most clauses, which was a good start. From there we were able to collect paradigms which showed what roles were played by the individual prefixes.

So, with any luck you should be able to pin down the main verbal elements of the first few sentences you collect. At this point, you will be ready to begin collecting full verbal paradigms. This can rapidly become an overwhelming business, as the number of possible variables involved in verbal agreement is truly remarkable. Verbs may agree morphologically with subjects and/or with objects, and this agreement may be triggered by any of a number of features. When you have four or five different features marked independently in the verbal morphology, collecting even one full paradigm can be a daunting task. Nida cites Barrow Eskimo as a language with particularly complex verbal paradigms: the subject-object paradigm for each transitive verb contains fifty-seven different forms (1946:182).

Each of the following sections introduces just one or two of the features that you may encounter working with your informant. By keeping these various notions separate in your mind and in your field notebook, you can avoid getting confused and making erroneous assumptions that may come back to haunt you.

5.2. Person
Person distinctions are fairly straightforward. Most—probably all—languages distinguish semantically between the first, second, and

third person. Of course, these distinctions are not reflected in the verbal morphology of every language. Using the paradigmatic approach, you should be able to determine relatively easily if person features are marked in your informant's language. Simply take a sentence that you have already collected, such as 'he walks', and substitute different subjects, such as 'you', or 'I', leaving the verb the same, and watching for any morphological changes. After you have collected a few forms with an intransitive verb, try a sentence with a transitive verb, such as 'she kicks the boy'. When working with transitive verbs, you may also wish to substitute different objects to see if the person features of the object are marked in the verbal morphology. Already, however, we see how quickly things can become complicated. We are now dealing not only with the person feature as a variable, but also with the subject/object distinction. For this reason, it is sometimes best to keep the object constant until you have a handle on subject-verb agreement.

5.3. Number

If person features are marked overtly in the verbal morphology of your informant's language, then it is likely that number is marked, too, as these two features often appear hand in hand. In a language such as Latin, for example, person and number features combine to create a full range of verbal endings (*-o/m, -s, -t, -mus, -tis, -nt*), corresponding to 1st singular, 2nd singular, 3rd singular, 1st plural, etc. When checking for subject-verb agreement, you will probably want to begin with singular subjects and then move on to plural subjects. The same strategy applies when checking for verbal agreement with objects. In addition to a singular/plural distinction, your informant's language may have a dual number, reserved for pairings of objects. Also, the first and second person plural forms may be divided into inclusive and exclusive forms. In other words, the verbal morphology may reflect, for example, whether the speaker is saying 'we, including you' or 'we, excluding you'.

5.4. Gender

Gender marking on verbs should not be confused with gender marking on nouns. A language which exhibits grammatical gender may show no gender markings in its verbal morphology. This is the case with German, for example. So, whether or not your informant's language has grammatical gender, you should be sure to check for gender distinctions in the verbal morphology. This involves substituting subjects (and objects, if you wish) of different genders for all possible persons and numbers. As odd as this may seem to an English speaker, there are many languages in which the verbal endings used by a male speaker differ from those used by a female speaker. Keep in mind that masculine, feminine, and neuter are not the only possible gender distinctions. There may also be verbal markings based on animacy, size, or shape, to name a few.

5.5. Negation

Negation figures heavily in the verbal morphology of many languages, including Armenian and most Bantu languages. Compare the following positive and negative pairs in Standard Western Armenian: kʰərɛtsʰi 'I wrote', tʃʰəkʰərɛtsʰi 'I didn't write'; gəkʰərɛm 'I write', tʃʰɛm kʰərɛr 'I don't write'. In such languages, the form of a negated verb is markedly different than the form of the same verb in the affirmative. It should not be difficult to figure out whether your informants' language works this way. You just need to collect a few identical sentences in the affirmative and in the negative, and compare them. If negation is marked on verbs in your informant's language, then you should collect as many paradigms as needed to figure out how negation works.

5.6. Tense/Aspect

So far, we have steered clear of tense and aspect. Tense and aspect form a complex and interesting part of the system of verbal morphology of many languages. They can also be extremely challenging to collect and analyze. For this reason, you will need to be especially well-prepared when working on tense and aspect. You should come to the session prepared with a list of sentences that you wish to elicit in each of the tenses that you are looking for. For a sentence such as 'they run', for example, you will want to have entries in your notebook for 'they ran', 'they will run', and whatever other tenses you may be looking for.

As always, communicating successfully with your informant is the most difficult task you face. Imagine that you wish to collect a sentence in the past tense; just giving a prompt in the past tense may not suffice. Because tense/aspect systems vary from language to language, informants often give translations in tenses other than the ones we expect. Working with our Gujarati informant—who does not speak English very well—we found that he usually translated our past-tense sentences into the present tense in Gujarati. In fact, he translated pretty much all of our prompts into the present tense, no matter what tense we gave him. To straighten things out, we had to add temporal adverbs like "today" or "yesterday" to our sentences. Consider the following excerpt from a session with our informant

Vaux:	How do you say 'I gave my wife her book'?
Informant:	mɑɾi pʌtni-ne teni tʃɔpɾi ɑpũ-tʃʰũ.
	[my wife-to her book I-give
	'I give my wife her book'.]
Vaux:	How do you say 'yesterday'?
Informant:	Today...uh...yesterday, gʌjkɑle.
Vaux:	Can you say gʌjkɑle mɑɾi pʌtnine teni
	tʃɔpɾi ɑpũ tʃʰũ ?

Informant: [correcting Vaux] gʌjkɑle mɑɾi pʌtnine teni
              tʃɔpɾi ɑpi hʌti. Means 'was'. ɑpũ tʃʰũ
              means 'now'.

Vaux: Ah.

Cooper: So how do you say 'I gave my wife the book' in
              the past?

Informant: mɑɾi pʌtni-ne (teni) tʃɔpɾi ɑpi hʌti.
              [my   wife-dat. (her)   book   gave I.was]

Even this is not a foolproof approach, because some
languages use temporal adverbs in place of changes in the tense of
the verb. In other words, a tense marker such as 'future' might
appear only when a word like "tomorrow" was not present. Cross-
linguistically, it is very common to indicate the future, at least
optionally, with a present tense form of the verb and an adverb,
rather than by way of an actual future tense. This is the case in many
Indo-European languages, including English, where *I leave
tomorrow* is another way to say 'I will leave tomorrow'.

Things can be even more confusing if your informant's
language makes a distinction in tense/aspect morphology which
English lacks. Take the case of Modern Western Armenian, where a
distinction is made in the perfect tense between "witnessed" and
"non-witnessed" events. If a speaker has personally witnessed an
event, then he or she uses a form such as (10a), but if the speaker
was not present for the event in question, only a form like (10b) is
appropriate.

(10)   a.   mɛɾʒɑdz ɛn
             'they refused'   (witnessed)

       b.   mɛɾʒɛɾ ɛn
             'they refused'   (non-witnessed)

It is easy to imagine an investigator collecting these two forms and having no idea why they were different. In most cases, the informant would not be able to explain the difference between the two forms, and so the investigator would be left very confused.

5.7. Voice

Use of the passive voice is not common to all languages, nor is it exclusively a morphological phenomenon. Nonetheless, you may wish to elicit some passive constructions in your work on verbal morphology. Note, however, that collecting data on passives may prove surprisingly difficult. Passives are often used in very specific, real-world contexts which are hard to create in a laboratory setting. Your informant may not see the difference between 'The cat catches the mouse', and 'The mouse is caught by the cat'. Also, informants often do not share linguists' willingness to see language as an abstract entity, and therefore resist producing utterances which they find nonsensical. To a linguist, a sentence such as 'I am being eaten by a purple dog' is perfectly acceptable, but an informant might reject the sentence on the grounds that there are no purple dogs, and that if there were, they would not eat humans.

Keep in mind also that passive morphology can sometimes overlap with other morphological phenomena. You might find, for example, that the passive marker is the same as the marker for intransitive verbs.

6. Collection techniques

In the paradigmatic approach, one generally begins with a single clause or sentence, and then makes substitutions or alterations to parts of this sentence in order to collect a full paradigm. So, if you have a sentence such as 'The man kicks the tree', and you are looking for morphological markings on 'kick', then substitute different subjects, objects, tenses and so forth in order to collect the desired forms. Ideally, the best strategy is to collect the whole paradigm for a given verb before starting in on a different verb. This can take a considerable amount of time, however, and can be terribly boring for the informant. You may want to break up the monotony at times by moving to another topic and then returning to your paradigm when the informant's interest has been revived.

By going through your elicitations one verb at a time, you make the crucial task of organizing your field notebook much easier. One of the keys to successful collection of verbal paradigms is keeping a well-organized notebook. The entries in your notebook should be organized around the basic sentences from which you are working. So, you may want to devote a certain amount of space in your notebook to each verb that you use. For example, you might have a page for the verb for 'to eat', another for 'to run', and so on. Depending on how far you wish to delve into the verbal morphology of your informants' languages—and depending on their attention spans—you may be collecting as few as three or as many as thirty paradigms for each verb you use, so the amount of space needed may vary. We have found it useful to have separate sections of the notebook for field notes and paradigms. This way you can neatly fill in your paradigms in one space, and make as many cluttered notes as you need elsewhere.

Alternatively, in some situations an investigator may be primarily interested in targeting the behavior of a single feature across a range of verbs. In this case, some modifications to the above approach must be made. Rather than having a one verb/one entry scheme, you may wish to organize your data according to the feature(s) you are particularly interested in. So, if you have found that the first person singular behaves oddly in your informant's language, and you want to focus on this phenomenon, then you may wish to collect the first person singular forms of many different verbs, one after another. These data could then comprise a whole entry in your notebook, as seen in (11b), as opposed to the more standard one verb/one entry approach, seen in (11a).

(11)   a. possible paradigm for 'run'   b. focusing on 1st sing.

I run	*I run*
you run	*I walk*
he runs	*I jump*
she runs	*I swim*
it runs	*I flee*
we run	*I ride*
you (pl.) run	*I sprint*
they run	*I go*

There are two different schools of thought on collecting paradigms, one favoring accuracy at the expense of efficiency, and the other favoring efficiency, perhaps at the expense of accuracy. Many linguists, including the present authors, prefer to move extremely cautiously when collecting paradigms, which means changing only one element of a sentence between one elicitation and the next. For example, we would follow up an elicitation such as 'The woman left yesterday', with 'we left yesterday', and then 'you (pl.) left yesterday', and so on. In each case, only the subject of the sentence is changed; everything else remains the same. This is as tightly controlled an experiment as one can conduct, given the fact that informants are decidedly human. The disadvantage of working this way is that one often has a limited amount of time with the informant, and this plodding approach necessarily reduces the amount of ground that one can cover. Also, the informant may become exceptionally bored when asked to repeat the same sentence over and over again with only one slight change each time.

The other school of thought on paradigm collection says that you should get as much data from the informant as possible within the limited time that you have. This means combating redundancy between elicitations by changing several sentential elements at a time. An investigator working this way might elicit (12a) and (12b) in succession, in order to eliminate unnecessary redundancies.

(12)   a.   'he **is** crying'

          b.   'the man from the village **was** crying'

At first glance, this experiment may look somewhat loosely controlled, but linguists who work this way would argue that this is not the case. The substitutions made between (12a) and (12b) are not random. Rather, the verb remains in the third person singular in both sentences, and only the tense of the verb is changed. The internal make-up of the subject is also altered, but this change should have no effect on the form of the verb, since the subject is still in the 3rd person singular. In this way, one can test for both the past tense and for noun phrase complements in one fell swoop. The key to collecting paradigms in this manner is not to lose track of what you are doing or become disorganized—having control over the experiment at all times is crucial. As always, thoughtful preparation ahead of time can eliminate a great deal of confusion during and after the actual elicitation session.

The main problem with this second, more expansive method is precisely that the experiment is not as tightly controlled as it could be. By using the sentences in (12), you open the door to possible misanalyses of the data. It might turn out, for example, that verbs agree differently with pronominal subjects (12a) than with full-NP subjects (12b) in the informant's language. An unsuspecting investigator would probably assume that the morphological differences in the verb between (12a) and (12b) were related exclusively to the change in tenses, and thereby miss the other distinction. Also, it is easy to miss important data using this method. The fact is that you never know where an interesting phenomenon is going to turn up, and so you need to be as thorough as possible. By using a more cautious method, in which only one element of the sentence is changed at a time, you can better protect yourself against missing data that you might need.

One other advantage to using the more cautious method, changing only one element at a time, is that the informant is more likely to catch on to what you are doing and then be able to help you out. When you change only one element in a sentence from one elicitation to the next, it is easy for the informant to see the pattern in what you are doing. If the informant observes, for example, that you always change the subject from one sentence to the next, then he or she may be able to quickly give you a whole paradigm with every different type of subject, thereby making your task much easier.

7. Texts

Some linguists use the paradigmatic approach only as a stepping stone toward text collection, which they consider the bread and butter of fieldwork. Text collection does not, of course, mean going to the library and looking up "texts" in the informant's language— there is a good chance that no such texts exist. Rather, text collection means asking the informant to relate a personal narrative, a traditional story, or something of this sort, and transcribing and analyzing the entire passage. Often, the informant's personal narrative will be the thrilling tale of what he had for breakfast that morning, or how he wrestled a particularly cagey pipe into place while fixing his toilet. Fear not; these stories can provide you with just as much good data as any entertaining anecdote would. Also, informants generally enjoy stories more than individual sentences.

When you collect a story, you put the informants in the driver's seat, which can be a lot of fun for them.

When collecting texts, you can hope to discover grammatical phenomena which would not be uncovered in collecting paradigms. For example, a tense or aspect distinction which would not come out in the course of an elicitation session might appear in a transcribed text. Collecting a whole text can be very difficult, however, particularly if one has little or no knowledge of the informant's language. Each word can become a perplexing puzzle when transcribing a text in an unfamiliar language. The informant is certain to grow bored, if not downright vexed, as it takes you several minutes to transcribe a single sentence. One linguist, who was not actually looking for a text at the time, described his difficulties with lengthy transcriptions when working with a Wauwana informant:

"How do you say 'I run' in your language?" The Indian was quiet for a while. First he looked down; then he looked out. Suddenly his face lit up as if struck by a sudden flash of inspiration. He spoke very rapidly. If I had been able to transcribe what he said, it would have spread across the page several times. I gulped and bravely started to write; but after a few syllables, I was already hopelessly bogged down.

"How did you say that?" With his repetition I added two more syllables, then bogged down again. When I asked for the third repetition, the informant began to waver and finally to change his story, and so I had to give up entirely. To my half self-justifying and half self-accusing, "But that surely doesn't all mean just 'I run'," he said, "Why of course not. It means I was sitting here with you; then I looked out of the door and saw a deer, so I quickly grabbed my spear and now I am running after it". Then, almost philosophically, he added to himself, "Only a fool would run for nothing." (Samarin 1967:37)

To combat this sort of difficulty, you can just record the story with a tape recorder and then try to transcribe it later, first on your own, and then with your informant's help. Once you have a story recorded and partially transcribed, your informant can actually be of great help in refining the transcription. In general, try to keep your stories short and simple, and make your transcription as narrow as possible, without boring the informant.

8. Warnings
There are certain difficulties that crop up again and again when working on verbal morphology. By alerting you to some of these potential problems, we hope to make your elicitation sessions more productive and less frustrating than some of ours have been.

• **Boredom—yours and theirs**. Collecting verbal paradigms is not an exciting business; few linguists go to bed dreaming of getting the pluperfect of 'to harvest'. Beware, however, that if you become too bored during your elicitation session, you may become careless.   After collecting paradigms which look identical for three verbs in a row, it is easy to assume that the fourth will be identical to the others, and then not to listen carefully to the forms that the informant actually produces.

Compared to the boredom of the informant, however, your boredom is likely to be negligible. You, at least, are in control of the situation and have a clear idea of both the purpose and direction of the exercise you are engaging in—not so for the informant. Famous field linguist Eugene Nida (1947) discusses this very problem:

"Repeating a word fifty times, as some field investigators have insisted upon, is of course boring; and without some understanding of what is expected

> any interest that the [informant] may have had
> originally is likely to wane. This is especially true
> with long, involved paradigms, which to us seem
> perfectly easy to recall, but for the informant these
> are sometimes quite a chore". (p. 138)

The informant's boredom can have a number of repercussions, including your receiving bad data because the informant's head is no longer in the game. One linguist, whose name shall remain undisclosed, was in the habit of sending e-mail messages to his informant containing 20 or 30 pages' worth of paradigms for translation (the informant's language was written with very transparent orthography, making e-mail a viable medium for elicitation). After a while, the linguist realized that the data he was receiving was unreliable; the informant was simply too bored and overwhelmed to render meaningful judgements.

We recommend avoiding marathon sessions with your informant. It is also best to mix things up a bit when collecting paradigms; try working on something else for a while and then return to them. In the meantime, you could give a little more time to some nagging question about phonology, for example, or try to collect a short text. Best of all, you can keep the informant's interest by making your sentences interesting. Use whatever you can to accomplish this. Throwing some local place names into your sentences might help, or using the names of friends, relatives or political figures, rather than just "John" and "Mary" could liven things up.

• **Beware of informants' glosses.** When collecting verbal paradigms, one often longs for a quick and easy morpheme-by-morpheme gloss of each sentence, especially of the verbal elements. Asking the informant for this information, however, may lead only to frustration.   Our Vank^h informant often confused us with his glosses.   For example, when asked the meaning of the morpheme -ɑ in the phrase iŋk^h-kɑl-æts-ɑ, meaning 'he bought', the informant first answered that it meant 'the'.   He then corrected himself, saying that it meant 'a', and then changed his mind again, arriving at 'one' as his final translation.   In fact, -ɑ is a clitic 3rd person singular copula, best translated as 'is'.   In a particularly extreme case, he once glossed the phrase nɑ hɑts^h-ɑ as 'he' or 'who'.   It means 'it/that is bread'.

In general, the glosses provided by informants are somewhat better for open-category morphemes (nouns, verbs, adjectives, etc.) than for closed-category morphemes (prepositions, articles, inflectional clitics, and so forth).

- **Watch for theme vowels and the like.** It is easy to be fooled by certain features of verbs which appear to be morphological phenomena, but are not.   A thematic vowel (THM.) which is associated with a certain class or group of verbs—sometimes called a "conjugation"—can look a lot like an inflectional morpheme.   Unless you control your experiments carefully, you can be lead into a faulty analysis.   Looking at the Polish data given below, for example, one sees that there is little difference, syntactically, between (13a) and (13b), and yet the vowel preceding the personal ending is different.   If you know the roots of these words, *czyt-* [tʃɪt] and *kup-*, and the personal ending, *-sz* [ʃ], then it is tough to explain what role these vowels play.   One might conclude that the vowel change is triggered by agreement with the direct object, for lack of a better hypothesis.   In fact, the two verbs simply belong to different conjugations.

(13) a. *ty*   *czytasz*   *ksiązkę*
         tɪ   tʃɪt-ɑ-ʃ   kʃõʃkə
         you   read-THM.-2nd.sg. book
         'You are reading a book'

   b.   *ty*   *kupujesz*   *samochod*
         tɪ   kup-uj-ɛʃ   samoxut
         you   buy-THM.-2nd.sg.   car
         'You are buying a car'

The sort of confusion sketched out above provides another argument in favor of a cautious approach to paradigm collection, in which only one element is changed from one elicitation to the next.

• **Watch out for special citation forms.** The citation form of a word or sentence is the form that a native speaker uses when asked to produce that word or sentence in isolation. For example, the citation form of the English verb which describes moving rapidly by foot is *(to) run*. In speech, one probably says *run* or *runs* or *running* more often than *(to) run*, but if your French teacher asks you "What does *courir* mean in English?" you still reply with the citation form: *(to) run*.

So, why is this a problem when working on verbal morphology? As we found out from our Vankʰ informant, in some languages the citation form for whole sentences is not the present tense. Whenever we asked our informant how to say something like 'I am running', he would respond with the equivalent of 'I ran'. Because the only way to determine the tense of the informant's response is by checking it against other data you have collected, it took us a while to figure out that this was going on.

- **Beware of hidden feature distinctions.** When I took Russian as an undergraduate, I remember being surprised to find that there is subject-verb agreement for gender in the 1st, 2nd and 3rd person in the past tense, but only in the third person in the other tenses. So, if you are cross-dressing in Russia, you had better only use the present and future tenses, lest you slip up and use the wrong agreement pattern in the past tense, thereby revealing your true identity.

  The point of all this is that certain feature distinctions may be dependent upon the values of other features. For example, number might be marked only in the present tense in your informant's language, or person might be marked only when the subject is singular. If you find in the course of collecting a paradigm that a certain feature, such as gender, is not marked, do not write this feature off and forget about it; it may pop up later in another paradigm where other feature values are different.

- **Beware of ergativity.** Absolutive/ergative systems work differently than the nominative/accusative systems many of us are used to. In languages of this type, subjects of transitive sentences are treated one way, while subjects of intransitive sentences and objects of transitive sentences are grouped together and treated differently. You should be aware of this phenomenon when studying verbal morphology. It is also important to note that your informant's language may use both a nominative/accusative system and an absolutive/ergative system. In many Indic languages, for example, an absolutive/ergative distinction is made in past tenses, but in the present and the future the distinction is nominative vs. accusative.

- **Don't trust negative evidence.** Just because you don't find a certain form does not mean that it doesn't exist. In some dialects of Armenian and Turkish, for example, plural markers can be omitted in certain contexts. In this case, it is easy to assume that there is no plural marker. Avoiding this mistake involves some degree of vigilance. You must always check for any forms that you suspect might exist, even if you see no evidence of them at first glance.

Suggested Readings

Readers who are interested in taxonomic morphology and the problems involved in breaking down words into individual morphemes can consult a range of books and articles in the structuralist tradition, including Harris 1942 and Nida 1948. For theoretical aspects of verbal morphology, one can consult the relevant portions of Spencer 1991 and Carstairs-McCarthy 1992. Pittman 1970 discusses the elicitation of paradigmatic data from texts. More advanced readers interested in theoretical aspects of verbal morphology should consult the relevant chapters of an introductory morphology text, such as Spencer 1991 or Carstairs-McCarthy 1992.

Exercises

1. Make up a list of English nouns which contains both 'count nouns' and 'mass nouns'. For example, *book* is a count noun, since you can say *two books*, while *dirt* is a mass noun—*two lumps of dirt*, but not **two dirts*. Elicit the corresponding forms from your informant and see how these concepts are treated in his or her language.

2. Collect a short text from your informant and go through it carefully, circling or underlining each noun or noun phrase. Try to identify the gender, number and case of each nominal element. If your prior work has shown you that some other feature, such as animacy or definiteness, is morphologically relevant, try to determine the feature values of these, too. Wherever you cannot identify all the feature values for a nominal element, go back and check it with further elicitations, so that you can fill out your analysis.

3. Collect two sets of nouns, belonging to two semantic classes (e.g. females and animals). See if you can identify any morphological features that distinguish the two.

4. Collect the full paradigm (singular, plural, and so on) for a noun in your informants' language. Discuss the techniques you used to collect the forms (including how you came up with carrier sentences you employed), and detail any difficulties that you encountered.

5. Choose a language other than English that you have some knowledge of, and practice writing out its verbal paradigms. Go through all the tenses, persons, numbers, genders, and so forth, creating as many distinct paradigms as you think you need to

capture the basics of verbal morphology in that language. You should pay particular attention to the way in which you organize and record your paradigms. Try to find a system which works well for you. This exercise should provide you with an idea of how to organize your notebook later on. (If you are not proficient in any language other than English, then just do the exercise using English.)

6. Try to collect a verbal paradigm in an obscure or unusual tense, one which you might not otherwise come across. Something like a past conditional—*She would have gone, if she could have*—ought to do the trick. The key here is to figure out how to elicit these forms. Try to come up with ways to explain or demonstrate to the informant what it is you are looking for.

7. Come up with an elementary morphological analysis of a verb or sentence and discuss it with your informant. Your analysis should include your own morpheme-by-morpheme gloss and a hypothesis about what features are marked by each morpheme. See what your informant thinks of your work. This should give you an idea of what your informant's attitude is toward linguistic inquiry and analysis. You may also get some impression of how much faith you can put in your informant's—and your own—glosses and analyses.

8. Try to find examples of periphrastic (compound) verbs. Which part of the verb is inflected, if any? Does this inflected portion of the verb behave like other, non-periphrastic, verbs in the informant's language, or is it somehow special? What restrictions are there on where the parts of the verb can occur, and what sorts of words or phrases can intervene between them?

Once again, the trick to this exercise is figuring out how to go about finding the desired forms.

9. Take a familiar verb from the informant's language, one for which you have not already collected a whole paradigm, and try to generate a paradigm on your own based on your notes. Test your forms out on the informant. If your predictions are correct, the informant may be quite impressed, and if they are not, you should be able to have a good laugh about it.

9　Analyzing sentence structure: Syntax

Operational tests, just as explanatory theories, must meet the condition of correspondence to introspective judgments.

Noam Chomsky
The Logical Basis of Linguistics

Studying syntax in the field requires techniques different from those used when working on phonology and morphology. Specifically, the investigator has to call upon the informant to make grammaticality judgements. This puts the informant in a new position. In addition to producing forms in his or her native tongue, the informant is now asked to play a somewhat more active role in the inquiry by deciding which sentences are acceptable, which are not, and what exactly is wrong with those that are not. The investigator's job is to obtain accurate and reliable grammaticality judgements from the informant, a task which requires patience, objectivity, and good preparation. The focus of this chapter will be on working with the informant in this way. At the end of the chapter, we talk about a handful of other syntactic phenomena that we have worked on at various points in the past or that we feel might be of particular interest to students working on syntax.

1. Grammaticality judgements

1.1. Starting out

Beginning linguists are often surprised to find that the business of making grammaticality judgements does not come naturally to everyone. There is a tendency among speakers to assume that all utterances are acceptable, or to assume that the distinction between grammatical and ungrammatical utterances is so obvious that no one would possibly want to study it. If you ask many informants, "Can you say X?" they tend to say that you can, even if X is really grammatically unacceptable. Because informants are generally unfamiliar with the process of making grammaticality judgments, their definition of acceptability can be too loose for your purposes. Furthermore, their eagerness to provide the answer that they think you want to hear can interfere with their judgement.

Fortunately, everyone is capable of making grammaticality judgements, given a bit of training. It is therefore the job of the investigator to explain, or better yet, demonstrate, what making grammaticality judgements is all about. You may start by highlighting the contrast between a grammatical sentence and an ungrammatical sentence in English. If, however, your informant does not speak English very well, then you will not get far with this tactic. The best approach is to come up with a sentence in your informant's language which is so clearly ungrammatical that this fact cannot be ignored. We had considerable success in this area with our Gujarati informant, as shown in the dialogue below. At this point in the session, we were trying to find out where the adverb gʌjkɑle 'yesterday' could be placed in a particular sentence.

Vaux: What about
            mɑɾi pʌtni-ne tɛni tʃɔpɾi gʌjkɑle   ɑpi-hʌti ?
            [my   wife-to   her   book   yesterday I.gave
            'I gave my wife her book yesterday']
Informant: They say it. No problem.
Vaux: And what about
            mɑɾi pʌtnine tɛni tʃɔpɾi ɑpi-hʌti gʌjkɑle ?
Informant: It's OK too. Anywhere.
Vaux: Can you say
            mɑɾi gʌjkɑle pʌtnine tɛni tʃɔpɾi ɑpi-hʌti ?
Informant: Yeah.
Vaux: You can?

Cooper: Wait, mɑɾi gʌjkɑle pʌtnine tɛni tʃɔpɾi
ɑpi-hʌti is OK?
Informant: No, no, no! not gʌjkɑle there.

Our informant appeared to get into a rut, thinking that all of our questions were designed to be answered "yes". This happens frequently, so we were careful to re-check the sentence that we did not expect to be grammatical. In this case it turned out that we were right.

We continued to work on grammaticality judgements throughout this session, which was very enjoyable, because we got to watch our informant discover new things about his language which he had probably never considered before. Among these was the notion that certain sentences are grammatically acceptable, while others are not.

Not all informants are as linguistically curious as our Gujarati speaker, and so you may find that, even at this point, your informants will consider this an unfruitful and mind-numbing enterprise. After all, the informants think to themselves, the distinction between grammatical and ungrammatical sentences should be obvious, right? To demonstrate better what you are getting at, try eliciting some sentences or phrases where the distribution between grammaticals and ungrammaticals is likely to be interesting. For example, it is a well-known fact that you can say *the big green shoe* in English, but not *the green big shoe*, although it is not entirely clear why. As it turns out, similar constraints on adjective ordering hold in many languages. So, try collecting an NP from your informant with a couple of adjectives in it, and then try switching around the order of the adjectives. If you are lucky, your informant will see that some orders are acceptable while others are not, and will begin to wonder why this is the case. If so, you are in good shape, because an informant who is interested in your work can be a great help.

1.2. Working with your informant

In an ideal world, all sentences would clearly be either grammatical or ungrammatical, and speakers would be able to identify them as such. Unfortunately, the world does not work this way; sentences populate a wide range of acceptability between perfect grammaticality and profound ungrammaticality. This potential ambiguity gives rise to at least two problems: training informants to identify nuances of grammaticality, as we just discussed, and identifying what causes a sentence to be ungrammatical if your informants can't.

Even if your informants have clear intuitions that a given sentence is ungrammatical, they may not be able to explain why, or they may even be deeming it ungrammatical for the "wrong" reasons (where by "wrong" we do not mean that the informants are mistaken, but rather that they are noticing flaws that are not relevant to the linguistic phenomenon you are interested in). Our Vank^h informant often judged sentences as marginal, unable to decide if they were really acceptable or not. Sometimes we suspected that his objections were not purely syntactic, as when he once proclaimed that a sentence I gave him was unacceptable because my "pronunciation was bad". On other occasions, however, we found that his judgements accurately reflected the status of the sentences we gave him. All languages have scales of acceptability: some sentences are good, some are bad, and some are on the border. Take, for example, the sentences in (1).

(1)   a.   How hot did you run the engine?

          b.   How coherent did you write the chapter?

          c.   How fresh did you drink the milk?

Many speakers find some or all of these sentences marginal, which is to say that they are not completely ungrammatical, but they also don't sound quite "right". Worse yet—and this comes up all the time in fieldwork—the same speaker may give different judgements on a sentence from one minute to the next. You may also find that from one session to the next, your informant's judgements on the same data will vary significantly. Do not despair. By asking your informant the right questions, you can iron out some of these inconsistencies and get at the information you want. On one occasion, for example, our Vank^h informant first judged a sentence ungrammatical, and then later changed his mind. When we pressed him for details, he said, "You can only say that if you really need to". This response, although not phrased in a very technical way, eventually allowed us to conclude that the particular topicalization pattern we were looking at was highly marked in his dialect.

One of the keys to getting reliable results from grammaticality judgements is finding out what exactly is wrong with a sentence that is judged unacceptable. This is not always as easy as it sounds. Very few informants are prepared to give answers like "Oh, that's probably an ECP violation", although this certainly would be convenient for the investigator. Still, most native speakers are able to point generally to the problem areas in sentences. Given a sentence such as *A rhinoceros is running through house my*, for example, most speakers can identify the *house my* element as being the source of trouble, as opposed to the subject or the verb. So, when your informant judges a sentence ungrammatical, you may ask him or her to tell you what is wrong with it. Also, it is often best to put the elicitation sentences in a real-world context, so that the judgements will be as comfortable as possible.

Some warnings regarding this approach are in order. First, the sentence that you give to the informant may be so fouled up that no specific part of it is easily identifiable as the trouble spot. There was a visiting scholar from Japan in our department who frequently asked me about "English" sentences which were so bizarre that I could not give him any clue as to what was wrong with them. One that sticks in my mind was *Which did Mary's reading in the library bother you?* Second, you must always keep in mind that your informant, no matter how well-meaning, can and will make mistakes, so you must take his or her analyses with a grain of salt.

Another point to consider is that grammatical sentences can be almost as much of a problem as ungrammatical ones, depending on what you are looking for. If your informant judges a sentence ungrammatical, then you can usually figure out what is wrong with the sentence, even if it takes a little work. Imagine, however, that you give your informant a sentence which, based on the patterns you have observed before, you feel certain will be ungrammatical. Much to your surprise, it is judged grammatical. You have to revise whatever hypothesis you were entertaining in order to account for this information, but you cannot simply ask the informant what is "right" about the sentence. This would accomplish nothing since, by definition, all parts of a grammatical sentence are "right".

As you begin to rely more heavily on grammaticality judgements from your informants, your own study of their language becomes more important. Of course, you will probably never learn a language well enough to give judgements yourself, but this is not the goal of such study. Rather, the goal is to develop a good enough understanding of the language to allow you to formulate sentences in that language which are useful for elicitation. If you want to check for subjacency effects, for example, you may begin by asking the informant to translate English sentences which involve extraction across two or more bounding nodes, but this will probably not get you very far. Your informant is not likely to understand your sentences, nor is he or she likely to translate them using the structures you had in mind. At some point, you will need to be able to come up with a sentence, in your informant's language, which is morphologically and syntactically well-formed with respect to all aspects of grammar other than subjacency. To do this, you need to know as much as possible about how the language really works. Otherwise, you might come up with a sentence which has the right clausal structure to test for subjacency, but which would be judged ungrammatical because of some morphological error. In this case, it would be difficult to know if there was actually a subjacency violation, or if something else had made the sentence ungrammatical.

1.3. A common misunderstanding

Linguists tend to take it for granted that language exists independently of its use as a tool for communication. Perhaps as an extension of this view, most linguists also assume that syntax is a system which operates somewhat, if not entirely, independently of semantics and pragmatics. Most informants, however, do not share these views. So, while a linguist would likely judge a nonsensical sentence such as *my telephone is eating a reprimand for lunch* to be grammatical, many informants would not. When working with grammaticality judgements, one must always keep this in mind. The informant's objections to a sentence may not be of the sort that the investigator is looking for. Our Vank[h] informant objected to our attempts to elicit passive constructions on just such grounds. A student asked him to say 'I am being killed by the bear' in his language, and he refused. "If the bear kills you, then you are dead", he explained. "You cannot talk". We then tried 'I am being attacked by the bear', to which he replied that if you are being attacked by a bear, then you are not in a position to talk about it. We tried several similar sentences, all with the same result, until we hit upon 'I am being watched by the bear', which he found acceptable. Such protests from the informant may at first appear ridiculous, or even mischievous, but by and large, they are not. Keep in mind that it is linguists who have the unorthodox view of language, not informants.

1.4. Common sense

Far too many linguists understand seemingly everything there is to know about syntactic theory, and even have a good idea of what to collect when working on syntax, but simply have no idea how to work with an informant on a personal level. There is no single strategy that can guarantee your getting reliable judgements out of an informant; you just have to use common sense. What this amounts to is knowing what effect your surroundings or, more importantly, your individual actions may have on the informant's state of mind and, by extension, his or her judgements.

A classic mistake is priming the informant. Investigators sometimes give informants a long series of sentences, all of the same basic form, all of which are grammatical, and then suddenly throw in an ungrammatical sentence. The combined effect of a string of grammatical sentences makes informants drop their guard. When an ungrammatical sentence finally comes along, they may perfunctorily judge it grammatical without even realizing that they are giving bad information (cf. Snyder 2000). An imagined session of this sort is given in (2).

(2)   **investigator's prompt**   **informant's judgement**
        I like the car   √
        I like the house   √
        I dislike the car   √
        I dislike the house   √
        I like to eat   √
        I like to drink   √
        I dislike to eat   √   (should be *)
        I dislike to drink   √   (should be *)

Of course, the same problem of priming can occur if you give the informant a string of similar ungrammatical sentences, followed by a grammatical one. Common sense says that the best way to go about things is to mix up sentence types and mix up grammaticals and ungrammaticals, in so far as possible—of course, you don't know for sure what the informant's judgements would be, or you wouldn't need an informant, but you can usually make an informed guess.

Another area in which common sense is crucial is in deciding how to pose your questions. Surprising as it may sound, we have seen more than one investigator ask an informant questions like "That must mean X, right?" or "This one is clearly unacceptable, isn't it?" The judgements given after an elicitation of this sort simply cannot be relied upon. Rules of politeness lead most people to respond in the affirmative to questions of this type, even if this is not a truthful answer. Our Vank[h] informant never contradicted students, no matter what crazy things they asked him. On one notable occasion, a student wanted to know what a certain morpheme, -*a*, meant. Unfortunately, the way she questioned the informant left her little hope of figuring it out. She asked, "-*a* means 'one' or 'a', right?" Of course, he agreed that it did. We later found out that -*a* is a clitic form of the copula.

Even though some informants are willing to contradict investigators on occasion, you cannot count on them to do so on a regular basis. It is therefore crucial that questions about the acceptability of sentences be phrased in as neutral a way as possible. Furthermore, if a sentence is judged unacceptable and you have a hunch as to where the problem might lie, try not to reveal this by way of asking leading questions. Rather than begin by asking "Is it unacceptable because the subject and verb don't agree?" for example, just ask "What is wrong with this sentence?" and see what sort of answer you get. If you then need to pinpoint a certain part of the sentence, try to do this without imparting too much of a bias into your questions. Also, have your informants describe situations in which the sentence could or could not be used.

Finally, it is important to keep something of a poker face when asking for grammaticality judgements. This can be surprisingly difficult, particularly if you are testing a hypothesis that you have grown somewhat attached to. Imagine that you have spent all night coming up with tests for dative subjects in the informant's language. The next day, you ask the informant to translate your first sentence, which you suspect will produce a dative subject. As you ask, you sit on the edge of your seat muttering "Please! Please! Please!" to yourself. When you are proven right, the temptation is to jump up from your seat, pump your fists and do a victory lap around the room. If you do this, however, you can pretty much forget about the rest the data you collect that day, because your informant is likely to tell you whatever he or she thinks you want to hear. Of course, few people actually get this excited about linguistic inquiry, but the point stands: you do not want to give your informant any more clues than you have to about what sort of response you want from an elicitation. This means keeping a straight face both while asking for a judgement, and after receiving the judgement.

1.5. When (not) to trust your informant

As mentioned above, an informant's grammaticality judgements should not always be taken at face value. Even linguistically knowledgeable informants can give incorrect judgements, sometimes because of the way an elicitation is phrased or the context in which it is given.

We managed, unwittingly, to illustrate this point perfectly when a student from Japan came into Vaux's office to ask a question about English syntax. In theory, we should be good native-speaker informants for English, but in this case, we gave our questioner some bad information, at least initially. She wanted to know about present continuous verb forms in English, and whether they could be used with repetitive actions. Specifically, her question was, "Can you say *I'm reading the paper every day?*" I immediately responded, "No way". My gut-level reaction was that there was something wrong with this sentence, and that it should be *I read the paper every day*.

Fortunately, she was persistent. She asked again if we were sure that there was no context in which one would say this, and Vaux was able to come up with one. In fact, there are at least two different contexts in which this sentence is perfectly acceptable, as outlined in (3a) and (3b).

(3)　　a.　　I can't believe I didn't even realize that Kennedy had been shot. From now on, *I'm reading the paper every day*.

　　　　b.　　My New Year's resolutions are holding up so far this year. I'm working out; I'm eating well; and *I'm reading the paper every day*.

In this case, I made an incorrect judgement because I did not immediately think of all the possible contexts in which this sentence might be uttered. In other cases, informants make bad judgements because they are simply not aware of the things they say. A good example of this is resumptive pronouns. When asked if they put a resumptive pronoun, *him*, in a sentence like *He's the kind of guy that you really like when you first meet (him)*, most English speakers say that they do not. Yet, there is no denying that one hears this sort of construction all the time.

So, if you find that your informant rejects a given sentence, but you have independent reasons to believe that it is actually grammatical, be persistent (but not in a leading way!). Just be careful not to be too confident of your own opinions, which is a problem many linguists (and others) suffer from. Remember that your own intuitions will not always be shared by others; an interesting example pointed out by Postal 1974 is the English sentence *I assume John to be the best candidate*, which I (and many other linguists before Postal) assumed was grammatical for all speakers of English, but is actually ungrammatical for a significant subgroup of the population.

2. Collection tricks for syntax

The two key techniques for working on syntax are elicitation through a common language, as discussed in the previous chapters, and grammaticality judgements of sentences in the informant's language, as discussed above.   It is sometimes the case, however, that elicitations and grammaticality judgements cannot provide you with all the information you need. Take, for example, the case of a group of aspiring linguists who were working with a Welsh informant. The students were interested in finding a sentence containing the simple present tense of 'to walk'. Whenever they asked the informant to translate 'she walks', however, he replied with a progressive form that actually means 'she is walking'.   They told him several times that the translations he gave them were not what they wanted, but to no avail, They tried creating sentences in Welsh of the sort they wanted, but they were not proficient enough in Welsh to force the construction out of the informant. Things eventually became so confused that the informant, in an attempt to help, concluded that he had misunderstood their directions, and proceeded to provide them with a list of every synonym for 'walk' that he could think of.

When this sort of thing happens, you need to find a way to show your informant what you are after. Anything you can come up with, including acting out the sentences in question, is fine if it helps get your meaning across. Working with our Vank[h] informant, we found that drawing pictures worked well. We discovered this trick when trying to get a handle on the thematic roles (θ-roles) in multiple wh-questions. When asked to translate 'Who eats what?' our informant provided us with the sentence hu hintʃʰ-ɑ otum? When we then asked him how to say 'What eats who?' he gave us exactly the same sentence. We found that no matter how we phrased our questions, he always gave us the same response. For independent reasons, we did not believe that this sentence could mean 'What eats who', and so we had to find a way to get at this meaning. Finally, we hit upon the idea of drawing pictures of the actors in the sentence and then drawing arrows to show the direction of the action. As soon as he saw what we were looking for, our informant gave us the sentence we needed: hintʃʰ huv-ɑ otum 'what eats who?' Although our system of drawing was rather primitive, it did the job.

3. Planning the session

Nothing makes for a more effective session with your informant than proper planning and preparation. This is especially true for syntax, where it is easy to stray off course and end up collecting pages full of virtually worthless data. You can minimize this danger by compiling ahead of time a list of all the sentences to be used during the session. Naturally, making up this sort of comprehensive game-plan requires a good deal of brainstorming.

The first thing to decide is what sort of sentences to include in your session. This depends on which syntactic phenomena you are interested in. If you want to work on wh-movement, topicalization, and reflexives, for example, then you need to make up independent sets of sentences to test each of these phenomena. This means having a group of sentences containing wh-words, a group containing reflexives, and so on.

Keep in mind when making up a sentence list that you have two testing methods at your disposal: elicitation through English (or another language that you and the informant both speak), and grammaticality judgements on sentences in your informant's language. Your sentence list should probably be based upon the elicitation technique. It should be made up of English sentences for your informant to translate into his or her language.

In many cases, however, you want to test for a subtle difference in meaning or grammaticality between two structurally different sentences. Elicitation through English is often not sufficient for this task, and so you have to switch gears and use grammaticality judgements on sentences in your informant's language. (This may also happen when searching for a construction for which there is no correlate in English, such as long-distance anaphors.) When checking for subtle contrasts between sentences in your informant's language, be sure to come up with sentences which are as similar to each other in grammatical and semantic content as possible, except where the phenomenon you are examining is concerned. In other words, your sentences should be "minimal pairs at the sentence level." (Schütze 1997:184) For example, if you were checking for semantic differences between regular pronouns and demonstrative pronouns (dem.) in German, the sentence pair in (4) would provide you with a more tightly-controlled experiment than the sentence pair in (5), because the sentences in (4) are all but identical, while those in (5) have little in common.

(4)   a.   *Ich   habe   **ihn**   noch   nicht   gesehen*
             I   have   him   yet   not   seen
             'I haven't seen him yet'

       b.   *Ich   habe   **den**   noch   nicht   gesehen*
             I   have   him (dem.)   yet   not   seen
             'I haven't seen him yet'

(5)   a.   *Wir   besuchen   **ihn**   morgen*
        we   visit   him   tomorrow
        'We're visiting him tomorrow'

    b.   *Mein Vater kennt   **den**   seit   zehn Jahren*
        my   father   knows   him (dem.)   since   ten   years
        'My father has known him for ten years'

Schütze 1997 points out that the semantic content of sentences can be very important when working with an informant: "...it is simply not true that people will rate all structurally identical sentences equally grammatical". Sentences which refer to a plausible state of affairs in the real world are often rated much more highly than those which stretch the informant's imagination too far. The example cited earlier in which our Vank[h] informant judged the sentence *I am being killed by the bear* unacceptable on practical grounds, illustrates this point nicely. For this reason, one should endeavor to make up sentences which describe plausible scenarios. It is also important, however, that the sentences not be so dull or unimaginative that the informant loses interest altogether.

Finally, it is important to number your sentence list, and to keep it with your notes after the session is over. During an elicitation session, you may not be able to get precise glosses for all your informant's sentences, and you may find later that you have forgotten what some of the things you transcribed actually meant. If you number your transcriptions, however, then you can always check them against the numbered sentences on your list, and find out what each sentence means in English.

4. A sample session

We will now demonstrate how to apply the principles we have discussed when working with a real informant. The bulk of the remainder of the chapter is devoted to recounting a session we conducted with our Gujarati informant. This session encapsulated many of the successes and difficulties that investigators often encounter, and so we feel it is particularly instructive.

We covered a number of topics during this session with our informant. Naturally, the session was not broken up into entirely discrete units, but rather one topic led to another, and so on. In the section below, however, the account of the session is divided into separate sub-sections, one for each major topic that we worked on.

4.1. Word order

We began our session by trying to learn something about word order in Gujarati. We already knew from previous sessions that Gujarati has a fairly strict—though not exceptionless—rule that the verb has to come at the end of the sentence. Our interest was in finding out to what extent the other parts of a sentence can be moved around, and what effect this movement might have on the meaning of the sentence. The first sentence we tried to elicit was *The weather is bad.*

We imagined that we would collect this sentence quickly, and then move on to re-ordering the various phrases and asking for grammaticality judgements. As is often the case in fieldwork, however, just getting started proved more difficult than anticipated. It actually took us about five minutes just to collect this one sentence. First, our informant just gave us different words for weather, three of them, in fact. He did not tell us that this was what he was doing, however, so we misanalyzed his responses. What we heard was:

Cooper: How do you say "The weather is bad"?
Informant: The weather is mosʌm.

Because our informant switches between languages a great deal, I first thought that mosʌm meant 'bad', and that he was saying "The weather is bad". In fact, mosʌm means 'season'.

Cooper:	So, what's the whole sentence?
Informant:	Uh...βataβʌrʌn is weather.[31] Uhh...abohʌβa.[32] βataβʌrʌn abohʌβa.

At this point, we had no way to know that abohʌva meant 'weather', and not 'is bad'. I assumed that the whole sentence was βataβʌrʌn abohʌβa.

Informant:	So, you say abohʌβa kʰʌrab tʃʰe.
	[weather bad is] kʰʌrab means 'bad'.

Only at this point did we finally figure out what was going on. We went back and found out that all three words—abohʌβa, βataβʌrʌn, and mosʌm—essentially meant 'weather', and from that we could figure out the full sentence. Unfortunately, we were unable to find any other grammatical word orders, no matter how many permutations of this basic sentence we tried. In the end, we gave up and decided to try a new sentence, figuring that a longer sentence might work better. Knowing when to give up on a particular line of inquiry is a valuable skill in linguistic fieldwork.

Next we tried the sentence *I gave my wife the book*, and our informant responded with the form in (6). This turned out to be an accurate translation of our elicitation. Better yet, this sentence ultimately led us to some very interesting information.

---

[31] Gala (n.d.) glosses vataβʌrʌn as 'atmosphere'. (Recall from chapter 5 that our informant generally pronounces as [β] (a voiced bilabial fricative) what is written as <v> in standard Gujarati.)

[32] Borrowed from a Persian word meaning 'climate'.

(6)   mɑɾi pʌtni-ne   tʃɔpɾi   apũ-tʃʰũ
        my   wife-dat.   book   give-past
        'I gave my wife the book'

Knowing that the verb probably could not move, we tried moving the word tʃɔpɾi to the beginning of the sentence, and leaving every thing else as it was: tʃɔpɾi mɑɾi pʌtni-ne apũ-tʃʰũ. Our informant rejected the proposed sentence rather sternly. From past experience, we knew that Gujarati word order was somewhat flexible, so this result was surprising. Vaux suspected that there was more to the story. From his experience with certain Turkic and Armenoid languages, he knew that some languages require that indefinite objects appear right before the verb, while objects with a modifier are free to move around. He changed the elicitation sentence slightly, adding a possessive modifier: *I gave my wife her book*. Our informant responded with the sentence in (7).

(7)   mɑɾi pʌtni-ne   tɛni   tʃɔpɾi   apũ-tʃʰũ
        my   wife-dat.   her   book   give-past
        'I gave my wife her book'

When we rearranged the terms in this sentence, putting tɛni tʃɔpɾi at the beginning, our informant judged the sentence acceptable. This demonstrates the importance of being thorough and persistent when working with an informant. Just because you fail to find evidence of a certain phenomenon the first time around does not mean that it does not exist.

4.2. Binding conditions

Binding is a very popular topic in generative linguistics. The interest centers around certain cross-linguistic generalizations that can be made about the distribution of three different types of noun phrases:

full noun phrases (full NPs), non-reflexive pronouns, often called simply 'pronouns', and reflexive pronouns, or 'reflexives'. When we elicited the sentence *I gave my wife her book* from our informant and began moving different terms around, we stumbled onto some interesting information regarding binding. Like its English counterpart, *her*, the Gujarati possessive pronoun, tɛni, can behave either as a reflexive or as a regular (non-reflexive) pronoun. This means that in a sentence such as *I gave my wife her book*, *her* can refer either to my wife's book, or to some other woman's book (although the former interpretation is generally preferred). Likewise, in (7), tɛni can have either of these two meanings.

When tɛni tʃɔpɾi is moved to the beginning of the sentence, however, as in (8), one of these interpretations is ruled out.

(8)   tɛni tʃɔpɾi mɑri pʌtni-ne ɑpũ-tʃʰũ
        'I gave my wife some other woman's book'
        *'I gave my wife her (own) book'

In (8), tɛni can only refer to some other woman, and not to 'my wife'. This result is actually predicted by the principles of binding which have been established by generative syntacticians. Syntacticians have theorized that a reflexive pronoun has to be c-commanded[33] by an antecedent—another noun phrase of some kind—contained within the same clause as the reflexive. In (7), this condition is met, since mɑri pʌtni-ne c-commands tɛni tʃɔpɾi. In

---

[33] C-command is a technical term referring to a specific relationship between nodes on a syntactic tree. The precise definition of c-command is not terribly important for our purposes, but some understanding of this concept may be useful. Basically, a syntactic node c-commands any other node which is its sister in a tree structure, and it also c-commands all nodes which are dominated by that sister node.

(8), however, the pronoun tɛni has no antecedent from which to get a reflexive interpretation, and so this interpretation is blocked.

Knowledge of theoretical syntax is often useful when studying syntax in the field. In this case, it allowed us to test for a phenomenon which we might otherwise never have come across. Furthermore, we were able to conduct this test quickly and efficiently, since we had a good idea of what the results would be. Beware, however, that relying too heavily on theoretical knowledge can seriously hinder you. It is important to remain open to all possibilities, even those which are judged theoretically impossible. You do not want to miss a great piece of data just because you assume that it cannot exist.

4.3. Relative clauses

Relative clauses are subordinate clauses which are introduced by a term, often a pronoun, which gets its reference from some term in a higher clause. Some examples are provided in (9).

(9) a. He sees the man *who is eating the fish*
     b. He sees the man *that (whom) the fish is eating*
     c. She likes the car *that has new tires*
     d. She likes the car *that Donna bought*

There is considerable variation across languages in terms of where relative clauses can occur, and in what order the terms within them can occur. In English, for example, relative clauses follow their antecedents, while in Japanese and Korean, they precede them. In many languages, it is possible to stack up a number of relative clauses, one after the other. English certainly allows this: *The man who lived in the house that was bought by the woman who ran for president died recently.*

We decided to try to elicit a few sentences with multiple relative clauses, in the hope that we could find evidence of resumptive pronouns. We did not realize just how much difficulty we would have collecting a sentence containing even one relative clause. As we found out, our informant, who speaks broken English, had never really learned to process English relative clauses as such. He simply interpreted them as two distinct thoughts connected in some way, perhaps temporally or causally. This wrought havoc on our attempts at elicitation, as shown below.

Cooper: How would you say 'this is the book that I gave to my wife'?

Informant: ɑ   tʃɔpɾi   hũ   mɑɾi   pʌtni-ne   ɑpis.[34]
[this book   I   my   wife-dat.   I.will.give]
'this' means ɑ.

Cooper: So this means, 'this book I give to my wife..'.

Vaux: 'I will give'.

[Note that our informant gave us a future-tense form, when the elicitation was actually in the past. This sort of thing is common.]

Cooper: Right. Um...OK...How would you say 'I am reading the book that I give to my wife'?

Informant: hũ   tʃɔpɾi   βãtʃis   pʌtʃʰi   mɑɾi   pʌtni-ne   ɑpis.
[I   book   I.will.read   after   my   wife-dat.   I.will.give]

Vaux: And what does that mean?

Informant: 'I will read the book, and after I will give to my wife'.

Vaux: I think it's 'I will read the book, and then I will give it to my wife'.

---

[34] The standard Gujarati form here is ɑpiʃ; as we discuss in section 5, our informant freely interchanges s and ʃ in his idiolect.

Informant: Yeah, that's it.
Cooper: Well, we're looking for something slightly different.
             (to informant) Imagine that Bert asks me 'What book are you reading?'.
Informant: [Translates this question so fast that we cannot transcribe it.]
Cooper: (laughing) Right, right. But imagine that he says, 'Hey, Justin, what book are you reading', and I say 'I'm reading the book that I gave to my wife'.
Informant: tʃɔpɾi βãtʃis pʌtʃʰi mɑɾi pʌtni-ne ɑpis. Same thing.
Vaux: We don't want pʌtʃʰi, though. We want 'the book **which** I gave to my wife'.

[Note that direct statements such as 'we don't want X' are interpreted as being very rude if one is addressing a native (or at least fluent) speaker of English, and therefore should be avoided. However, it is often counterproductive to employ formulaic expressions of politeness with informants who do not speak English very well, because they will generally be unable to parse the grammatical structure and pragmatic significance of phrases like *would you mind telling me how to say X?*. Straightforward expressions like *I want X* or *tell me X* can be much more successful in such situations, because the informants are more likely to recognize the words and the constructions, and in all likelihood will not know that these constructions are considered rude among native speakers. (Just be sure that you don't get carried away by the form of your sentences and actually become rude to your informants!)]

Informant: [no response.]
Cooper: Let's think of a different example, maybe. (long pause.)
             Let's say there's a man, and he kisses my wife, right?
Informant: It's no good.

Cooper: I know, so I'm angry, so I'm gonna kill him. So let's say, 'I kill the man who kissed my wife'.

Informant: me[35] tʌne mɑɾio kɑɾʌn mɑɾi pʌtni-ne tʃumbʌn kʌɾe-tʃʰe.

Cooper: So, what does this mean?

Informant: Means, 'I kill him, because he kiss to my wife'.

Cooper: Oh, OK. What's kɑɾʌn?

Informant: 'because'. Oh, no. Same problem, ah? You don't want the 'because'?

Vaux: Right. We want 'The man who kissed my wife'.

Informant: hū te   mɑnʌs-ne mɑɾi nɑkiʃ   dʒe mɑɾi

             [I   that man-dat.   my   will.kill who my]

             pʌtni-ne   tʃumbʌn   tʃʰe.

             [wife-dat.   kiss   does]

             ['I will kill the man who kisses my wife'.]

Vaux: Yeah, that looks like it.

Finally, after all that trouble, we had found a relative clause. We decided to put resumptive pronouns, our initial topic of interest, on the back burner for a while. Resumptive pronouns usually occur when two or more relative clauses pile up, and we were not sure that we could successfully collect such a sentence. More importantly, however, we had stumbled on another interesting topic: ergativity.

4.4. Ergativity

Linguists have done a good deal of work on languages with nominative/accusative case systems, as opposed to the more familiar (to most English speakers) ergative/absolutive system. Roughly speaking, languages with an absolutive/ergative case system mark

---

[35] This pronoun is <mẽ> in the official Gujarati orthography, but our informant pronounces a non-nasalized [e].

subjects of transitive sentences with one case—the ergative—while marking both direct objects of transitive sentences and subjects of intransitives with another case—the absolutive. Some languages, including many in the Indic family, have what is called a *split-ergative* system, in which a nominative/accusative system is used in some tenses, and an ergative/absolutive system is used in others.

We were therefore not surprised to find that Gujarati is a split-ergative language. This came up right at the end of our long search for a relative clause. When we finally collected the sentence me manʌse mari pʌtnine tʃumbʌn kʌɾio me tʌne marina kʰjo, 'I killed the man who kissed my wife', we noticed that the subject of the main clause was me, and not the usual 1st person singular subject pronoun, hũ. "Where's hũ?" I asked. "me", our informant replied. "me means 'I'."

Vaux surmised that me was an oblique form of the 1st person singular pronoun, and that this was probably due to the presence of a split-ergative system. To check, we asked our informant if hũ would be acceptable in this sentence, in place of me. He judged the sentence completely ungrammatical with hũ as the subject of the main clause.

The behavior of subject pronouns of intransitive sentences was very interesting. Based on the standard model of ergative/absolutive systems, we expected me not to be acceptable as the subject of an intransitive sentence, since it is the form used as the subject of transitive sentences. However, we suspected that unergative and unaccusative verbs might behave differently, and therefore elicited some sentences containing verbs of these two types.[36] As it turned out, our informant said that me was acceptable

---

[36] Comrie (1981:59) notes that some languages can use either ergative or absolutive case for intransitive subjects, depending on how volitional the action is. Transitive verbs can also show this variation, depending on how agentive the verb is (118).

as the subject of a sentence such as me tʌɾio hʌto 'I swam, but that hữ was the preferred form, at least in his idiolect.

Unfortunately, we cannot trust our results completely on this matter, because I made the serious mistake of asking several leading questions. As mentioned in previous chapters, there are few things worse than asking an informant a question of the type "This is like X, right?" and yet I made this mistake several times during this portion of our session, as shown in the transcript below. It is difficult to keep these sorts of questions from slipping out, but we recommend that you try, and we hope that you do better than I did.

Cooper: How do you say 'I swim'?
Informant: Right now? hữ tʌɾutʃʰũ . 'I am swimming'.
Cooper: How do you say 'I swam'?
Informant: Ummm... hữ tʌɾio hʌto.
Cooper: Can you say me tʌɾio hʌto?
Informant: Yeah, this OK too.
Vaux: Aha!
Informant   But, almost the people use the hữ, means 'I'. Sometime, in the village, the people use the me too, me words. But in the town, the people words hữ.

[For more on our informant's odd use of *almost* and other English terms, see section 5.]

Vaux: Can you use me?
Informant: No. I use the hữ...and the me. Both.
Vaux: So, can you say me tʌɾio hʌto?
Informant: Yes. The same meaning.
Cooper: Is it OK, or not as good?
Informant: hữ is better. hữ tʌɾio hʌto. me tʌɾio hʌto.   Same meaning.

Cooper: But hũ is better, right?
Informant: hũ is better.

It seems likely that my leading questions corrupted our data, at least somewhat. In this case, the best option is to return to this topic another day. Before we move on, though, notice that our informant said that Gujarati speakers normally use nominative subjects (e.g. hũ) with verbs like 'swim', but "villagers" sometimes use an oblique subject (e.g. me). Taken at face value, this is an indication of dialectal variation in Gujarati. However, you must treat such assessments with extreme caution, and be sure to confirm them with the relevant speakers (in this case, one would want to see if any villagers actually use the me construction). In our experience, statements of the sort that our informant made are often simply another way of saying "I personally don't find the sentence grammatical".

5. The informant's English

Over the course of a number of sessions with our Gujarati informant, we have honed our ability to interpret his English. This has proven useful for several reasons. First, our communication with him during the sessions has become more efficient, since we at least know what he is saying, even if he does not always understand us. Second, we have found that he actually can actually provide us with detailed information, including sophisticated analyses, about Gujarati, if only we can figure out what he is saying.

The key to understanding our informant has been the tape recorder. Listening to recordings of our sessions, we have picked up on all sorts of things that he says. For example, at one point in one of our sessions, he said "tʃʰe means 'is' and hʌto/hʌti means 'was male and female'." At the time he said it, this comment did not make sense. Re-playing the tape, however, we realized that this was actually an accurate analysis of his system of auxiliary verbs. tʃʰe is a present auxiliary meaning something like 'is' or 'does', while hʌto and hʌti are the past tense forms of this auxiliary. The former carries masculine inflection, and the latter feminine, hence our informant's comment that they meant "male and female". Reviewing this same tape, we realized that he used the words "front", "back" and "middle" to mean "future", "past" and "present", respectively.

One of the more amusing features of our informant's English is his use of the words "almost" and "always". He consistently uses "almost" to mean either 'everyone' or 'always', as in *Almost the people use Hindi words*, meaning 'everyone (always) uses Hindi words'. "Always", meanwhile, has a different meaning for him: namely, 'sometimes'.

On the phonetic/phonological front, we have had to get used to the fact that our informant does not distinguish between [v], [β], and [w], nor between [s] and [ʃ]. He once said to us, for example, *In India, somebody sit over there, outside*, and then began laughing uproariously. At first, we found this fact rather unremarkable. People sit outside everywhere, right? Then we realized that he meant that people defecate in the streets. Getting accustomed to the quirks of our informant's English has generally made our job as investigators much more enjoyable.

Still, informants' idiosyncrasies in English can always cause trouble, no matter how well you become accustomed to their idiolects. Even now, we cannot trust our Gujarati informant's glosses of his own sentences, because he rarely puts his English translation in the same tense as the original Gujarati sentence.

It is especially important that you take your informant's English skills into account when working on questions, reported speech, and related topics. An informant who speaks broken English is not likely to catch the difference between, for example, *She said she was leaving* and *She said, "I'm leaving"*. Your informant may also not know when you are asking a question, and when you are making a statement. We have a Japanese colleague who, despite speaking excellent English, has never quite mastered English question formation. As a result, when she says something like *This is your copy of the assignment*, one never knows if this is a statement or a question. You should try to identify any such oddities that you can find in your informants' English, so that you will be able to understand them better.

6. Further syntactic phenomena

6.1. Exceptional case marking

This is an excellent phenomenon to investigate when working with an informant, because the situations in which exceptional case-marking occurs are very similar cross-linguistically. This means that if you provide the informant with an English sentence containing ECM, his or her translation of that sentence is likely to provide you with the desired form, if it exists, without you having to do a great deal of coaxing and prodding. ECM occurs when a transitive verb case-marks the subject of a lower clause. ECM is common in English, as seen in (10), and in other Indo-European languages, such as Latin (11). It is also found in many non-Indo-European languages, such as Japanese (12).

(10)   a.   *I expect him to be there.*
       b.   **I expect he to be there.*
       c.   *I expect that he/*him will be there.*

(11)   a.   *Dico   poetam   stultum   esse*
            I.say   poet.acc.   stupid.acc.   be
            'I declare the poet to be stupid'

b. **Dico poeta stultus esse*

    I.say   poet.nom. stupid.nom. be

(12)   a. *John-ga   Mary-o   bizin-da-to   omotteiru*

          John-nom. Mary-acc. beauty-cop.-comp. think

          'John thinks Mary is beautiful'

       b. **John-ga   Mary-ga   bizin-da-to   omotteiru*

          John-nom. Mary-nom. beauty-cop.-comp. think

In (10a), *him* is the subject of the infinitival clause *him to be there*, but it is case-marked by *expect*, and so it occurs in the accusative rather than the nominative. The same process applies in (11a), where *poetam*, which is the subject of the infinitival clause, is in the accusative because it receives its case from *dico*, the tensed verb of the main clause. In (12a), *Mary-o* is the subject of the complement clause, but it receives its case from *omotteiru*, the verb of the main clause.

ECM generally occurs with verbs such as *think, believe, declare, say, perceive,* and a handful of others. Keep in mind that familiarity with the verbal morphology of the informant's language is very useful when checking for ECM. You want to be able to identify infinitives, if they exist, and you want to know which subjects or objects agree with which finite verbs.

6.2. Null subjects and null objects

It is a well-known fact that subjects may be omitted, under certain circumstances, in many of the world's languages. Languages such as Italian, Spanish and Polish—and Gujarati, for that matter—allow null subjects with tensed verbs. In Polish, therefore, one typically uses a form such as (13a), rather than (13b), unless you want to say that it is specifically *you* who understands, and not anyone else.

(13)   a.   *Rozumiem.*
                understand (1st. sg. pres.)
                'I understand'
       b.   *Ja rozumiem.*
                I understand (1st. sg. pres.)
                'I understand'

Some languages, such as Korean, allow both null subjects and null objects, provided that the referents of both are retrievable from the discourse. So, in response to a question such as judʒin-i pɑp tʃo-ɑ-hɛ? "Does Eugene like rice?" one could respond tʃo-ɑ-hɛ, meaning simply "likes". Clearly, coming up with appropriate contexts for null subjects and objects is crucial to finding out if your informant's language allows them.

It is worth noting that, cross-linguistically, certain types of constructions appear with null subjects more often than others. One example of this is impersonal constructions, especially those associated with the weather. So, in many languages, "it is raining" is expressed simply as *Rains*. Another example involves sentences where there is likely to be a semantically empty subject, such as existentials: *There is a gun on the table*. English happens to add the expletive *there* in such cases, but many languages do not. Even if your informant's language does not appear to allow null-subjects in 'regular' sentences, you should inquire as to how some of these other constructions are handled.

6.3. Topicalization

Topicalization involves extracting a syntactic element from its original location in a clause and moving it to some designated site, such as the beginning of the clause, in order to show its special status. An example from English would be *Barry White, I'm a big fan of*, where the deep-structure is presumed to be *I'm a big fan of*

Barry White. In this case, *Barry White* is topicalized because the speaker wishes to place emphasis on this element.

The easiest way to elicit topicalized structures is to come up with sentences in which a certain element bears contrastive stress. This often involves giving the informant a sentence or two providing context before you ask for a translation of the sentence you are interested in. For example, you might begin by explaining that some person (give him or her a name!) likes cars and likes motorcycles. Then you ask the informant how to say that this person does not like bicycles, with stress on *bicycles*. Typically, the informant will respond with a sentence in which *bicycles* is topicalized.

It should be noted that in some languages, topicalization is not marked by movement, and so this elicitation strategy is by no means foolproof. In fact, when working with our Gujarati informant, we were unable to find any evidence of topicalization at all. This may have had something to do with our informant's chatty nature, however. I began my line of questioning by asking him how to say "I like movies", and he gave me a translation, along with a word-by-word gloss. When I followed up by asking him how to say "I don't like books", he responded by saying "Oh, yes, sometimes books bad. Sometimes naked picture books. You know, naked girls! My daughter, she like to read all the books, but my son, no like read books". By the time we got back on track and he came up with a translation for "I don't like books", the moment was lost, as was the sense of contrastive stress that I was trying to highlight. I tried a few similar sentence pairs, but was unable to find any evidence of topicalization, either morphologically or syntactically. This brings up an interesting point about fieldwork, which is that while one can easily prove the existence of a given phenomenon in a language, it is all but impossible to prove the non-existence of a phenomenon. Just because I could not find evidence of topicalization in Gujarati does not mean that it does not exist. Indeed, one could work for months, or conceivably years, on this very topic, searching all the time for an example of topicalization, and still not be able to prove that no such example existed. There is always the possibility that the construction is there somewhere, and you have simply failed to elicit it.

7. Trouble spots

As is the case with any sub-field of linguistics, there are certain pitfalls involved in working on syntax. Below are some of the traps that we have fallen into, or heard of others falling into.

- **Don't get cocky!** The more proficient you become at speaking and understanding the informant's language, the less likely you are to misanalyze one of the speaker's grammaticality judgements. You will also find that you can use your own knowledge of the informant's language very effectively to produce novel utterances for the informant to judge. Do not assume, though, that you know if a given construction will be grammatical or not, just because a similar construction was judged a certain way; linguists often extrapolate incorrectly. You should also keep in mind that forcing a construction out of the informant by way of elicitations in his or her language can be a risky technique. One linguist told me about a case in which he was doing elicitations in Irish, and was laboring to find a crucial, yet subtle, contrast in meaning related to extraction. He had reason to suspect that this contrast existed, but could not pinpoint it. Because the contrast he was looking for did not exist in English, elicitation through English was not getting him anywhere. He then provided the informant with two sentences in Irish which he hoped would highlight the contrast he had in mind. To his delight, the informant judged one of them ungrammatical, just as the linguist had predicted. He wrote up his results and presented them in a paper at a conference. Only later did he find out that the informant had judged the sentence unacceptable because of a simple grammatical error unrelated to the phenomenon the linguist was looking at.

- **Keep it interesting.** As mentioned at the beginning of this chapter, native speakers of a language often assume that the distinction between grammatical and ungrammatical utterances in their language is completely obvious. Even if you are successful in demonstrating that this is not the case, your informant may still become bored after giving you judgement after judgement on what appear to be meaningless sentences. Take, for example, the session that Vaux had with a native speaker of Western Armenian. This informant was not very forthcoming with information on null objects, because he thought that null objects were always grammatical, as in (14a). By coming up with a sentence (14b) in which a null object was not acceptable, however, Vaux managed to catch the informant's interest.

(14) a. hagopʰə tʰaranɛn kʰirkʰ-mə arav jɛv
      (*aniga, *iŋkʰə)   indzi   dəvav
      Hagop   shelf (abl.) book-a   took   and
      it   me.dat.   gave
      'Hagop took a book from the shelf and gave (*it) to me'

   b. hagopʰə kʰirkʰə ajrɛtsʰ pʰajtsʰ aramə
      *(an(iga)) gartʰal gərtsʰav
      Hagop   book   burned but   Aram
      it   read   was.able
      'Hagop burned the book, but Aram was able to read *(it)'

- **Going off track.** Because syntax provides the investigator with so many opportunities to come up with theoretical analyses during the course of a session, there is always the danger of straying too far away from one's sentence list. It is very tempting to run with a hypothesis that you have just come up with, and to test it fully right then and there. This sometimes leads to long sequences of elicitations which are not very fruitful. Many linguists find that when they come up with a great idea in the middle of a session, they do best by jotting it down in a notebook, putting a star next to it, and moving on. After the session is over, they have time to sit down and think of sentences for elicitation that will test their hypotheses effectively. These can then be included in the sentence list for the next session. Of course, there are also advantages to continuing with a given topic when you are on a roll, and so some linguists prefer to use the sentence list primarily as a starting point from which to launch spontaneous inquiries. For one thing, this may help you avoid priming the informant, since your elicitations will be somewhat random. As always, common sense is your best guide.

- **Beware of drink.** We noted in the introduction that the importance of food and drink cannot be underestimated when working on linguistics in the field. This is certainly true. Alcohol, in particular, is good for befriending the informant, and for building up trust between the investigator and the informant. Unfortunately, it is generally not as useful during actual work sessions. As one syntactician noted to me, "the problem with people who are drinking is that they are often drunk". When you are trying to work actively with the informant, and are relying on him or her for grammaticality judgements, you should both be relatively sober.

- **Keep your head about you.** A typical elicitation session involves spending most of one's time frantically writing down everything the informant says, just trying to get all the words on the page before they disappear forever. This is especially true for syntax, where the informant is likely to be spewing out whole sentences in rapid succession. Under these circumstances, it is OK to sacrifice some accuracy in your transcription, as long as you are getting everything on tape. The key is to keep thinking during the session, and to keep formulating questions that will lead to topics of interest.

  Working with our Gujarati informant, who is a prodigious talker, I fell into the trap of writing furiously without thinking. The trouble began when, in one of the more bizarre moments of my life, our informant turned to me at the beginning of one of our sessions and said "I love you". At first I was dumbfounded, but then he immediately gave the Gujarati translation of the sentence, and followed this up by explaining that I needed to know how to say "I love you" if I wanted to talk to pretty Gujarati girls. I had just about recovered when he gave me another sentence, which I diligently transcribed as *ja ti amu*, which is roughly how he said it. I asked him what this sentence meant, and he said that it also meant 'I love you'. This made no sense! How could two sentences meaning the same thing be so completely different? Fortunately, Vaux had kept his thinking cap on in the midst of this madness, and so he explained: 'It's Spanish'. Our informant concurred; he had learned some Spanish and was just trying it out on me. (The actual Spanish phrase is *yo te amo*.)

Suggested Readings

Blackwell, A., E. Bates, and D. Fisher. 1996. The time course of grammaticality judgment. Language and Cognitive Processes 11.4:337-406.

Brame, Michael. 1987. Ungrammatical Notes, 13: A Taller Man Than My Mother. Linguistic Analysis 17.1-2:99-109.

Comrie, Bernard and Norval Smith. 1977. Lingua Descriptive Studies: Questionnaire. Lingua 42:1-72.

Cowper, Elizabeth. 1992. A Concise Introduction to Syntactic Theory: The Government-Binding Approach. Chicago: University of Chicago Press.

Gibson, Edward and James Thomas. 1999. Memory Limitations and Structural Forgetting: The Perception of Complex Ungrammatical Sentences as Grammatical. Language & Cognitive Processes 14.3:225-48.

Haegeman, Liliane. 1994. Introduction to Government and Binding Theory, second edition. Oxford: Blackwell.

Hinds, John. 1981. The Interpretation of Ungrammatical Utterances. In Florian Coulmas, ed., A Festschrift for the Native Speaker, 221-235. The Hague: Mouton.

Hiramatsu, Kazuko and Diane Lillo-Martin. 1998. Children Who Judge Ungrammatical What They Produce. Annabel Greenhill, Mary Hughes, Heather Littlefield, and Hugh Walsh, eds., Proceedings of the 22nd Annual Boston University Conference on Language Development, 337-47. Somerville, MA: Cascadilla.

Householder, Fred. 1973. On Arguments from Asterisks. Foundations of Language 10:365-376.

Makkai, Valerie. 1975. 'Pretty Damn Seldom...': On the Grammaticality of Ungrammatical Utterances. Columbia, SC: Hornbeam.

Nagata, Hiroshi. 1989. Repetition Effect in Judgments of Grammaticality of Sentences: Examination with Ungrammatical Sentences. Perceptual & Motor Skills 68.1:275-282.

Otero, Carlos. 1972. Acceptable Ungrammatical Sentences in Spanish. Linguistic Inquiry 3:233-42.

Payne, Thomas. 1997. Describing Morphosyntax: A guide for field linguists. New York: Cambridge University Press.

Pittman, Richard. 1970. On eliciting transformations in Vietnamese. In Alan Healey, ed., Translator's field guide, 379-390. Ukarumpa: Summer Institute of Linguistics.

Sampson, Geoffrey. 1987. Evidence against the 'Grammatical'/ 'Ungrammatical' Distinction. In Willem Meijs, ed., Corpus Linguistics and Beyond, 219-226. Amsterdam: Rodopi.

Schütze, Carson. 1996. The Empirical Base of Linguistics. Chicago: University of Chicago Press.

Schwarte, Barbara. 1974. Intuitions of grammaticality and the 'law of contrast'. Studies in the Linguistic Sciences 4:1:198.

Spencer, N. 1973. Differences Between Linguists and Nonlinguists in Intuitions of Grammaticality-Acceptability. Journal of Psycholinguistic Research 2.2:83-98.

Tillery, Jan. 2000. The reliability and validity of linguistic self-reports. Southern Journal of Linguistics 24.1:55-68.

Exercises

1. Collect a short text from the informant, something no more than a few sentences long. Be sure to get a good gloss for all of the words. Use what you know about the grammar of the informant's language to re-write the passage, altering the word order and clause structure wherever possible. For example, take a sentence such as *He leaves on the train tomorrow*, and re-write it as *He leaves tomorrow on the train*. At the next session, read your modified passage to the informant, and see what he or she thinks. No doubt, some of the things you expected to be grammatical will turn out not to be, and you may find out about some interesting grammatical rules in the process.

2. Collect and transcribe a pair of independent, yet related, clauses, such as *They have a lot of money* and *They cannot afford a house*. Ask the informant to combine these clauses into a single sentence, something like *Although they have a lot of money, they cannot afford a house*. Transcribe the new sentence that the informant gives you, and then try this out with some other pairs of clauses. This should give you some clues about coordination and subordination in the informant's language. Keep in mind that you may have difficulty explaining to the informant what you are after, and may have to come up with a creative way to explain yourself.

3. Give your informants some sentences which are clearly ungrammatical and see how they react. See what sort of explanations they give for their reactions, and try to determine whether their explanations can be trusted.

4. Collect a sentence which you expect to have an ambiguous meaning, and see if your informant picks up on the ambiguity.

This can be tricky, since what is ambiguous in English may not be ambiguous in your informant's language. One possibility would be a sentence like *He likes his wife*, where *his* may or may not refer to the same person as *He*.

5. Look over the sentence list given at the end of this chapter. Think of improvements that could be made, and come up with your own revised sentence list for testing wh-movement. For example, you could add some sentences that include negation.

6. Think of ways to test for negative polarity items in your informant's language. Negative polarity items are words or phrases whose occurrence is triggered by the presence of negation. Typically, these words have counterparts which occur in positive contexts. For example, we use *anybody* in negative contexts in English, and *nobody* in positive ones (there are exceptions, of course): *He knows nobody*, vs. *He doesn't know anybody*. Many languages have negative polarity items; the trick is to figure out how to elicit them. Try to collect some, and discuss the problems you encounter in doing so.

7. Ask your informant to translate some English sentences containing quantifiers such as *all, many, few, several, none/no*. See if there are any generalizations to be made about where quantifiers appear within a clause. In English, for example, *all* can occur pre-verbally, as in *we all love new cars*, while most other quantifiers cannot: **we several love new cars*. Both *all* and *several* can immediately precede a full noun phrase, however, as in *we love all new cars* and *we love several new cars*. Check to see if quantifiers can be moved around in your informants' language, and study what effect this has on the meaning of the sentences involved. Finally, try asking the

informant to give you the same sentences, but in the negative, and see what effect negation has on the quantifiers.

Sample Sentence List

Provided below is a sentence list used by a Celtological colleague in an elicitation session focusing on wh-movement. This list is not meant to limit you in your choice of sentences; rather, we merely hope to give you an idea of the form a sentence list may take.

1. Who sings Welsh songs?
2. Who does Megan like?
3. Who likes Megan?
4. Whose book is this?
5. Who did you give the book to?
6. Who does Megan study with other than Ioan?
7. Who are you going to the pub with?

8. Where do you live?
9. Where do you work?
10. Where does Megan study?
11. Where is a good place to dance?

12. What is your name?
13. What did you eat?
14. What time is it now?
15. What color do you like?
16. What (kind of) tea do you like?
17. What language do you speak other than French?

18. Which one do you like?
19. Which one is yours?

20. How many bottles of whisky do you have?
21. How many people are present in this room?
22. How do you go to the pub?

23. What will Megan do after she graduates?
24. When did Megan say that she would come?
25. Where did Megan say that she wanted to go?
26. Where should I go to drink beer?

10 Studying language use: Pragmatics

Linguists strive to develop grammars which are general and simple, and which ideally cover as much data as possible. This often involves abstracting away from the data somewhat, ignoring informants' qualifications such as "you can say that, but only if you're really angry at someone". However, tidbits like this are an essential part of a language, whether you are studying the use of language in society or subtleties of theoretical syntax. Since linguists do not have direct access to the linguistic knowledge that speakers have in their heads, they must by necessity study the use of language in the real world, which includes not only published texts and recorded narratives, but also elicitations of grammaticality judgements and even introspective reflections on one's own linguistic competence. Ideally, these performative aspects of language will directly reflect speakers' linguistic competence, but any number of pragmatic factors can interfere, especially when one is conducting fieldwork. William Labov (1972, 1994) has identified what he calls the *observer's paradox*: the things that the linguist most wants to examine—normal speech patterns—are disrupted when the informants are conscious of being observed.

In this chapter we discuss some ways of compensating for the observer's paradox, and we consider some basic pragmatic factors that play a role in linguistic performance. We have grouped together under the heading "Pragmatics" topics that one would probably not address when writing up a grammar, but which can reveal a great deal about an informant's language and culture. We deal with "real-world" pragmatics, rather than theoretical pragmatic topics such as the ways in which languages reinforce stereotypes, utility and function, and so on. This chapter therefore contains information about some of the most important practical aspects of learning or studying a language: how to introduce yourself, how to avoid offending people within their own culture, and so forth.

1. Methods

There are certain challenges involved in working on pragmatics. One of these is that the phenomena you are interested in studying may only come up in certain situations. Imagine, for example, that you are interested in studying exclamations of anger in your informant's language. You might ask your informant, "What do you say when you drop something on your foot?" Unless the event is actually re-created, however, your informant may be reluctant to produce the forms you are looking for, particularly if they are considered vulgar or impolite. The truth is that I usually say something like *motherf**king shit!* when I injure myself, but I am reluctant to admit this in my more cool-headed moments.

Another difficulty is that real speech generally occurs in the form of conversation, and yet most of the time, we have only one informant. It can be difficult to elicit certain pragmatic phenomena when the informant has only himself or herself to talk to (assuming that the fieldworker is not a fluent speaker of the informant's language). One of the challenges of studying pragmatic phenomena is getting the informant to produce natural speech in a less than natural setting.

Finally, studying pragmatics can be difficult because of the "denial" factor. Individuals are often unaware that they produce certain words or forms in their utterances, and when it is pointed out to them, they deny it. Incidentally, this behavior is not restricted to informants with no linguistic training. Most English speakers, including linguists, say things all the time that they do not admit to saying. For example, in certain situations, English speakers often leave out the indefinite article *a/an* before a noun phrase containing an adjective. Specifically, in a sentence like *That's a fascinating observation*, speakers sometimes begin with the intention of saying *That's fascinating*, and then they tack on the *observation* midway through the sentence, with the result that the final string is *That's fascinating observation*. Vaux does this all the time, and yet he continues to deny it. Another thing that English speakers do, without being aware of it, is begin sentences with a combination of a "yeah" and a "no": *yeah-no*. An example of this is shown in the sample dialog below (1).

(1) A: I really admire Brandon. He's so honest and sincere.
     B: Yeah...no...He's a great guy—absolutely.

Speakers of American English, particularly young ones, use this "yeah...no" form all the time, and yet they often deny doing so, if asked. Your informants may also deny saying things that they have just said, but fortunately, you will have it all on tape! Beware, however, that even when you play their voices back to them, they may not acquiesce. Sometimes our informants have simply claimed that they made a mistake, even if they used a given word or construction numerous times during the course of a session. Some such "mistakes" are indeed speech errors, which all humans make on a regular basis; you should be sure to note these down and correct them appropriately. (To yourself! Never try to correct your informants; they will already be worried enough about speaking "correctly" in front of a linguist.) Other "mistakes" can actually be grammatically correct, but deemed unacceptable by your informants for other reasons. We once recorded a long folk tale from our Abkhaz informant, only to have him correct almost every sentence that he had uttered. It turned out that what he did not like was a particular clitic g^jə which he had sprinkled liberally throughout the original narrative. Further questioning revealed that the g^jə had no clearly identifiable meaning, but its usage was grammatically correct; the informant simply felt that it was too conversational to be canonized in the "official" transcription of the story. The issue with this clitic was therefore not one of grammaticality, but rather of *register*, a phenomenon we discuss in more detail in chapter 11.

2. Topics

2.1. *Watch your mouth!*

One of our favorite topics is curses. All languages seem to have them, and they are invariably fun to study. Collecting swear words can be tricky, however, because you are at your informants' mercy. If they do not want to produce any swear words, then you could be in trouble. It can help to know what sorts of terms are likely to be obscene or offensive. If you can get your informants started thinking along these lines, then lots of good data is sure to follow.

In fact, there are cross-linguistic generalizations to be made about swear words. Some of the most common candidates for swear word status are sexual acts, sexual organs, defecation, urination, and certain animals (dogs, pigs, etc.) and family members. English has swear words, of varying degrees of vulgarity, fitting into all of these categories. This does not mean that swear words are identical across cultures. Many insults in German hinge on pigs (*Schwein*, *Sau* and compounds), for example, while some of ours are based on female dogs (*son-of-a-bitch*). One common category of swear words in which English is somewhat impoverished is religious terminology. We do have *damn*, but this is nothing compared to some other languages. In Quebecois French, for example, most of the worst swear words are religious terms: *tabernacle* (tabernacle), *vierge* (virgin), *hostie* (Host), *sacrament* (sacrament), and so on (cf. Proteau 1996:138-9).

There are also rules about using bad words that apply in many cultures: swearing is generally not tolerated in front of parents or other elders, nor is it acceptable in formal social settings. Many people believe that women swear less than men (see section 2.4 below). You should find out as much as you can about restrictions on swearing in your informant's language. When is swearing permissible? When is it not? Who does and does not swear?

Needless to say, these are touchy issues, and your informant may not wish to divulge a great deal of information. In fact, some people are simply never comfortable with bad words, no matter what the situation. We have a Japanese friend, for example, who refuses to produce a certain Japanese word for genitalia, even though she knows that we know the word, and that it is meaningless to us. She simply cannot bear to make those sounds in that order. If you have an informant who is truly this reserved, it may ultimately not be worth studying swear words at great length. If, on the other hand, your informant enjoys "potty talk" then you could be in business. You may find yourself bowled over with more information about swear words and when to use them than you had ever hoped for.

Our Gujarati informant proved to be very talkative where swear words are concerned. He gave us detailed descriptions and translations of every term we mentioned to him, as well as volunteering facts about India to provide us with some cultural background. For example, when we were talking about swear words involving defecation, he told us a great deal about going to the bathroom in his village. He explained that people do not use toilet paper; rather, they wash themselves with water. The funniest part of our conversation came when he said *Sometimes people have big bowels and use the water.* This seemed like altogether too much information, until we realized that *bowel* was his pronunciation of "bowl", and that he merely meant that people used bowls full of water to clean themselves.

Many informants are neither as reserved as our Japanese friend nor as candid as our Gujarati informant. They are not entirely uncomfortable with this topic, but they need a little encouragement to get them going. The situation in which it is most likely to be difficult to collect curses and related information is when the fieldworker and the informant are not of the same gender, especially when the fieldworker is male and the informant is female. If you find yourself in such a situation, you should of course be very careful not to pressure or embarrass your informant. However, there are ways to encourage informants to produce swear words without feeling pressured or embarrassed.   One is to make use of the "laboratory setting", which for once is an asset rather than a liability. When working with a linguist, people are often willing to produce even the foulest of swear words, the thought of which would otherwise make them blanch, because they know that what they say does not really "count". They are not in their native speech community, nor are they really talking to anyone, so they feel they can get away with producing otherwise unacceptable words. Another way to encourage your informants is to ask them to tell you a story about a time when they saw someone get really mad and curse another person out, or a story involving something scatological or racy.

There is more to studying swearing, however, than collecting a list of words. You should also find out when individual words are used, and when they are not. Invariably, certain swear words are more vulgar than others, and are therefore only appropriate in certain situations. Take the English words *crap* and *shit*, for example. They mean the same thing, and yet there are situations in which only one of the two is acceptable. Most of us would not want to say *shit* in front of our grandmothers. By the same token, it would be somewhat strange to say *crap* in the middle of a highly competitive game of football, when you could say *shit*.

Your informant should be able to tell you which words are only somewhat vulgar, and which are truly vulgar. You may even want to come up with a ranking of swear words, from the least offensive to the most offensive. Working from this list, you can find out exactly which words can be used in which situations, and by whom.

2.2. *Age differences*[37]

There are many interesting things to study involving age differences between speakers. As we all know, languages change over time, and so it can be rewarding to compare the speech of younger and older speakers. Once again, however, there is the problem that most of us have only one informant to work with. Still, your informant may be aware of certain changes in his or her language, especially in terms of slang and other popular terms. Our Gujarati informant frequently tells us which words are typical of the younger generation and which are used by older people. He told us, for example, that younger Gujarati speakers use the word pɑpi to mean 'father', while older ones say bɑpu-dʒi or pitɑ-dʒi. (One of our other Gujarati friends stated that pɑpi can be used by any child to address his or her father, but is not actually a Gujarati word.) To take another example, most English speakers are aware that *cool* is a term used primarily by younger people, while *swell* is preferred by the older generations, if anyone.

In most languages, the relative ages of speakers also has an active effect on the forms one uses in conversation. In English, the effect is minimal, but it is still observable. In a conversation between two people of substantially different ages (15 years or more, perhaps) the younger person would be unlikely to use many imperatives. It would seem odd for a 25-year-old to say to a 50-year-old, *Tell me all about yourself,* while this would be a perfectly reasonable request going in the other direction. As most of us know,

---

[37] See also chapters 11 and 12, where we discuss this topic in greater detail in the context of dialectology and historical linguistics.

age plays a somewhat larger role in many European languages, which use a different 2nd person pronoun depending on the age and status of the other speaker. In East Asian languages such as Japanese and Korean, the age of the speakers involved in a conversation has a drastic effect on many aspects of speech. In Korean, for example, speakers are obliged in every sentence to choose from among a number of verb forms which correspond to a hierarchy of politeness and deference. How much linguistic deference is shown toward another person depends in large part upon that person's age, and so the age of the speakers actually determines what "honorific markers" are used. Many languages have a system somewhat similar to the Korean and Japanese model, although most are not as complex.

The trick as an investigator is to figure out how to elicit this information. You may ask your informant directly how age affects the way people talk to each other, but this will not always give you all the information you need. One good tactic is to present your informant with an imaginary scenario involving a handful of people of different ages and statuses. We recommend including as much detail in your scenario as possible. Draw the imaginary actors on a blackboard if you have one, and include as much relevant information as you can about each one. For example, you might want to draw a man with a hat and a briefcase, and a child with a toy doll, and then write their ages underneath them. Then ask your informant how each of these actors would say things certain things to each other. For example, how would the child ask the man to give him a dollar? How would the man greet the child, or how would he say goodbye?

If you are of a substantially different age than your informant, you may also wish to make use of this fact. Try asking your informant how he or she would say some sentence to you, and then ask how you would be expected to say the same sentence to him or her. You may wish to choose a sentence which has some sort of implicit command or request, as these are the sorts of utterances where politeness forms are highlighted. When eliciting this sort of contrast, though, beware that people have a tendency to say "they're the same!", without thinking carefully about the similarities and differences involved. If this happens to you, make sure to walk your informants through the possible nuances of difference that you are looking for, before you accept that the forms are actually the same.

A side effect of the role that age differences play in speech is that it is often necessary for speakers to know how old their interlocutors are. In languages where age is important in determining politeness forms, such as Korean, it is often not considered rude to ask someone outright "how old are you?". You may want to see if this question is considered impolite in your informant's language, as it is in English, for example. If so, why? And if not, then under what circumstances is it acceptable?

2.3. Introductions

Most languages have certain codified ways in which speakers go about introducing themselves to each other when they meet for the first time. It can be interesting to study both the actual words used, such as "hi, my name is Wendy", and also the choice of what information gets passed between people when they meet. For example, there are subtle differences in American English between *hi*, *hey*, and *hello*: *hey* is too casual to be used with most older people, while *hello* is fairly formal.

Most of the time, people ask a few questions of each other when they meet. Within a community of speakers, the questions asked vary little from speaker to speaker, or from introduction to introduction. They serve to provide speakers with precisely the information that is needed to carry on a comfortable conversation in their language and culture. In English, for example, we usually try to find out what someone's name is, and possibly their occupation. We choose to ask these things because, to talk to someone comfortably in English, you need to know his or her name, and you often need to know what he or she does. It is hard to know what to talk about if you do not know what tone to use with your conversation partners, nor where they stand relative to you in terms of age, occupation, and so forth. The questions asked at a first meeting between speakers of your informant's language may be different. It might turn out, for example, that speakers of this language are not terribly concerned with the names of their conversational partners, but are more interested in where they are from, or whether or not they are married. If this is the case, then it tells you something about your informant's culture, as well as his or her language.

If your informant were Korean, for example, you would find that introductions are carried out very differently in Korean than in English. As mentioned above, it is a virtual necessity when speaking Korean that you know how old your conversational partners are. If you do not have this information, you are likely to use the wrong politeness forms, which can lead to uneasiness at best and serious insult at worst. As a result, it is considered perfectly normal to ask someone, upon meeting them, "What year were you born?" This question goes along with a host of other standard questions, such as "Where are you from?"; "What do you do for a living?"; and "Where did you go to school?" Answering all these questions allows the speakers to size each other up, and figure out how much linguistic respect should be accorded to each speaker.

If you have only one informant, you may want to construct a hypothetical meeting between two or more people in order to collect data on introductions. Your speaker is likely to know most or all of the appropriate greetings, so this should not be too difficult. Ask your informant how the people would greet each other, if they were meeting for the first time. What sorts of questions would they ask of each other, and what would be appropriate responses? Imagine, for example, a meeting among three English speakers: a male high school student, a female college student, and a female professor. The two students would probably greet each other with "Hey", and an exchange of names, possibly without even shaking hands. They would probably ask each other where they went to school, and they might even reveal their ages. By contrast, each student would almost certainly say "Hello" or "Hi" to the professor, shake hands, and perhaps ask her polite questions about her job. Neither student would dream of asking the professor her age. This is the sort of information that you can collect from your informant using an imagined scenario.

2.4. Gender[38]

Many linguists study differences in the way men and women talk. This is an interesting topic, one which almost everyone seems to enjoy discussing. The problem with studying "genderlect" is figuring out how to get information about the speech of both men and women out of a single informant who, presumably, represents only one of the two basic human genders. At best, a female informant is likely to know how women talk, and how men talk around women. She cannot reasonably be expected to know how men talk when no women are present, just as a male informant cannot have first-hand knowledge of conversation among females. Nonetheless, we decided to tackle the genderlect issue with our Gujarati informant, and we found that he was able to give us some valuable information.

We started by asking our informant if there were any words in Gujarati that men would use and women would not, or vice versa. As is often the case, this direct approach was not terribly successful: our informant told us that everyone uses the same words in India,

---

[38] See also chapter 11, where this topic is examined in greater detail.

and that there is no difference between men and women where swearing or taboo topics are concerned. After a moment's reflection, he changed his tune, saying that women "never" use bad words in India. Neither of these answers sounded entirely plausible, so we had to do some more investigation.

First we covered defecation and urination. We suspected that men would talk more freely about these matters than women. The first term that our informant gave us for defecation was sʌɳɖas, which literally means 'toilet'. When we asked him, he said that that this word was used by both genders. Unfortunately, we had a considerable amount of difficulty explaining to our informant what we were interested in studying. As a result, he changed his story a number of times, depending on how we phrased our questions, and we had trouble getting reliable information. After collecting the word for 'toilet', we managed to collect some terms which seemed a bit less polite. These were ʌgʰβʌ dʒɑu tʃʰũ, meaning 'I am taking a shit' (literally 'I am going shit'), and pesab[39] kʌɾβa dʒɑu tʃʰũ, meaning 'I am taking a piss' (literally 'I am going to do piss'). Our informant first said that these expressions could also be used by both genders, but later said they were only used by men. We also collected the word *gu*, which is a noun meaning 'shit' or 'turd'. Once again, our informant first told us that everyone used this word, but then he later said that women would actually be unlikely to say it.

We kept trying to get detailed information on what terms men and women could and could not use, but it seemed that our informant did not really see what we were getting at. Finally, we came up with an example from English which demonstrated what kind of information we were interested in:

---

[39] The standard Gujarati form is peʃab 'urine', which is a loan from a Persian word that literally means 'front-water'; note that our informant again uses s for ʃ.

Cooper: So, I might say *I'm going to take a shit*, but a woman would be more likely to say *I'm going to the bathroom*. A woman would probably not say *I'm going to take a shit*.

Informant: Yeah, same thing in India.

Cooper: Like what, for example?

Informant: Woman, he want to go to bathroom, he say hũdʒɑu tʃʰũ.

[Note that our informant here uses *he* to mean *she*. In fact, he seems to switch freely between the two.]

Cooper: What does dʒɑu tʃʰũ mean?

Informant: dʒɑu tʃʰũ means 'going'.

This sentence, hũ dʒɑu tʃʰũ, literally means 'I am going', but it is used to avoid talking directly about the process of defecating (or urinating). When our informant saw what we were interested in, he gave us some more information. He told us that there are certain words that women prefer to use when talking about defecation and urination because they are considered polite: *eki*, meaning 'pee-pee', and *beki*, meaning 'poo-poo'.[40] This was precisely what we were looking for. When we went back and asked him if women would say some of the sentences he had given us before, involving seemingly more vulgar words, he said "Right words, right sentence, but woman never talk like that".

Of course, women's and men's speech can differ in many ways, not only where peeing and pooping are concerned. There are a number of topics that you may wish to explore with your informants.

---

[40] *eki* literally means 'an odd number', and *beki* means 'an even number'; the pair is thus a rhyming version of English 'number one' and 'number two'.

Ask your informant about words for genitalia and sex acts, for example.[41] See if he or she can think of any words or terms that people would use only among members of their same sex. Another good test for genderlect is words for 'man' and 'woman'. In most cultures, there are many terms for both of these concepts, some of them pejorative and some not so. Take English, for example, which refers to males with a number of words, such as *boy, guy, man, fellow, chap, dude,* and so on. Some of these words correspond to certain age ranges, others to personality types or subcultures. On the female side, we have an interesting situation in which there is no term that fits neatly in the age scale between *girl* and *woman*: *gal* is awkward and antiquated for many speakers, while *chick* is somewhat pejorative. See if your informant's language has a similarly large range of words for men and women, and try to get a handle on the nuances in meaning of some of the terms.

You may also want to see if men and women have different words for men and women. This is not an uncommon situation. Very few English-speaking women would use the word *broad,* for example, while most men would not refer to other men as *hunks.* Even the words that men and women use for family members may be different. In Korean, for example, a woman calls her older sister on:i, while a man calls his older sister nuna. With any luck, one or more of these subjects will bring out some differences in the way men and women speak in your informant's speech community. Once you have hit upon one such example, you can expect that others will follow more easily.

---

[41] Obviously these topics must be approached with extreme caution, as you want to avoid embarrassing or harassing your informants.

2.5. I said "No!"

The fact is that speakers generally try to avoid saying things like "No!" in response to a request for something, unless they have to. Most languages have some strategy for expressing delicately that you do not wish to do what someone else wishes you to do. In America, for example, we often just say "yes" and then duck out at the first opportunity, or neglect to call back, or whatever it takes. We have all heard people say (or said ourselves) "Yeah, sure, I'll come over tomorrow", while having no intention of doing so. See if you can get your informant to tell you how this is done in his or her language.

The strategies used to avoid speaking directly or conveying bad news can be fascinating. Sometimes they are so ritualized that they become idiomatic, and do not make much sense unless you are a member of the native-speaker community. Take the example of Japanese. Printed below is a transcription of a short conversation in Japanese, with both literal and free-form translations of each line (2).

(2) A: kombaŋ utʃi   e   iraʃːai-masɛn   ka ?
          tonight house to come-want   Q.
          'Do you want to come over to my house tonight?'

     B: tjotːo...
          a little
          'Not really'.

     A: soː oʃːara-zuni doːzo iraʃite kudasai
          so   say-without please come   please
          'Don't say that. Come on over!'

     B: ie. hontoː ni...
          no   really
          'No. Really'.

In the second line, Speaker B says tjotːo, which translates as 'a little'. In this context, however, it actually means 'no', whereas for an English speaker it would mean something slightly different. Speaker A persists and asks again, at which point Speaker A has no choice but to actually say 'no'.

Incidentally, Speaker B's persistence may not be unjustified; there are many cultures in which you have to insist on something once or twice before your offer or request is taken seriously. Consider, for example, the ritual that people go through to decide who pays when dining out. Typically, a guest or a younger person has to make at least one token offer to pay, sometimes two or more. The host or older person then insists on picking up the check over the protests of the other diner or diners. There is even a certain pattern that these conversations follow, which we have attempted to reproduce in (3). (Speaker A is the younger guest and Speaker B is the older host who extended the initial invitation to dine out.)

(3)   (check arrives)
         A: I'll take that.
         B: Oh, no. I've got it.
         A: Are you sure?
         B: Absolutely. I insist.
         A: Well, OK, but I'll get it next time.
         B: Sounds good.

See what strategies are employed to resolve conflicts of interest, either real or ritualized, in your informant's language. Speakers may simply say "No, that's not what I want", or they may even say "Yes" and then go on and do what they wanted to do anyway. You can collect this information by creating an imaginary scenario in which two speakers have to wrestle with these issues.

2.6. Hellos and goodbyes

It is always interesting to know how people greet each other in a language, and how they take leave of each other. In many cases, greetings are highly situational. If you bump into someone you know on the street, for example, you might just nod and say *Hey*. In other circumstances, this would be strange, even unacceptable. When going to visit a professor in his or her office, you are expected to say something a little more formal than *Hey*, even if it is only *Hi*.

Getting reliable information on greetings can be tough. People often think that they say one thing, when in fact they say another. If asked how to greet someone in English, I would recommend saying *Hello*. In fact, I probably go weeks without saying *Hello*. I always say *Hey*, *Hi*, or something of that sort. Our Gujarati informant showed us a textbook from India which he used to learn English. In the textbook, typical English greetings are given, such as *Good afternoon, my daughter*; *Good day to you, sir*; and *Excuse me for being late, beg my apologies*.

If possible, you should try to listen in on two or more speakers of your informant's language, and see how they greet each other. This is often not feasible, however, so will have to get at this information some other way, such as by creating an imaginary scene with several people greeting each other and having your informant act out the roles of the interlocutors.

In most languages, there are many different greetings. You should try to collect as many of these as you can. There might be several different words for *Hello* and *Goodbye*, each appropriate in some situations but not in others. For example, your informant's language may have a greeting which is said by the stationary party to the party arriving on the scene, and another greeting said by the arriving party. In Armenian, there are two different types of goodbyes, as shown in (4).

(4)   a.   mənɑs   pʰɑɾov
              stay   well
              'goodbye' (to someone who is staying behind)

       b.   jɛɾtʰɑs   pʰɑɾov
              go   well
              'goodbye' (to someone who is leaving)

There are many other types of greetings to check for. How do people greet each other on the telephone, for example? In German, one says *Auf Wiedersehen* when parting ways in person, and *Auf Wiederhören* when hanging up the telephone. In English, *see you later* sounds fine in face-to-face conversation, but is a bit odd in phone conversations and written correspondence. Your informant's language may have special words or phrases used only to greet family members and close friends. There may also be codified ways of saying 'hello' and 'goodbye' in impersonal settings, such as in a place of business. As usual, the most difficult task facing you is conveying to your informant what you are looking for. Once he or she gets the picture, coming up with a number of forms should be fairly easy.

2.7. *Expressions of anger or delight*

Expressions of disappointment, anger, or happiness can be fun to study. Interestingly, people choose which expression of anger or delight to use depending on all sorts of pragmatic factors. This is surprising, since you might reasonably expect that when someone stubs his toe and yells *OUCH!*, he does not care, at that moment, who is listening. In reality, this is almost never the case. Even when people are truly overcome with emotion, they are usually aware of who is listening to them and adjust their speech accordingly. For example, many people swear like sailors around their friends, but when they are at work and the boss is watching, they control themselves. Even if they run headfirst into a doorway, they remember to say *Shoot!* and not *Shit!*

You should be able to collect some expressions of joy and anger just by asking your informant what people say when certain things happen to them. Try to get as many as you can. The key is then to find out in what situations these different words or expressions are used. Your informant may tell you that he or she just says whatever springs to mind in the heat of the moment, but this is probably not true, especially with expressions of anger. Try to describe in detail some situations in which you imagine that the use of a strong exclamation of anger might be frowned upon, and see if your informant agrees with you. What sorts of factors come into play?

It is often interesting to find out if these expressions have any cultural significance. Some may be gibberish, such as the English expression *dagnabbit!*, but others may refer to well-known cultural reference points, such as the equally beloved *Jesus H. Christ!* Some of the phrases you learn are likely to be idiomatic, but your informant may be able to explain what they mean, at least to some extent.

2.8. Taboos

As we all know, most languages and cultures have certain taboos, topics which cannot be discussed in polite society. Taboos are different from swear words in that the social uneasiness surrounds an entire topic, and not just an individual word. Of course, many swear words are related to taboo topics, such as words for sexual intercourse and defecation. Still, the effect of a taboo goes beyond that of mere swear words: many people consider it unacceptable to talk about death in certain situations, for example, regardless of the specific words one uses.

In some cases, taboos can be so strong that a topic can scarcely be talked about at all, regardless of the social setting. Certain sexual acts and terms for sexual organs are treated this way in much of the English-speaking world. There are often taboos associated with death, sex, relieving oneself (notice the euphemism), and religion or religious figures. Others are less predictable, however. Certain animals or foods may be taboo, or certain numbers.

The basic approach for collecting information on taboos is the same as for collecting swear words (see section 3). With our Gujarati informant, we actually began by collecting swear words, and then moved on to taboo topics. He volunteered some information in this area, including telling us the word for menstruation or, as he put it, "monthly problem".

Perhaps the greatest potential problem with taboos is stumbling upon them unwittingly. If you set out to collect information on taboos, then you can expect that your informants may become somewhat uncomfortable. If, however, you are trying to collect information on some other phenomenon, and you happen to hit upon a taboo topic, the results can be confusing and damaging. There are societies, for example—including many Muslim societies—in which people simply do not talk about dogs, except in the most disparaging terms. Working with an informant from such a society, it would be easy to hit upon a taboo without meaning to do so. This could offend your informant and corrupt your data at the same time. If you asked your informant to translate the sentence *The dog bites the man*, he or she would be likely to give you an inaccurate translation in order to avoid saying the word *dog*, or simply to avoid the topic altogether.

Samarin discusses a number of taboos which investigators have run across in doing linguistic fieldwork. One of the most interesting of these is found among the Ata people of the Philippines, who have a taboo against humans engaging in any unnatural or illogical behavior towards other living things. This taboo prohibits things like talking to dogs, as well as making statements which ascribe human characteristics to animals (Samarin 1967:143). It is easy to see how this last restriction could cause problems for an investigator, since linguists occasionally collect sentences like *The pig is feeding her baby*, which could be seen to raise pigs to human status.

2.9. Discourse markers

It is often hard to tell in conversation when someone wants to talk, when they are done talking, or whose turn it is to talk next. To sort all of this out, speakers employ a wide variety of discourse markers. When someone wants to take a turn in conversation, for example, he or she may say *So...* and then begin talking.

Attempting to elicit information on discourse markers directly is not likely to work. Speakers are generally unaware that they use discourse markers, and when it is pointed out to them, they sometimes deny it. You can collect some good data, however, simply by recording a story from your informant. During the course of the narration, you informant is likely to throw in a few discourse markers. Among other things, check to see what your informant does during pauses. In most languages, there is a certain word or sound, such as English *umm*, Spanish em, Turkish ʃej, Western Armenian pʰɑn,[42] etc., which is typically used to fill pauses in a monologue.

Of course, the best data can be obtained by recording a conversation between your informant and another speaker. If you are fortunate enough to arrange this, then be sure to look at turn-

---

[42] The Turkish and Armenian forms literally mean 'thing', but are used in essentially the same contexts as *umm* and *uhh*.

taking strategies. How do speakers indicate that they are through speaking, for example? In English, we often end sentences with *you know?* or with an *or...* that sort of tails off, indicating that it is someone else's turn to speak. Also, how do your informants indicate a desire to begin speaking? Pay attention to body language, as well as what is actually said.

3. Challenges and warnings

- **The classroom setting.** We have mentioned at several points in this chapter that one can actually use the laboratory setting as an asset in collecting swear words, taboo items, and other naughty bits. This can backfire, however, particularly when the setting is not merely an office with one or two investigators, but a classroom full of students. Sometimes informants are unwilling to talk about socially uncomfortable topics in front of a room full of people, particularly if some of those people are of a different gender than the informant.

  If your informant is reluctant to loosen up in front of an entire class, then a change of strategy may be appropriate. We have found that working to prepare the informant beforehand can be helpful. The professor, or one of the students, can meet with the informant before class and begin talking about whatever topic you wish to discuss, so that the informant will be "in the mood" when class begins. Also, you may wish to have only that one person (student or professor) ask questions during class, at least at the beginning, so that the informant gets the sense of a private interview with observers, rather than a mass interrogation. If this also fails, then it may be necessary to set up individual appointments, so that those students who are interested in taboos can meet with the informant privately.

- **Beware of honorific markers.** Certain pragmatic factors cannot be ignored if you are studying a language with a system of honorific markers. Specifically, you have to be aware of differences in age and social status between you and your informant, because producing a sentence correctly depends on taking these factors into consideration. As a result, you may not be able to repeat sentences back to your informant to see if you transcribed them correctly, because when you repeat the sentence, you will be using the wrong honorific markers. For example, when I was in Korea, I practiced my Korean with the woman who owned the house I was staying in. She was much older than I was, so I would use the most polite verb forms possible. Things got confusing when I would say something, like *I am hungry,* and she would respond with an echo question, like *You're hungry?* Inevitably, the verb form in her echo question would be different from the verb form I had used. I would think that I had made a grammatical mistake, so I would say the sentence again with the verb form she had used. Unfortunately, this was the form reserved for talking to younger people—which is why she had used it in the first place—so I was actually insulting her without knowing it.

Suggested Readings

Levinsohn, Stephen. 1983. Pragmatics. Cambridge: Cambridge University Press.

Levinsohn, Stephen. 1994. Field procedures for the analysis of participant reference in a monologue discourse. In Stephen Levinsohn, ed., Discourse features of ten languages of West-Central Africa, 109-121. Dallas: Summer Institute of Linguistics and the University of Texas at Arlington.

Mey, Jacob. 1993. Pragmatics: An Introduction. Oxford: Blackwell.

Wardhaugh, Ronald. 1985. How Conversation Works. Oxford: Blackwell.

Exercises

1. Come up with a way to find out what questions speakers of your
    informant's language ask each other when they meet. You may
    wish to create a little skit for your informant to act out. See if
    you can figure out what effect the answers to these questions
    might have on the conversation that follows.

2. Make a list of things that you could say that would be
    'appropriate' vs. 'rude' vs. 'truly offensive' in a given situation.
    For example, asking people you just met to tell you their names
    is fine, while asking them how old they are is rude, at least in
    America. Asking "what are those scars on your face?" is likely
    to be rude in almost any culture. See what similarities or
    differences exist between your language and your informant's
    language regarding this sort of scale of acceptability. You may
    also wish to see how things might change in different social
    situations.

3. Given the sterile nature of a classroom setting, think of ways to
    go about collecting taboo terms and swear words. What can you
    do to put the informant in the right mood to talk about these
    touchy subjects? Also, try your techniques out both in a one-on-
    one session with your informant, if possible, and see if this
    changes the results you get.

4. Collect a list of insulting terms for people, such as 'ugly
    man/woman', or 'promiscuous man/woman', and have the
    informant rank them in terms of nastiness and meanness. Which
    ones would your informant be willing to use, and under what
    circumstances? Which ones can be combined with each other,
    and what effect does this have on the overall power of the insult?

5. Collect an introductory dialog from your informant and act it out in class (in your informant's language).

6. If a textbook or phrasebook of your informants' language is available, find the place where they present greetings and, with the help of your informants, figure out the following:
   - When can these particular greetings be used, and when are they inappropriate?
   - Does anyone actually use these particular greetings, or are they outdated or fictitious?

11 Studying language variation: Sociolinguistics

Our fine dictionary words are mere dead sounds to the uneducated, which fail to awaken in their minds any living and breathing reality. So they call up new ones for themselves, mostly of a grotesque order, certainly, but as full of life and spirit as a brigade of shoe-blacks.

G. P. Marsh
Lectures on the English Language (1860)

You can be a little ungrammatical if you come from the right part of the country.

Robert Frost

In this chapter we concentrate on the collection of data involving linguistic variation. This variation can depend on a number of factors, including location, age, gender, ethnicity, and social class. Since language is a central means of delimiting individual and group identity, and differentiaton of this sort is one of the main preoccupations of humans, linguistic variation is rampant in all human cultures. However, this does not entail that it is easy to collect data from your informants involving linguistic variation. Though individuals typically know a great deal about the ways in which their language varies according to gender, region, and so on, it can be quite difficult to produce this sort of information on demand, particularly under the watchful and expectant eye of a linguist. Even when such information is forthcoming, it must be evaluated very carefully for reliability, for reasons we'll see below. Nevertheless, given the tips we present in this chapter, it should be possible for you to collect a wide variety of useful linguistic variation from your informants.

1. Methodology

In this section we address three basic challenges that inevitably arise when one attempts to collect dialect data:

- Identifying informants who are likely to provide useful dialect information, and persuading them to help you.
- Eliciting dialect data successfully, in face of the fact that most speakers feel that they have no non-standard linguistic features.
- Making informants comfortable with the interview situation and the fact that they speak a non-standard dialect.

1.1. Selecting informants

No individuals speak a 100% pure "standard" dialect of their language, though most people that you ask will insist that they do. This variation can be attributed to two main causes:

- **No national language academy or other standardizing force controls every single component of a language**. For example, the French academy has nothing to say about what one calls the *sunshower*, or about the full range of meanings of the word *chat* (one of which is 'cat'; others are unprintable here). Individual grammars will therefore vary significantly in these unlegislated areas (and even in legislated areas; witness the French academy's failed attempts to eradicate English loans such as *Walkman*, *weekend*, and so on).

- **Speakers are not consciously aware of some components of their languages**. As we saw in chapter 7, English speakers who are not linguists are unaware that they pronounce *t* in many different ways, including [tʰ] in *tar*, [t] in *star*, and [ɾ] in *butter*. Since speakers are unaware of differences of this type (which can be lexical, morphological, and syntactic as well as phonetic and phonological), they will not necessarily alter them to conform to the "standard".

Given that all individuals possess at least some nonstandard features, in theory you should be able to collect dialect data from anyone. However, the real world is not so simple. For one thing, you may be interested in a specific dialect, rather than whatever non-standard features a given individual might happen to have. Furthermore, it can be extremely difficult to identify the linguistic nooks and crannies where an individual speaker differs from the norm. For these reasons, it is generally a good idea to seek out specific types of informants who are more likely to provide the sort of dialect information that you want.

If you are looking for "traditional" dialects—i.e. the dialects associated with given regions in literature and in the popular imagination—you can save time by going directly to certain classes of people who are relatively likely to speak non-standard dialects where differences are abundant and easily noticeable. These include villagers, firemen, policemen, workers in local stores and factories, farmers, and individuals who have not had significant amounts of schooling. This latter category includes younger speakers, who studies have shown to be less likely than older speakers to have been affected by normative pressures in schooling (Wells 1982:496).

The same goes for people above sixty or seventy years of age, who generally predate the introduction of standardized nationwide schooling in most countries, and therefore are less likely to have been indoctrinated in the "standard" language of their country. Another advantage to working with older speakers is pointed out by Wright in the introduction to his *English Dialect Grammar*:

"Again, it is certain that dialect speakers in extreme old
age revert to the dialect as it existed in their youth. Two
years ago I visited an old woman in a Yorkshire village,
whom I had known intimately for forty-eight years, and
for at least half of that time had been in daily intercourse
with her. I found that whereas she formerly said deǝ,
uǝm for 'day', 'home', she now said *dê, ôm,* and some
of her other vowel-sounds had been changed in a similar
manner". (Wright 1905:vii)

   A third important advantage of working with older speakers
is that they are (obviously) more likely to preserve older linguistic
forms and constructions. One of the things we hear most often when
conducting dialect research with informants is "only old people say
that"; therefore, if you want to collect archaic or otherwise non-
standard forms of a language, it is in your best interest to work with
older individuals.

   It is also a good idea to collect data from both men and
women, because one gender or the other is often more likely to
preserve dialect forms. In a survey of New Englanders, for example,
Miller 1953 found that 84% of the men used [æ] in *ask* , compared to
only 27% of the women. The other 73% of the women employed the
older pronunciation of *ask*, [ɑsk]. It is not always the women who
are more conservative, however.   Several sociolinguist studies
suggest that middle-class women tend to adopt the norms of the
"standard" language (and thus middle-class men are more
conservative than their female counterparts), whereas working-class
men spearhead changes away from the standard (and thus are less
conservative than their female counterparts). We are not entirely
convinced by this generalization, but the fact remains that one gender
or the other is often conservative with respect to a given linguistic

feature, and you should allow for this in your fieldwork by interviewing both men and women if possible.

1.2. Eliciting dialect information

Once you have recruited some individuals who you believe to speak a non-standard dialect, the challenge is to collect dialect data from them successfully. This is often harder than it sounds, because, as we mentioned earlier, most people believe that they speak just like everyone else. Even if they acknowledge that they speak a dialect, it may be difficult for them to come up with good examples on the spot. For these reasons, you need to be prepared to ask specific kinds of questions in particular ways in order to collect your data successfully and efficiently.

If you are having trouble conveying to your informants the concept that not all individuals in a community speak in the same way, it can be helpful to try out a number of tricky syntactic constructions on them. In our experience, asking informants for grammaticality judgements on complicated clause types often produces exchanges like the following:

Linguist: Can you say this?
Informant: *I* can't, but some other people do.

At this point, you can indicate to your informants that this is the sort of information that you are looking for. Inquire further about the sorts of people who do allow the construction in question, and you may well hit on a legitimate case of dialectal variation.

If you are collecting variation in grammaticality judgements, beware of confusing *idiolectal* and *dialectal* variation. Dialectal variation is systematic, being shared by an entire speech community. Idiolectal variation, on the other hand, is characteristic only of individual speakers. Before you label something as a dialect feature, make sure to ascertain that it is used by a discrete group of speakers.

If your informants are still reticent, it can also be extremely effective to speak—or at least try to speak—in your informants' dialect. The following anecdote from Joseph Wright's *English Dialect Grammar* illustrates this perfectly:

> "The working classes speak quite differently among themselves than when speaking to strangers or educated people, and it is no easy matter for an outsider to induce them to speak pure dialect, unless the outsider happens to be a dialect speaker himself. An excellent example of this came before me the other day in a Westmoreland village. A man said to me: ðə rɔːdz ə dəːti[43], and I said to him, duənt jə seː up iər ət t'riɑdz əz muki?[44]   With a bright smile on his face he replied: wi diu, and forthwith he began to speak the dialect in its pure form". (Wright 1905:vii)

A similar story is told about the great Armenologist and dialectologist Hrachea Adjarian, who would go into tiny Armenian villages and try to pass himself off as a native by speaking the local dialect; legend has it that more often than not he was successful.

Wright's technique can also be used to identify dialect speakers who for one reason or another are reluctant to own up to the fact that they speak a non-standard dialect. I once got wind of a fellow from the Abkhazian city of Gagra, who I suspected might be one of the immigrants to that area from the Armenian enclave of Hamshen in northeastern Turkey. When I called him on the telephone, he (as expected) stated reservedly that he was Russian. A

---

[43] i.e. "the roads are dirty".
[44] i.e. "don't you say up 'ere 'at t'roads is mooky?"

few more pointed questions about the Armenian community in Gagra failed to yield any results, so I then took the bull by the horns and asked him a few questions in the Hamshen dialect. He promptly cheered up, admitted that he belonged to the Hamshen community, and volunteered to help me study the dialect.

1.3. Making your informants feel comfortable

These anecdotes segue nicely into our next point, which involves dealing with informants who feel uncomfortable in the interview situation. Robert Frost's quote at the beginning of this chapter illustrates two important principles of dialect studies: (i) possessing non-standard dialect forms can give the speaker a modicum of prestige and an exotic air in certain situations; on the other hand, (ii) many non-standard forms and usages are highly stigmatized. Both of these principles can be observed in most large American universities, where certain dialects (especially middle and upper-class New York, Southern, and British) are tolerated and even cherished, whereas others (especially Midwestern, Boston, and working-class New York) are so highly stigmatized that any student who speaks one of them is quickly forced by peer pressure to adopt the standard dialect. It is vital to understand the importance of these two principles when conducting dialectological or sociolinguistic fieldwork, because they will color every response that your informants provide, and if you don't deal with them properly, your informants may give you no information at all.

When working with speakers of non-standard dialects, the problem you will most often encounter is the conviction that their dialect is inferior to the standard language. This feeling is encapsulated in Frost's implication that non-standard varieties of speech are "ungrammatical". In most literate societies, school children are taught that only one form of language—the one conveyed in their textbooks—is grammatical; all other forms of speech are incorrect, used only by the the uneducated and the stupid. As a result, informants will typically be unwilling to use their non-standard dialect with you, because they feel that by doing so they would come across as uneducated and stupid. This problem is further compounded by the universal misconception that linguists are nothing more than high-level grammar teachers, whose job consists of learning languages and correcting people's grammar.

In order to get any dialect research done, you will have to persuade your informants that their variety of speech is not inferior, and that you are not going to correct them. This is not so difficult if you do not speak the same language as your informants, because in this situation it is generally clear to them that you will not realize the sociolinguistic significance (within their own speech community) of the fact that they are speaking in a nonstandard dialect.

If, on the other hand, you do speak the same language as your informants, you will actually need to convince them that their dialect is acceptable. It is always helpful, of course, to state this fact flat out; however, this is typically not enough. We always try to give our informants specific examples that illustrate how no one dialect is superior to another; one such example that is often effective involves copula deletion in African-American Vernacular English (Ebonics), which is presented nicely by Labov (1972) and Pinker (1994). (Note, though, that it is best to use an example from your informants' own language, if possible.) Non-linguists generally assume on the basis of utterances such as *we bad* (meaning 'we are bad') that speakers of Ebonics have a deficient grasp of English, and this is why they "fail" to insert the verb *are* in sentences of this type. In fact, closer inspection reveals that the Ebonics scheme for dealing with copular verbs is just as systematic as the one employed in standard English. The situation is as follows:

- Where standard English allows contraction (*we're bad*, etc.), Ebonics allows deletion (*we Ø bad*);
- Where standard English does *not* allow contraction (**I* wonder where he's*), Ebonics does not allow deletion (**I* wonder where he Ø*).

This example demonstrates that the grammatical system of Ebonics is just as logical as that of standard English, and it cannot be maintained that Ebonics is in any way deficient or inferior.

Another way to approach this issue that you may find fruitful involves discussing with your informants cases of dialectal variation that clearly do not reflect relative superiority, better education, and so on. Many good examples of this type can be found in the realm of vocabulary. For example, many inhabitants of the Boston sphere of influence say *potato puffs* for what most Americans call *tater tots*, a sort of fried potato concoction served in cafeterias. Is either of these forms superior to the other in any way? Clearly not: neither is shorter than the other; neither has a clearer relationship to the object being referred to; neither is borrowed from a high prestige language; neither is clearly older than the other; etc.

It is also important to persuade your informants of the validity of non-standard dialects by means of your own behavior. If they see that you treat their non-standard dialect with respect, and find in it the same sorts of interesting linguistic phenomena that occur in the standard dialect, your informants are more likely to begin respecting their dialect as well.

You can further this process by stressing the ways in which your informants' dialect is particularly interesting. The sorts of superficial linguistic features that non-linguists generally appreciate include archaism, humor, and originality, so you may want to find examples of these types to mention to your informants. To give you an idea of what I mean, here are some representative anecdotes that I have used when working with informants who speak non-standard dialects of Armenian:

Archaism: Did you know that your dialect is the only variety of Armenian that preserves the Classical Armenian present tense formation from 1500 years ago? (Said to a speaker of Basra dialect)

Humor: In my opinion, your way of referring to rain falling when the sun is shining as a *sparrow's wedding* is much more interesting than our calling it a *sunshower* in English. (Said to a speaker of Homshetsma)

Originality: I think it's fascinating that your language has more vowels than any other known human language. (Said to a speaker of Musaler dialect)

If all of the techniques just described fail, you can still remedy your informants' reticence by putting them in a situation where they feel comfortable and forget to feel embarrassed about their speech. Labov and his students found it helpful when working with young Ebonics speakers to bring up taboo topics like 'drinking pee', which would focus the children on the humor of the taboo concept itself, and distract them from the fact that they were being interviewed by grown men in an artificial social situation.

2. What to collect

With these methodological preliminaries in mind, let us now turn to the question of what to collect from your informants. We stated at the beginning of this chapter that a language can vary in terms of a wide assortment of variables. If you are interested in a particular type of linguistic variable, then you should skip down to our discussion of that variable below. If you are simply interested in general linguistic variation, on the other hand, you should look into variables such as the following:

- gender
- age
- class
- location
- register

In the next few sections we briefly consider each of these topics in turn.

2.1. Gender

We believe it is safe to say that all languages have gender-based linguistic differences. In American English, for example, it is acceptable for women—but not generally for men—to refer to a man as *cute*. (Note that this is not for homophobic reasons; it is quite acceptable for a man to say that another man is *good-looking* or *handsome*.) Along similar lines, American women generally refer to the act of urinating as *peeing*, whereas men prefer to use *pissing*; conversely, women rarely use *piss* and men rarely use *pee*. Since we already discussed this issue in a previous chapter, we will not go into it further here.

2.2. Age

Age-based variation can be quite important, as we've already seen. Variation of this type generally falls into one of three categories:

1. Forms used by older people, which are lost or disappearing among younger speakers. An example of this type is the word *davenport*, which I remember my grandparents using, but is no longer used by Americans of younger generations.

2. Forms tied to disappearing technologies, concepts, etc. The use of *icebox* for *refrigerator* and of *horseless carriage* for *car* are typical examples of this type.

3. Forms used by only one age group for other reasons. Languages typically have terms of address that are only used by young people when speaking to older people (e.g. *pops*), by older people when speaking to young people (*sonny*), and so on. Furthermore, slang (*cool, raunchy*) and extremely saucy language (*shithead, dickwad*) tend to be used much more often by younger speakers.

Age-based variation of types 2 and 3 is relatively easy to collect, especially if you provide your informants with a few examples of the sort listed above. Type 1 variation is harder to collect, but you can make the task easier by giving your informants some specific examples like *davenport* and *wireless* (meaning "radio"), which may help to trigger their memories. We have also found it helpful to go through a dictionary or word list with informants; this almost always produces responses like "we don't say this anymore", "only my grandmother would say this", and so on. Sometimes it is not entirely clear which type a given linguistic variable belongs to: the use of *eh* for 'what?' is identified in the American imagination with old people who are hard of hearing, suggesting type 3 affiliation, but it also happens to be one of the preferred ways of expressing 'what?' in British English, suggesting that *eh* may actually belong to type 1. We will return to the topic of age-based varation in the next chapter, when we discuss the collection of historical data.

2.3. Class

Like age-based differences, class-based differences can be related to several different factors:

- **Lifestyle**. Different social classes are exposed to different objects, different activities, and different concepts, and their language invariably reflects this. A member of the upper class, for example, is more likely to use terms like *dumb waiter, the help*, and other such concepts linked to money and privilege. By the same token, members of less monied classes are more likely to be familiar with terms such as *party barn* and *brew thru* (both of which denote drive-through liquor stores in different parts of the United States).

- **Mobility**. Sociolinguists generally believe that lower classes are more likely to show regional linguistic variation, because members of the upper class are more likely to move from place to place, go away to school, travel, and engage in other similar activities that expose them to different forms of speech. Taking the term 'mobility' in another sense, members of the middle class are generally considered to be more likely to speak the standard dialect than upper and lower class individuals, because they are the most interested in moving up the socio-economic ladder, and feel that this cannot be done without speaking the standard language.

- **Education**. For reasons that should be self-evident, highly educated individuals are significantly more likely to pepper their speech with highbrow expressions, typically drawn from foreign languages, as in 'she has a certain *je ne sais quoi*' (French), and 'oh, dear—I fear I shall have to consort with the *hoi polloi* again tomorrow' (Greek). (This of course does not hold for foreign languages with which people of all classes are in contact: saying *adios* for 'goodbye' is not considered highbrow in the United States, for example.) Furthermore, as we have already mentioned, uneducated speakers are more likely to preserve non-standard dialect features that are beaten out of one in school.

- **Pretentiousness**. When one belongs to a higher social class, sometimes a simpler or more transparent form simply won't do. In English, for example, the words *parlor* and *living room* refer to the same room in a house for most speakers (excluding those who do not know the word *parlor*, and those who are wealthy enough to have both a living room and a parlor in their house). For most speakers the formation of *parlor* is opaque: it does not have any obvious internal morphological structure, nor is it clearly borrowed from any particular language. The derivation of *living room*, on the other hand, is completely transparent: it is the room in which one lives. We feel that the relative transparency of words like *living room* plays a role in their correlation with social class: they tend to be associated with lower social classes, whereas more opaque forms like *parlor* that are felt to have a more exotic flavor tend to be used more by speakers belonging to higher social classes. (An amusing example of this appears in the episode of *The Simpsons* where Moe berates Homer for using a word as pretentious as *garage*. Shocked that this would be considered highbrow, Homer asks, "What do you call it then?" "A car hole," replies Moe.)

  The same can be said for truncations—abbreviated forms such as *limo* are much more likely to be used by speakers of lower social classes (and in more informal situations), whereas their full forms (*limousine*, etc.) are more likely to be used by speakers belonging to higher social classes, and in more formal situations.

- **Etiquette**. Social classes differ in what they consider to be acceptable behavior in different social situations, and this has a significant effect on their linguistic behavior. To illustrate, consider the case of mildly taboo body parts. The higher the social class (and the more formal the register), the less acceptable it is to refer to such body parts in public. As a result, one is forced in these touchier situations to use milder words. Languages typically have a wide array of vocabulary items referring to taboo body parts, ranked by degree of sauciness. A partial list of the English terms referring to the *buttocks* runs as follows (from least saucy to most saucy): *backside-derriere/behind/rear end-rump-butt-tush-arse-ass-booty*. (Other terms can only be used in very special contexts, such as *fanny*, which is generally used only by older American speakers (q.v. chapter 12), and *buttocks*, which is only used in extremely formal situations.) Speakers select from this hierarchical list according to the requirements of their social class and the formality of the situation.

• **History**. Sometimes class-based variation is grounded in nothing more than historical chance. Pairs such as *couch/sofa* and *jelly/jam* (where the second member of each pair is associated with higher social prestige) are completely arbitrary from a synchronic perspective. A particularly striking example involves the terms for *bathroom* in English: the relatively high-prestige forms *washroom* and *bathroom* are both periphrastic (they talk their way around the actual bodily actions involved), but the relatively low-prestige forms *toilet*, *can*, *head*, and *john* are just as obtuse—*toilet*, for example, was originally a term for a cloth cover for a small table!

Collecting all six types of class-based variation will obviously be difficult if you have only one informant, or if all of your informants are from the same social class. However, speakers typically have a good idea of how members of other social classes speak, and they may well produce some examples of this type for you, especially if you trigger their memory via concrete examples of the sort given above.

2.4. Location

> *From the outset, I was amazed that scholars were for the most part going off to distant corners of the country to look for works of folk poetry when a living tradition of folklore was to be found around Moscow and even within the city limits. So I began to collect Moscow legends and choral and ritual songs that had remained alive in the backyards of the city: the bits of rhyme and the interminable and unchanging songs hummed on the edges of Moscow, the popular beliefs and deeply rooted superstitions, the proverbs and formulas that embellished conversation, the counting rhymes and riddles of the children of Moscow...It is worth noting that in our collective research and recording of popular works, we always insisted on working in an area close to the capital.*
>
> Roman Jakobson
> *Jakobson-Pomorska Dialgoues*

The next sort of linguistic variation that we'd like to consider involves differences based on location. This is the domain of traditional dialectology, and can be extremely interesting for both fieldworkers and informants. Furthermore, collecting regional dialect data can be very easy. No special tricks or interrogation devices are required, for example, to ascertain from only a few Americans the range of expressions for the tiny gray bug that rolls up into a sphere when you touch it: *doodlebug* (which appears to be limited to Texas, Louisiana, and parts of Georgia and South Carolina), *pill bug* (the form used in the American Heritage Dictionary), *roly poly, sow bug, potato bug, cannonball, basketball bug*. In our experience Americans immediately know what bug is being referred to, and just as quickly know their word for it (except

Northeasterners, who have no word for this creature, even though they exist in the Northeast).

Similarly, if you ask a set of Armenians how to say 'I carry' in their language, you'll immediately get the following responses:

bɛɾɛm	(Iraq)
gəpʰɛɾɛm	(Standard Western Armenian)
bɛɾumɛm	(Standard Eastern Armenian)
bɛɾɛlisim	(Ardvin; northeastern Turkey)
bɛɾɑdzim	(Karchevan; southern Armenia)
bɛɾɛlim	(Maragha; Iran)
pɛɾɑsəm	(Hädrut; Azerbaijan)
pʰeimgu	(Homshetsma; northeastern Turkey)
hɑpiɾim	(Kesab; Syria)

Informants will occasionally produce the Standard Armenian form first (e.g. a Kesab Armenian might initially produce gəpʰɛɾɛm rather than hɑpiɾim), but they invariably know the local form as well. The challenge arises not with common forms like the present tense of core verbs (cf. the discussion of Russian stress patterns in chapter 12), but rather with less common words and constructions. (As we stated earlier, this does not include less common words and constructions that do not have a "standard" form, such as the sunshower; these typically show regional variation.) How can one deal with cases like this, where informants often do not know or use nonstandard forms? This is part of the larger problem of what to do when no meaty dialect information is forthcoming from one's informants.

In these situations, one has recourse to songs, poems, and so on, which often have useful dialect bits. Imagine that you are interviewing Paul McCartney in order to collect data on Scouse, the dialect of the Merseyside region, but his many years spent dealing with speakers of standard British and American English are interfering with his native Liverpool dialect. By pulling out an older Beatles tune such as "I Saw Her Standing There", one can find all sorts of Liverpudlian linguistic features. Consider the following rhyme from the song (cf. Trudgill 1990:69-70):

> *Oh we danced through the night,*
> *And we held each other tight,*
> *And before too long I fell in love with **her**.*
> *Now I'll never dance with another,*
> *Since I saw her standing **there**.*

In standard English, these two words do not rhyme: the vowel in *her* is [ɹ], while the vowel in *there* is [ɛ]. On the other hand, in Scouse, and in the Beatles' pronunciation, these two words both are pronounced with [ɛ]. One can find many such dialectal features in Beatles songs; another example in the lexical domain is *somerset* 'somersault', which occurs in "Being for the Benefit of Mr. Kite".

Now consider the following lines from a traditional English nursery song that my mother used to sing to me:

> *Ride a Cock horse to Banbury **Cross***
> *To see a fine lady upon a white **horse***

Note that *Cross* in line 1 rhymes with *horse* in line 2. To standard American ears, it makes no sense to rhyme *Cross* [kʰɹɒs] with *horse* [hɔɹs]. The rhyme also fails to make sense in standard British English, wherein *cross* is pronounced [kʰɹɒs] and *horse* is pronounced [hɔːs].[45] Since it is clear from the rest of the song that

---

[45] Note, however, that Gilbert and Sullivan play on the apparent rhyme of *often* (Standard British [ɒfən] and *orphan* (Standard British [ɔːfən]) in their

these two lines should rhyme, we can infer that at least one of these two words must have been pronounced differently at the time and place the song was created. Both words originally had a short *o*, but they cannot have rhymed until the *r* was deleted in horse. We know that the sound change that deleted *r* when not followed by a vowel only appeared in the fifteenth century; before that time, *horse* would have been pronounced in roughly the same way that it is in standard American English today.

Let us assume, then, that the lyrics to the song were written after the *r*-deletion rule appeared in the language, but before the changes that made *Cross* no longer rhyme with *horse*. Alternately, the lyrics to the song could have been composed in an area where the vowels in the two words are the same. A cursory inspection of Wright's *English Dialect Grammar* reveals that the two words in fact rhyme in the following traditional dialects:

east Dorset	(kʰrɑːs/hɑːs)
Westmoreland, Isle of Man	(kʰrɔs/hɔs)
west Somerset	(kʰrɔːs/hɔːs)
eastern New England[46]	(kʰɹɒs/hɒs)

We can rule out the Isle of Man and New England dialects as sources of this particular nursery rhyme, since the Isle of Man is too far away and New England was not yet settled by the English in the sixteenth century. The other dialects above remain legitimate possibilities. At

---

operetta *HMS Pinafore*—"I am an orphan". "When you say orphan, do you mean *orphan*, 'a child who has lost his parents', or *often* 'frequently'?"

[46] Traditional wisdom maintains that the New England dialects are based on those of East Anglia in England, but Wright does not list any East Anglian dialects wherein *cross* and *horse* rhyme. This particular rhyme is also found in what we call the "Hoss dialect"—i.e. the varieties of (western?) American English where *horse* is pronounced as what is popularly written <hoss>.

any rate, the point that is relevant for our present discussion is that songs of this type often contain tidbits of dialectological interest, and it is therefore in your interest to collect songs, poems, nursery rhymes, and so on from your informants if you are interested in dialect variation.

Another possibility is raised by the presence of a related older German form *hross*, which in fact is preserved as *ross* in the traditional dialects of southern Germany, as you can see in the map below (König 1978:210).

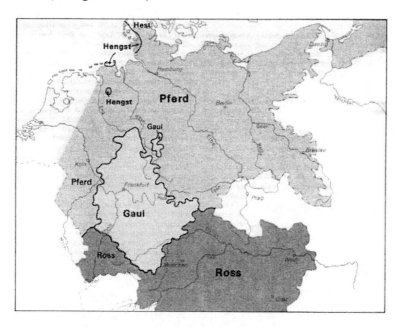

German dialect words for 'horse'

Another helpful aid in collecting traditional dialect data is the manual for collection of dialect forms. These exist for many languages, and contain questions specifically tailored to elicit salient dialect information efficiently. Some useful dialect manuals and atlases include Gillieron and Edmont 1902-10 (French), García de

Diego 1946 (Spanish), Redard 1960 (Iranian), Avanesov and Orlova 1964 (Russian), Wolff 1969 (Abuan), Pederson 1974 (Southern American), Muradjan et al. 1977 (Armenian), Heine and Mohlig 1980 (Kenya), Breen 1981 (Mayi), Lastra de Suárez 1986 (Nahuatl), and Upton, Sanderson, and Widdowson 1987 (British English).

We have found dialect manuals like these to be extremely helpful when working with informants. On many occasions, individuals who have insisted that they speak only the standard form of their language, or have been unable to think of any nonstandard forms, suddenly come alive when presented with examples from the dialect manual for their language. The main problem with this approach is that the dialect manual for one language can't always be used with other languages: the words that show interesting regional variation are not always the same from language to language; different cultures employ different implements and value different concepts; different lands have different flora and fauna; and so on. Even if you are using the manual for a language group to which your informants' dialect belongs, it sometimes will not work. The Armenian dialect manual (Muradjan et al. 1977), for example, does not work very well with the Muslim Armenians from northeastern Turkey, because are not familiar with Standard Armenian and therefore do not recognize the headwords for each dialect form. Another potential drawback of dialect manuals is that they normally are traditionally oriented and therefore non-theoretical; as a result, they generally concentrate on vocabulary and morphology, and pay little or no attention to syntax. This is not a problem for non-theoretical linguists, of course, but can be quite frustrating for theoreticians.

2.5. Register

One final sort of linguistic variation that we would like to discuss involves **register**, a variety of language that is defined according to its use in different social situations (formal, informal, written, etc.). Speakers always control many different registers, and you should try to collect samples of each if possible, because each is likely to show different points of linguistic interest. In American English, for example, the interesting constructions *a whole nother*, *didn't use(d) to*, and *as good of* show up only in informal registers, as in the following fragments of dialogue:

| informal | *I like Bio, but Econ's a whole nother story.* |
| formal | *I like my Biology course, but my Economics course is an entirely different story.* |

| informal | *Nah, she doesn't like me. At least, she didn't used to like me...* |
| formal | *No, she does not like me. At least, she did not like me before now...* |

| informal | *I'm not taking that easy of classes this term.* |
| formal | *I am not taking such easy courses this term.* |

These examples also demonstrate that contraction is generally mandatory in informal registers, and even to a certain extent in formal spoken registers; however, it is frowned upon in formal written registers, such as the one in which we are currently writing. To take another example, the statement *I do not like you* is eminently acceptable in an academic paper and in children's books, but it is utterly unacceptable in spoken registers of English (unless the *not* is stressed).

Clearly, then, there are many potential rewards to be reaped from the collection of register-based linguistic variation. The problem is that it is extremely difficult to control what register individuals use in an interview situation; typically they will use some sort of formal, careful register. Once they are in this register, it can be very hard to get your informants to use a different register, or even to come up with examples of things they might say in another register. The best way to deal with this problem is to record speakers in natural speech environments: talking with their siblings or close friends, talking with their children, writing a letter, and so on. If you are not able to do recordings in the field like this, the next best option is to involve more than one speaker in your interview sessions, and ask them to act out conversations designed to elicit different registers. For example, you might ask your informants to improvise a dialogue between a doctor and a patient, or between two students, and so forth.

3. Dialect information and how to collect it

In this section we'd like to return to the general problem of how to collect dialect data. It's acceptable to cut to the chase with your informants, and directly ask them questions like the following:

- Does your language have any dialects? (Or, if they don't know what a dialect is, "do people speak your language differently in different parts of the country?")
- Can you tell where someone is from in your country by the way they speak? How?
- Are there any words or expressions that men use but women do not, or vice versa?

However, as we hinted at earlier, informants are typically unable to describe dialect differences in any useful way. Individuals are often aware that different dialects of their language exist, and will tell you as much, but when asked to characterize these dialects, they typically say things like "they talk faster", "they sound guttural", "they talk through their noses", and so on. A Yakut speaker I worked with several years ago volunteered that her language contained two dialects, and even executed lengthy renditions of them. When asked to describe in more specific terms how the two dialects differed, though, her response was that one was "sing-song" and the other was "monotonous". This is a popular characterization of dialects by non-linguists. To take just two of many more such examples, one of my Armenian informants described the Jerusalem dialect (after hearing it for the first time) as having a sing-song quality relative to standard Armenian. Similarly, a cab driver originally from Manhattan recently asserted to me that people speak differently in each borough of New York City; when asked for examples, he replied "it's the melody".

The two most common descriptions of others' speech are "nasal" and "sing-songy". If I had a dollar for every time someone has described someone else's speech variety to me in this way I wouldn't have to be writing this book. It isn't just simpletons who use such terms, either; Isaac Asimov, for example, describes a dialect as nasal and sing-songy in his 1985 book *Robots and Empire*. In addition to being phonetically inaccurate, such descriptions are also harmfully value-laden, as Holliday 2002:188 points out when discussing a student's analysis of Chinese stage productions. The student writes "In Chinese television and stage shows there are usually...a man in a tight-fitting white blazer and a girl in a large flouncy ballroom gown...They take turns to speak with a sing-song intonation, the man in a low dignified tone and the woman in a high-pitched nasal whine." Holliday responds that "when Grace presented this extract at a research seminar...other people there...saw in it culturalist language which Grace had clearly not intended, but which is in fact there...'sing-song' and 'high-pitched nasal whine' represent [the student's] own derogatory spin on events which are not normally considered to be derogatory."

The point here is not to devolve into cultural criticism, but rather to suggest that descriptions of speech as "nasal", "sing-songy", and the like are typically not objective observations of linguistic realities, but instead are manifestations of deeply entrenched cultural biases that have no basis in anything relevant to a linguist.

To be fair, the description of a dialect as "sing-song" can be linguistically significant, referring for example to the fact that the dialect in question makes systematic tonal distinctions, whereas other dialects of the language do not. However, our suspicion is that the "sing-song" description normally refers to the fact that the dialect in question simply has a different system of discourse intonation than other dialects do. This is well worth studying, but is beyond the scope of most Field Methods courses and also outside the range of interests of most linguists.

The other feature most commonly attributed to dialects (and also to foreign languages) is that their speakers talk quickly. Consider the following description of the Tsugaru dialect of Japanese, taken from a website dealing with Japanese dialects. (The original URL http://www.ifnet.or.jp/~eichi/Tsugaru.html is not currently working; all grammatical errors are preserved from the original site.):

> "In Tsugaru, they don't speak so much but when they speak something it's very fast. Actually they don't spend a lot of time speaking, because they never want to open their mouth in cold air. So conversations must be short..."

To combat these popular notions of how dialects differ, you should provide your informants with specific examples of legitimate dialect differences, in order to give them an idea of what you're looking for. Make sure to start with linguistic differences that will make sense to your informants, such as vocabulary differences, different morphemes, and so on. Individuals are often consciously aware of linguistic differences based on religion, region, class, etc., so they are likely to get the idea if you mention specific examples of any of these types. Here are some examples of simple, easily understandable dialect differences that one might mention to an Irish person when trying to collect information about Irish English dialects:

Religion	Catholics say <h> as [heːtʃ] ("haitch"), whereas Protestants say [eːtʃ].
Region	People in Northern Ireland use *stoned* for 'drunk', and say *what about you* for 'how are you'.
Gender	Men pronounce *Jesus* as [dʒeːzəs]; women tend to use [dʒiːzəs].
	Only men say *me ol' one* for 'my mom' and *me ol' lad* for 'my dad'.

If you don't know of any good dialect variants from your informants' language, try giving them examples from your own language or from some other language they know. This may not be as effective as examples from their own language, but can still work quite well.

If none of these tricks work, you can still elicit linguistic variation in many cases simply by asking the right sorts of questions. Start with things that normally vary within a language, such as the word for 'shit'; men will typically use a different form for this than women do.

Another trick requires a bit of linguistic sophistication: if you know that the language you're studying has a certain linguistic rule, try presenting your informants with hypothetical forms that fail to undergo the rule. Sometimes they will simply deem these forms ungrammatical, but occasionally they will respond that the forms you asked about are actually used in another dialect, and you can go on from there.

One final trick for collecting dialect and idiolect data is to bring together two or more speakers, and ask them for grammaticality judgements or any other sort of linguistic information. You'll be surprised at how often they will disagree with each other! Take down each of the variants your informants produce, and ask each of them what he or she thinks about the forms produced by the other speakers. A variant of this technique involves having your informants read a text or listen to a recording of another person, and asking them to translate it. Whenever your informants come across a word or construction that they do not know, they will probably attribute the offending item to old people, or young people, or regional dialect difference. At this point you can discuss with them the significance of dialect variation, and try to find out if your informants know of any other similar differences in their language. We once used this trick to good effect with an informant who insisted that Armenian had only two dialects, and he spoke both of them. We then showed him a text written in the dialect of a town only a short distance from his, and he was completely unable to read it. Next we played him a videotape of a dialect spoken at the opposite end of the Armenian world, and he was unable to make head or tail of it. At this point he admitted that Armenian seemed to have many dialects, and from then on he became more open to the fact that his forms were not always the standard ones.

If none of these tricks are working, be patient; often the best tidbits pop up serendipitously during sessions that aren't designed to elicit dialect data. All languages are rife with dialect variation, and this variation will inevitably rise to the surface on occasion. Furthermore, don't get discouraged if your informants can't think of something on a particular occasion. People remember different things on different occasions; try your question again in the future, and you may well get better results.

To wrap up this section, we'd like to give you a concrete example of the sort of things you'll encounter when you ask an informant about dialects. The following is a transcription of what transpired when we tried to collect some information on regional dialects from our Gujarati informant. We have appended comments on the progress of the interview where appropriate.

Q: *Do you know if there are any different varieties of Gujarati, that are spoken in different towns, for example?*

A: Oh, different town, oh yeah. hɛdo hɛdo. We say "I wanna go", we say "go go". So in Guzarati we say tʃɑlo. The people almost use, they say tʃɑlo. In the small town and another state the same in the Guzarat, but different town, the people call hɛdo hɛdo...The people no say tʃɑlo—always use the hɛdo in the Rajasthan. In Guzarat, Amdabad, Surat, over there the people say tʃɑlo. In some town the people say hɛdo—the same meaning.

[At this point we form the interim hypothesis that the imperative "go!" is tʃɑlo in the big cities in Gujarat (Surat, Ahmadabad), but in Rajasthan and some villages in Gujarat the form is hɛdo.]

Q: *Do you think that* hɛdo *and* tʃɑlo *are related? Are they the same word, just pronounced differently?*

[This question has the advantage of getting right to the point, and showing respect for the informant's opinion; however, it has the disadvantage of being a leading question, and what the informant responds therefore may not be reliable.]

A: Oh no. They mean same, but different words.

[Our interim conclusion is that the words are not pronunciational variants of each other, but we should await further evidence before drawing a final conclusion.]

Q: *Are there any differences in pronunciation between different areas, like saying* s *instead of* h, *or* h *instead of* tʃ?

[We asked this because he had mentioned such differences before but had not remembered them yet in this session; we were hoping that this time around he might remember more specific information about the distribution of these dialect variables.]

A: Yeah, is tʃʰʌɾi is a knife—in my town the people say tʃʰʌɾi. But in the village people say sʌɾi. And the town name is suɾʌt, but in the village people say tʃʰuɾʌt.

[Inspection of a dictionary reveals that tʃʰʌɾi is in fact the standard Gujarati word for a small knife; sʌɾi must be a dialect variant, though we thus far do not know its distribution. We may be able to refine this information at a later date with more pointed questions. As for suɾʌt (the city of Surat), we suspect that tʃʰuɾʌt may be a hypercorrection, either on the part of our informant or of the villagers to which he refers. Addressing this question will require further work.]

4. Traps and pitfalls

> *This forty-year-old Abkhazian...is aware of the Bzyp dialect...but does not actually admit that Abkhaz has any dialects: according to him, there are only those who speak well—and this is what is called Bzyp—and those whose language is corrupt or vulgar.*

Georges Dumézil, describing one of his informants

All sorts of traps and quagmires await the field linguist who attempts to collect dialect data. The most common trap of this sort appears as soon as one begins to ask informants about the dialects spoken by others or by themselves: they almost always insist that everyone speaks their language in exactly the same way, and their language has no dialects. However, we can guarantee that this is wrong; in fact, we would go so far as to say that there is no language that does not have any dialects. There are always differences between speakers and between communities, and if you know the right questions to ask you should be able to find them. Since we have already touched on these issues in sections 1.1 and 1.2, we will not elaborate on them here.

The next potential problem is that even if your informants acknowledge that dialects exist within their language, and that they themselves speak a dialect of that language, they may still be unaware or unwilling to admit that their grammar contains a particular phenomenon in which you're interested. My brother, for example, refuses to this day to acknowledge the fact that he pronounces *milk* with an Illinois accent—[mɛlk]—even though it is quite clear to the rest of the family.

Our next problem is much more insidious: sometimes speakers will have a very definitive answer to your question, but this answer happens to be wrong. For example, individuals often have the wrong idea of where specific dialect features are used. One of our friends, a Chicagoan, once pointed out that the term *jagoff* 'jerk' was used only in Chicago. Intrigued by this observation, we set out to ask a number of people from Chicago and elsewhere whether they knew the word *jagoff*. The responses we received resoundingly confirmed our friend's generalization: all of the Chicagoans we surveyed were familiar with the term, and none of the non-Chicagoans. Imagine our surprise, then, when a search of the Web for uses of *jagoff* turned up a site devoted to Pittsburgh dialect, which proclaimed that *jagoff* was a word used only in Pittsburgh! Further consultation with the *Dictionary of American Regional English* (III, p. 97) revealed that the word is primarily characteristic of Pennsylvania.

We can learn at least two lessons from this experience: first, don't always believe everything you read, even in trusted sources (in this case, DARE completely missed the Chicago usage of *jagoff*); second, don't always believe your informants' intuitions. Always be sure to check and double check every linguistic tidbit that you hear or read; you never know when you may turn up unexpected refutation or modification of your analysis.

The same sort of problem arose with the word *bubbler*, which means drinking fountain in parts of the Northeast (especially around Boston) and in parts of the Midwest (especially Wisconsin). Many Bostonians and Wisconsonians we have worked with have readily identified *bubbler* as a shibboleth of their respective regions, and all were shocked to hear that the term was used in the other region. Even DARE (I, p. 403) is not entirely reliable on this issue: it states that *bubbler* is especially used in Wisconsin, and makes no mention of it being used in Massachusetts.

The intuitions of linguists can also be wrong in these matters. To take a particularly damning set of examples, one of the present authors was convinced that the term *johnny cake*, which refers to a kind of cornmeal bread, was used only in the South of the

United States; but the DARE linguistic survey reveals that it is used almost exclusively in the North (III, p. 154). His co-author was not infallible, either: he was under the impression that *bain't* (a variant of *ain't*) was characteristic of nineteenth-century African-American English, but it in fact is a very old British dialectal form, which was also used in Newfoundland.

Your informants may also have incorrect ideas about what the distinctive features of their dialects actually are. Most people when asked about the Boston dialect will respond with something like "pahk ya cah in Hahvahd Yahd" [pʰɑːk jə kʰɑː ɪn hɑːvəd jɑːd]. The line of thinking here is that Bostonians simply "drop their r's", changing a word like *car* [kʰɑɹ] into [kʰɑː]. In reality, *r*-deletion generally affects the quality of the preceding vowel, so for example *car* is actually pronounced by most Bostonians as [kʰaː], with a slightly fronted and raised a (not ɑ). Another common incorrect description of Boston dialect is that "it inserts *r* in all the wrong places". People—including native speakers of Boston dialect—most often say that this involves inserting *r*'s at the end of words; *The Boston Dictionary*, for example, has numerous entries such as *piazzer* 'front porch', *otter* 'ought to', and *nanner* 'father's mother'. In fact, these words are *not* pronounced with a final *r*, but rather with a final schwa: [pʰiætsə], [ɒɾə], [nænə], etc. The correct generalization is that *r*-insertion occurs only when one of the vowels {ɑ ɒ æ ə ɔ ʌ} is followed by another vowel. This description is relatively easy to come up with when one tests the pronunciation of a few words in Boston dialect, but for some reason people always seem to produce the fallacy of *r*-insertion at the end of words. You should always be on the lookout for this sort of incorrect generalization when working with informants; be sure to test their generalizations in as many different linguistic environments as possible (before different vowels and consonants, and so on).

Even if your informants have accurate information in their heads, it may come out in a misleading way, due to idiosyncrasies such as speech defects, speech errors, and so on. For example, when our Gujarati informant stated that villagers in Gujarat say sʌmnʌ instead of tʃʰʌmnʌ for 'fish', we were not immediately sure whether he meant sʌmnʌ or ʃʌmnʌ, because (as we mentioned in chapter 9) he freely varies in his English pronunciation between s and ʃ. Similarly, if one hears Barbara Walters or Elmer Fudd produce a [w], it is not immediately clear whether they are trying to produce a [w], an [r], or an [l] (cf. chapter 7). One way to guard against this sort of problem is to have your informants write down the forms in question, or to show them your transcriptions to make sure that they are correct.

Finally, you should be careful when collecting lexical items, because similar items can easily be confused. For example, there are several different little crustaceans that look and act almost exactly the same, including the doodlebug mentioned in section 2. People tend to confuse or conflate similar creatures like these, which can contaminate your data. My students readily label as *pill bug, sow bug*—or whatever their favorite term is—the critter that I call a *doodlebug*. However, reality is not necessarily so simple, because for example the pill bug and the sow bug are two different bugs, according to the *American Heritage Dictionary*. Caution must also be exercised when comparing these terms across different areas, because they can have slightly or radically different meanings; for example, *doodlebug* refers to the larva of an ant lion or a tiger beetle in parts of the South, and to a dung beetle in the Carolinas (DARE II, pp. 134-5).

Suggested Readings

Bailey, Guy and Jan Tillery. 1999. The Rutledge Effect: The Impact of Interviewers on Survey Results in Linguistics. American Speech 74.4:389-402.

Bailey, Guy and Margie Dyer. 1992. An Approach to Sampling in Dialectology. American Speech 67.1:3-20.

Cassidy, Frederick and Audrey Duckert. 1970. A Method for Collecting Dialect, second edition. American Dialect Society 20.

König, Werner. 1978. dtv-Atlas zur deutschen Sprache: Tafeln und Texte. München: Deutscher Taschenbuch Verlag.

Kurath, Hans. 1968. The Investigation of Urban Speech. American Dialect Society 49.

Labov, William. 1972a. Some principles of linguistic methodology. Language in Society 1:97-120.

Labov, William. 1984. Field methods of the project on linguistic change and variation. In John Baugh and J. Sherzer, eds., Language in use. Readings in sociolinguistics, 28-53. Englewood Cliffs: Prentice-Hall.

Linn, Michael. 1983. Informant Selection in Dialectology. American Speech 58:225-43.

Maynor, Natalie. Grammatical Judgments in "LANE". American Speech 57:228-31.

McDavid, Raven. 1985. Eliciting: Direct, Indirect, and Oblique. American Speech 60:309-17.

Mufwene, Salikoko. 1997. The ecology of Gullah's survival. American Speech 72.1:69-83.

Pederson, Lee, et alii. 1974. A Manual for dialect research in the Southern States, second edition. Tuscaloosa: University of Alabama Press.

Shuy, Roger. 1968. Field techniques in an urban language study. Urban language series 3. Washington: Center for Applied Linguistics.

Wilson, George. 1944. Instructions to Collectors of Dialect. Greensboro, NC: American Dialect Society.

Wolfram, Walt, and Ralph Fasold. 1974. Field methods in the study of social dialects. In Walt Wolfram and Ralph Fasold, eds., The study of social dialects in American English. Englewood Cliffs, NJ: Prentice-Hall.

Wolfson, Nessa. 1976. Speech events and natural speech: Some implications for sociolinguistic methodology. Language in Society 5:189-209.

Exercises

1. If the language of your informants has already been described in the literature, ask your informants whether there are any dialects within their language, and how these dialects differ. Compare the answer you receive to what is said in the published descriptions. If the published sources have more complete dialect information, discuss how you might have altered or revised your original questions to come closer to the level of detail contained in the published sources.

2. Compile a list of dialect differences in your own language, then find one or more published descriptions of dialects of your language and see how your list compares to the published information. Discuss how you might prompt your informants to think of the sorts of dialect details that you yourself did not think of when creating your list.

3. Go through a dictionary and collect and discuss five words for which your pronunciation differs from the one provided.

4. Go through an old (i.e. pre-WWII) dictionary and collect and discuss five words where your pronunciation differs from the one given in the dictionary, or where you consider the word to be archaic, no longer in use, or to have changed meaning.

12 Reconstructing the linguistic past: Historical Linguistics

The first thing which strikes one on studying linguistic facts is that the language user is unaware of their succession in time.

It is clear that the synchronic point of view takes precedence over the diachronic, since for the community of language users that is the one and only reality.

Ferdinand de Saussure
Course in General Linguistics

1. Introduction

Saussure's assertion that speakers do not know the history of their language is largely true but not entirely. Most individuals have noticed differences between their own way of speaking and that of their parents, grandparents, and other elders, and in many cases cultures preserve traditions about older forms of their language. We can use this historical memory—taken with a grain of salt, as we'll detail below—to help us reconstruct the history of the language we are studying.

I remember, for example, that my mother's parents referred to the couch on their back porch as a *davenport*, a term that has subsequently fallen out of general usage among English speakers below a certain age. They also referred to one's rear end as the *fanny*, and were fond of introducing certain types of propositions with *why*— "Why, I just don't know about you, Bert Richard", and so on. Both of these usages have now almost completely disappeared from the English language. By collecting information of this sort from your informants, you can begin to build a picture of earlier forms of their language.

In addition to remembering particular features of our elders' speech, we typically have some sense of what is archaic in our

351

language. For example, most English speakers—including those who have not studied the history of the language—are aware that forms such as *prithee*, *yon*, and *thee* were once used in the language, though now they are not used in everyday speech. The fieldworker must be careful in collecting information of this sort, because speakers do not always use archaic features in a historically correct manner: TV sitcoms, for example, often use historically inaccurate forms such as "I goest", "I goeth", and so on when imitating archaic speech. (The character Dylan on *Beverly Hills 90210* once said "yes, thou doth", to take one example.) Furthermore, it is important for the fieldworker to remember that archaic speech is not necessarily the same as old people's speech; *forsooth*, for example, is archaic but not a feature of the speech of (recent) older generations. This demonstrates that speakers' recollections of archaic speech can enable us to reach back much farther into the past than we can go with older people's speech: whereas *davenport* only disappeared from common usage in the past few decades, the last (non-ironic) attestation of *forsooth* in *The Oxford English Dictionary* is from 1880, and it was probably moribund long before then.

Another way that one can often get at older forms of a language is via underlying forms (q.v. chapter 7), because as one linguist once put it, "yesterday's surface forms are today's underlying representations". In other words, the underlying representations of words in the synchronic grammar of a language typically reflect the surface pronunciations of older stages of the language (whereas the surface forms of the modern language generally reflect more recent innovations). For example, phonologists assume that the underlying form of the word for "head" in modern Russian is /golov/, even though this never actually appears in any surface forms (cf. [gəlɑˈvɑ] 'head (nominative)', [gɑˈlof] 'head (genitive plural)', [ˈgoləvu] 'head (accusative singular)'). This underlying form *golov*, which we postulate for reasons entirely independent of the history of the language, happens in fact to coincide with the surface form of "head" at an earlier stage in the history of Russian, before it developed rules changing unstressed o to ɑ or ə. This correlation between synchronic underlying forms and historical surface forms does not always hold, but is sufficiently common that you may well be able to make use of it in your historical fieldwork.

Thus far we have considered some ways in which elders, archaisms, and underlying forms can help in accessing the history of a language. In the next section we turn to more specific suggestions for the sorts of linguistic information of historical import that you can collect, and in section 3 we suggest ways in which to collect this information successfully. Finally, in section 4 we point out some common traps and pitfalls that can beset historical fieldworkers.

2. What to collect

When you are trying to collect linguistic data that will provide insight into the history of a language, the key is to remember the words of the French linguist Antoine Meillet: *look for forms that no longer make sense* (cf. Meillet 1924:41). The reason for this is that newer forms in a language tend to "make sense": they take productive prefixes and suffixes (q.v. chapters 8); in the case of compound words, their subparts and their meanings are readily identifiable; in the case of phrases, idioms, and sayings, it is clear how the individual words combine to give the sense of the entire collocation; and so on. However, these sensible mappings between form, function, and meaning can be obscured by the ravages of time, as sound changes mutate the original pronunciation of words, semantic changes alter their meanings, and so on. When we come across a form that does not "make sense", it is highly likely that this form can tell us something about the history of the language, and specifically about the linguistic changes that have applied to this form since it last "made sense".

2.1. Words that don't make sense

Consider the cranberry. All English speakers have the intuition that this word is formed from *berry* plus the morpheme *cran-*, which on its own does not have any readily identifiable meaning (though thanks to the folks at Ocean Spray it now has the sense of "a product made in part from cranberries", as in *Cranapple, Crancherry, Crangrape*, etc.). Here we have a prime case of what Meillet was talking about, because the morpheme *cran-* makes no sense; let us now see if we can make some sense of this form by delving into the history of English. If we root around the lexicon a bit, just about the closest word to *cran* that we find is *crane*. Emboldening ourselves to hypothesize (on the basis of systematic parallels such as *James* [dʒeɪmz] vs. *Jamison* [dʒæmɪsən]), we can conjecture that *cran* is in fact a descendant of *crane*, which has been transmogrified and frozen by the whims of the English language. What we have, then, is a berry that has been named after either a large piece of machinery, or a long-legged bird known for frequenting bogs. It is of course highly unlikely that the cranberry was named after the piece of machinery, because a) the two objects have no common form or function; b) there has not been enough time for **craneberry* to develop into *cranberry* between the invention of the crane and the present day. On the other hand, the crane of the aviary persuasion and the cranberry do have something in common: association with bogs. We hypothesize, then, that the cranberry was originally called *craneberry*, reflecting the fact that this particular berry is found in areas frequented by cranes. As it turns out, this hypothesis indeed reflects the actual history of the word.[47]

It will not always be possible for you to carry out this sort of reasoning with idiosyncratic forms that you have collected, of course. Furthermore, with most languages you won't be able to verify your hypotheses, due to the lack of historical records for these languages. However, we have often found it useful to see if our informants have any ideas about the origins of these idiosyncratic forms. As we mentioned above, speakers often have some knowledge of the history of their language by virtue of remembering forms used by their elders, so it is quite possible that they will have some idea of the provenance of the forms in which you are interested. Even if your informants do not have any accurate historical information, we encourage the collection of folk etymologies for the forms in question, because these always shed light on speakers' analysis of their own language (which can subsequently prompt hypercorrections and reanalyses, such as *sparrowgrass* from *asparagus*), and sometimes may even reveal legitimate morsels of the history of the language.

2.2. Formations that don't make sense

Another place to look for forms that don't make sense is in non-productive morphological categories. English, for example, has a large number of non-productive plural formations (*oxen, children, brethren, kine; geese, mice, lice; sheep, deer, fish*; etc.), past tense formations (*went, bought, sank*, etc.). Many of these have regular biforms, such as *oxes, brothers*, and *cows*; whenever you run into a pair of this type, where one member is regular (e.g. *brothers*) and the other is irregular (*brethren*), it is a safe bet that the irregular form

---

[47] Onions 1966, on the other hand, suggests that the word may have been borrowed from German *Kranbeere*, in which the composition is more clear; cf. *Kran* 'crane'.

reflects an earlier state of the language. (Exceptions are few and far between, such as the past tense of *dive*, which originally was the regular form *dived* but has become the irregular form *dove* for many English speakers; another interesting case is *skun*, the past tense of the verb *skin* in some nonstandard varieties of American English, and similarly *snuck*, the new past tense form of *sneak*.) In the case of *brethren*, we can in fact identify two schemes that at one time in the history of English were commonly used to pluralize nouns: one involved altering one or more vowels of the base word (*brother* → *brethr-*; cf. also *geese*, *mice*, etc.); the other involved adding the suffix *–(e)n* (*brethr-* → *brethren*; cf. also *kine*, *oxen*, etc.). We can see that both of these formations are quite old from the fact that they also show up in German and other languages closely related to English (and they have not borrowed these from English, or vice versa).

With both the idiosyncratic words and the non-productive morphological categories discussed above, the question arises of how to identify these needles of linguistic history in the enormous haystack of words, morphemes, phrases, idioms, collocations, and so on that make up a language. Fortunately, the forces that control language change have conspired to make this task relatively easy. Every idiosyncratic form in a language taxes the memory of its speakers more so than regular forms do; for example, learning the plural of *child* requires four extra bits of information:

(1)   i.   add *ren*.
       ii.   *ren* is a suffix (i.e. added to the end of the word).
       iii.   change the vowel of the base word from [ɑj] to [ɪ].
       iv.   do not add the regular plural ending.

Forming the plural of *dog*, on the other hand, requires no special information; the combination {*dog* + PLURAL} automatically produces the correct output *dogs*.

In a sense, then, we get the plural *dogs* for free, whereas the plural *children* requires English speakers to memorize four extra pieces of information. What enables speakers to keep track of all this extra information? Well, we all know from personal experience that memory goes hand-in-hand with repetition; we are much more likely to remember things that we see or use frequently than we are to remember things that never come up. The same generalization seems to hold for language: we are much more likely to remember idiosyncratic information for words that we see and use all the time than we are for obscure words. What this entails is that core words in a language—*dog*, *mother*, and so on—are significantly more likely to retain archaic linguistic features than peripheral words like *caboose* and *flange* are. A classic illustration of this phenomenon can be found in the Russian accentual system, where 98.2% of nouns have a fixed accent and only 0.8% of nouns have mobile (idiosyncratic) accent (Zaliznjak 1967). As the preceding discussion leads us to expect, the mobile accent type preserves an older state of the language, whereas the fixed accent type, which is fully productive and requires no special memorization, represents a newer pattern in the language. Interestingly, though—and unfortunately for individuals learning Russian—the 0.8% of nouns that have idiosyncratic accent also happen to be the most commonly used words in the entire language!

For historically-oriented field linguists, on the other hand, this distribution is very convenient. In order to find forms that no longer make sense in the synchronic linguistic system of the language, it is not necessary to root around the remote corners of the lexicon; these forms will generally pop up automatically when one collects the basic vocabulary and morphology of the language.

2.3. *Collocations that don't make sense*

Our next source of historical material is longer strings of words that habitually go together, yet do not entirely make sense for one reason or another. Examples of this type can be poems, sayings, songs, idioms, curses, ritual utterances, phrases, and so on.

Let's start with an idiomatic verb phrase. One occasionally hears Princeton undergraduates referring to *dropping the P bomb*, as in "I was talking to my dad's friend, and as soon as I dropped the P bomb, he offered me a job for the summer". As one can infer from this example, "dropping the P bomb" involves telling someone that you are a student at Princeton University; however, one cannot deduce this meaning from the meanings of the words from which the phrase is built. *Dropping the P bomb* thus presents us with another case of Meillet's sort, because this phrase makes no sense in the synchronic grammar of English. We can provisionally conclude, then, that this phrase will tell us something about the history of the language, if we ask the right questions.

In this particular case we don't need to look very far, because the history of *dropping the P bomb* is very recent. In fact, the origins of this phrase are so new that English speakers still use the original constructions. These of course are *dropping the A bomb* and *dropping the H bomb*, which refer respectively to the atom bomb and the hydrogen bomb. The original phrase *dropping the H bomb* was quickly appropriated by self-conscious Harvard students in order to express the act of telling someone that they go to Harvard. In this form, the phrase (which is still extremely popular among Harvard undergraduates) is quite sensible, because it metaphorically captures both the power of the original bomb (insofar as dropping the H(arvard) bomb has an immediate effect on a prospective mate or employer) and its negative connotations (insofar as attending Harvard College, and especially mentioning that fact in polite conversation, are sources of intense annoyance for many decent folk). However, Harvard doesn't exist in a vacuum, so it is not surprising that its pet phrase was quickly taken up by rival schools, yielding phrases that have lost their tie to the original context, such as *dropping the P bomb.*

Songs and poems are another excellent source of historical material, because their relatively rigid structure and their dependence on rhyme and meter frequently result in the preservation of older linguistic forms, or at least clear clues regarding the prior existence of these forms. Take for example the English word *have*, which is pronounced [hæv], though based on the spelling we might expect it to be pronounced [hɛɪv], rhyming with *save*, *grave*, and so on (cf. *behave*, which is spelled just like *have* but rhymes with *save*). We might consider this mismatch between the spelling and the pronunciation to simply be yet another quirk of English orthography, were it not for evidence such as the following rhymes:

(2)   *What is this world? what asketh men to **have**?*
        *Now with his love, now in his colde **grave***
        Allone, with-outen any companye.
        [Chaucer, *The Knightes Tale* (c. 1390), lines 2777-2779]

(3)   *'Tis true he grants the people all they **crave**,*
        *And more perhaps than subjects ought to **have**:*
        For lavish grants suppose a monarch tame,
        And more his goodness than his wit proclaim.
        [Dryden, *Absalom and Achitophel* (1681), lines 383-386]

These poems, which rhyme *have/grave* and *have/crave* respectively, suggest that at least until the late 17th century *have* was in fact pronounced like *grave*, *crave*, and so on. This supposition is further corroborated by the Scots equivalent *hae* 'have', which is still pronounced with the original vowel, [heː].

The preceding discussion demonstrates that poems and other rhymed compositions can preserve traces of earlier stages of a language. If you are interested in studying the history of your informants' language, it is therefore a good idea to collect rhymed material of this sort. Once you have collected a rhymed composition, look for word pairs that should rhyme but in fact do not, like *have* and *grave* in the Chaucer passage above. Collect as many such rhymes as you can, and once you have a critical mass you can begin to form hypotheses about the linguistic history of the anomalous forms, just as we hypothesized here that *have* was once pronounced [hev].

Poetic meter can also be useful in reconstructing linguistic history. Consider for example the following excerpt from the Sanskrit text of the Rigveda, the first stanza of hymn 71 of book 8. The hymn was originally composed about three millennia ago, but for most of that time was only preserved in oral form. When it was finally written down sometime in the first millennium A.D., it was pronounced as follows:

(4) tvɑ́m no ɑgne mɑ́hob^{h}ih   O Agni[48], with your mighty wealth
    pɑːhí víʃvɑsjɑː ɑ́rɑːteh   Protect us from all malignity
    utɑ́ dviʂó mɑ́rtjɑsjɑ   And from all mortal hatred.

The stanza is composed in a meter called gɑːjɑtriː, wherein each stanza consists of three lines, each consisting of eight syllables. Note, though, that in this particular stanza both line 1 and line 3 appear to contain only 7 syllables:

---

[48] The Fire God in Vedic religion.

(5)

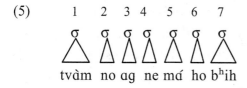

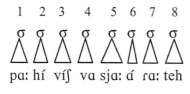

It is reasonable to hypothesize that all three lines originally contained eight syllables, and that the first and third lines each subsequently lost a single syllable. Our challenge then is to see if we can determine the nature of these deleted syllables. Until positive evidence forces us to assume otherwise, it is logical to hypothesize that a minimum of information was lost between the time that the stanza was composed and the time it was written down. The smallest amount of phonetic material that can be deleted and thereby lead to deletion of an entire syllable is a vowel, as in $C_1V_i.C_2V_{ii}.C_3V_{iii} \rightarrow C_1V_iC_2.C_3V_{iii}$ (where the period "." denotes a syllable boundary). Let us therefore assume that a single vowel has been deleted in line 1, and likewise in line 3. Where would these vowels have been located? A prime suspect is the word tvàm in line 1, which contains the unusual ` accent. This accent, which is called *svarita* in Sanskrit, results from the combination of a high tone and a low tone on a single vowel, as can be seen in the formation of tanvàm 'body-accusative' and sò-dʰamáh 'he is the worst'. Let us begin by examining the derivation of tanvám, bearing in mind that accented vowels bear a high tone (H), and unaccented vowels bear a low tone (L). The underlying form of tanvám is as follows:

(6)   L H   L
        | | |
      tanú:-   +   -am
      'body'   'accusative'

The form in (6a) undergoes a rule that changes high vowels (i and u) to glides (y and v respectively) before vowels, producing tanvám. Since consonants cannot bear tones in Sanskrit, the high tone that was linked to the u is delinked from the v (7a). Rather than simply disappearing, though, the high tone then links to the adjacent vowel a (7b). The a is now linked to two tones, a high tone followed by a low tone (7c), which as we stated above is interpreted as a *svarita* accent.

(7)

a.

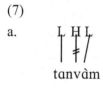

tanvám

b.   LH L
          | \|
        tánvàm

c.   LH L
          | \
        tánvàm

Consider now the derivation of sò-dʰamɑ́h 'he is the worst', which in a sense is the mirror image of the derivation of tɑnvɑ̀m. The underlying form of the phrase is given in (8).

(8)
```
     H                    L        L H
     |                    |        | |
    sɑ́- +    s     +    ɑ-   + dʰamɑ́- +    -s
    'he' 'nominative' 'negative' 'worst' 'nominative'
```

For reasons that do not concern us here, the nominative ending -ɑs becomes -o before a word beginning in ɑ-, yielding (9a). This then triggers a rule that deletes an ɑ after an o (9b). As in (7b), though, the tone that was linked to the deleted vowel does not itself delete (9c), but instead attaches to an adjacent vowel, in this case the preceding o (9d). This again produces a vowel linked to a high tone and a low tone (9e), which is interpreted as a svarita accent ` on the o in sò-dʰamɑ́h.

(9)

a.
```
    H L    L   H
    | |    |   /
    | |    |  /
    so-ɑ-dʰamɑ-s
```

b.
```
    H L   L   H
    | ⸻   |   \
    | ⸻   |    \
    so-ɑ-dʰamɑ-s
```

c.
```
    H L   L   H
    |     |   /
    |     |  /
    so-ɑ-dʰamɑ-s
```

d.   H L   L   H

so- -dʰama-s

e.   H L   L   H

so- -dʰama-s

In light of the facts in (6) through (9), it seems reasonable to assume that the svarita accent in tvȁm also results from vowel deletion or glide formation. This assumption would have the desirable result of accounting both for the otherwise mysterious svarita accent, and for the lack of a syllable in the poetic line. We happen to know that the stem of the second person singular pronoun in Sanskrit is tú- (cf. the dative form tú-bʰjam), so we can then postulate an original nominative form tú-am. The u in this form then undergoes prevocalic glide formation, just like the uː in tanvȁm, and the high tone of the original then shifts to the following a, producing the desired form tvȕm, with svarita accent.

Though we won't go into the details here, further elements of Sanskrit phonology suggest that Vedic Sanskrit (the language in which the hymn was originally composed) did not allow glides to occur after sequences of two consonants or after a long vowel followed by one or more consonants. This enables us to predict that the missing vowel in line 3 occurred in the form martjasja, which must originally have been martiasja, since the glide y was not allowed after the two-consonant sequence -rt-.

With these deductions in hand, we can now reconstruct the original version of the stanza as follows; note that each line now contains the expected eight syllables.

(10)   túam no ɑgne mɑ́hobʰih

pɑːhí víʃvɑsjɑː ɑ́rɑːteh

utɑ́ dviṣɑ́ mɑ́rtiɑsjɑ

By taking this stanza of an archaic hymn, identifying the elements of it that do not make sense, and trying to explain these elements, we have learned something not only about the hymn itself, but also about the structure of the language at two periods in its history. The same sorts of techniques can be applied to any language, provided that the material you collect contains elements that do not make sense in the synchronic grammar of the language.

The same sorts of facts can often be gleaned from songs, which of course are structurally quite similar to poems, by and large. Recall our children's song from chapter 11, repeated here:

(11)   *Ride a cock horse to Banbury Cross*

To see a fine lady upon a white horse

Rings on her fingers and bells on her toes

And she shall have music wherever she goes

The modern Banbury Cross

The first couplet contains several archaic items of linguistic interest. First of all we have *cock horse*, which is an archaic term for a toy horse; to the best of our knowledge, this term is no longer in common usage. Next we have the place name *Banbury Cross*, which refers to a large monument erected at a crossroads in the southern English town of Banbury.[49]

Though the sense of this collocation is still fairly transparent, it no longer makes sense (especially in the United States) to name a place *Cross* in English, unless it refers to an already-existing place by that name.

Finally, we note the usage of *upon*, which is now considered archaic in modern (American) English; the preferred form nowadays would be *on*. (Note, incidentally, that this same archaic word is preserved in the fixed phrase that begins fairy tales in English, *once upon a time...*, demonstrating that folk tales can also be an excellent source of linguistic archaism.)

This case study clearly shows how useful songs can be in reconstructing the history of a language. By taking only two lines of a children's song, we were able not only to draw an inference about the original pronunciation of two words (see the discussion of *Cross* and *horse* in chapter 11), but also to identify three archaic usages that

---

[49] Interestingly, the original Banbury Cross was destroyed in 1600, and the present-day replacement was not erected until 1859. This enables us to surmise that the song was composed before 1600, given that a) one would be relatively unlikely to see fine ladies upon white horses in Banbury after 1859, b) the rhyme between *Cross* and *horse* must have disappeared long before 1859. The composition of the poem must also postdate the appearance of *r*-deletion in English, or else *Cross* and *horse* would not rhyme; this places the creation of the poem sometime between the fifteenth century and 1600. The earliest reference to the poem is in 1725. It has been suggested (cf. Opie and Opie 1951) that the 'fine lady' of the song may have been Lady Godiva or Queen Elizabeth I (d. 1603). Opie and Opie 1951 also mention a theory that the use of "bells on her toes" points to the fifteenth century, when this style of dress was in fashion.

are no longer current in modern English but must have been at the time the song was composed.

Sometimes it happens that a song or poem will preserve linguistic information without actually maintaining the original words. Consider the following counting rhyme from Homshetsma (Vaux, LaPorta, and Tucker 1996):

(12) mɛg, tʰɛɹone pʰɛɹg   one, a mattock outside
     ɛɹgus, tʰɛɹone tʃʰapʰa   two, a hoe outside
     jijɛkʰ, govu tʰɛkʰ   three, a cow's placenta
     tʃʰoɹs, dzile noɹs   four, sparse corn sprouts
     hiŋg, tʰɛɹone di(ŋ)g   five, a sack outside
     vɛtsʰ, kʰɛnafin tʰɛtsʰ six, smelly air in the outhouse
     oχte, dolabin tʰuχte   seven, sheet of paper in the cupboard
     utʰe, tʰɛɹone tʰutʰe   eight, the mulberry outside
     ine, valan hine   nine, the old pants
     dase, tʰaɹkʰin tʰase   ten, the bowl on the shelf

Homshetsma is closely related to Armenian, but due to the conversion of its speakers to Islam between the sixteenth and twentieth centuries and its many centuries of isolation from the rest of the Armenian-speaking world, it is no longer mutually intelligible with Armenian, and has absorbed a great deal of Turkish phonology, syntax, and vocabulary.

The Turkish influence appears even in this counting rhyme, which is quite old and conservative. It should be clear from the structure of the poem that each line begins with a numeral and ends with a word rhyming with that numeral: jijɛkʰ '3' : tʰɛkʰ 'placenta', dase '10' : tʰase 'cup', etc. In this light the second line is very odd, because ɛɹgus '2' does not even come close to rhyming with tʃʰapʰa 'hoe'. Given that tʃʰapʰa is the only word in this conservative text to be borrowed from Turkish[50] (cf. Turkish *çapa* 'hoe'), one immediately suspects that the Turkish form has been substituted for an original Armenian word that rhymed with ɛɪgus. Furthermore, it is highly likely that this word meant 'hoe' or something similar. (Unfortunately, we thus far have been unable to identify an appropriate candidate.)

What this intriguing Homshetsma case shows us is that language can be like footprints. Just as footprints tell us a great deal about the long-gone feet that made them, in the same way we can use songs, poems, and so on to reconstruct pieces of the history of a language, even if the actual pieces are no longer there.

The same sort of reasoning that we have used in the preceding pages with poems, songs, and folk tales can also be applied to more prosaic collocations that do not appear in poetic contexts. Consider the construction that I heard recently while walking past a bar in Watertown, Massachusetts at closing time: *where the fuck are my keys?!* Now, all English speakers above a certain age know the meaning of *fuck*, but most would be hard-pressed to explain how it made its way into this type of construction. Most people would agree that the word *fuck* can function both as a verb ("man, the IRS really fucked me last year") and as an exclamation ("Fuck! I forgot to pay my taxes again!"), but in *where the fuck are my keys*, it appears to be acting as a noun. One's first reaction might be to say that one can simply insert swear words wherever one likes in English, but this obviously is too powerful a theory: though one can say *where in hell are my keys*, **where in fuck are my keys* is impossible; **where the shit are my keys* sounds equally bad.

---

[50] dolɑb and vɑlɑ are borrowed from Persian, and kʰɛnɑf is originally Arabic, but the Armenians were in contact with these languages long before the Turks arrived in Turkey, so loans from Arabic and Persian do not compromise the antiquity of the text.

Here again, we have in *where the fuck are my keys* an expression that makes no sense in the synchronic grammar of English, and hence is a prime candidate for revealing some vignette in the history of our language. As with *dropping the P bomb*, the history of *where the fuck are my keys* is short enough that we can actually reconstruct it armed only with one or two expressions that still survive (at least marginally) in modern English. It seems here that the starting point is the construction "where in hell is/are ____?", which one can still hear said in certain situations. In this construction, the prepositional phrase *in hell* makes sense as the complement of *where*, and the entire phrase is a logical expression of the fact that the speaker cannot find something important anywhere on this earth, and is enraged by this to the point of obscenity. The *where in hell is _* construction must have then spawned the *where in the hell is _* construction, though it is not clear to us how the *the* came into the picture (it also mysteriously appears in constructions such as *shut the fuck up*; perhaps it is imported from the expression *where in the world is/are _*, which itself may be the antecedent of the *where in hell is _* construction). The next stage in the development of this construction was to drop the *in*, yielding *where the hell is _*; replacement of *hell* by *fuck* then gave the desired expression *where the fuck is _*. It is interesting that the stages of this development are relatively clear, even though the motivations for several of the steps in the derivation are entirely unclear; for example, why should the *in* drop from *where in the hell is _*? Note that the *where in hell is* construction gives rise to at least one further construction which no longer makes synchronic sense, exemplified in comedian Dennis Miller's recent rant *why in the fuck aren't more kids watching my program?!* (The Dennis Miller Show, HBO, April 3, 1998.) The progression has gone even further in the slang of certain youths, in the expression *fuck you doin'?!*, which not only has replaced *hell* with *fuck*, but also has deleted *what (in) the*.[51]

Lingering briefly on the topic of obscenities, one can also exploit curses that at first glance seem to make no sense whatsoever, such as *Judas Priest!* (not to be confused with the rock band), *Jiminy Cricket!* (not to be confused with the Disney character), and *Jeezum Crow* (used in parts of the northeastern United States). Though all of these curses are now moribund in English, they were used until qite recently as relatively mild expressions of astonishment, annoyance, etc. Note that neither of these expressions makes any literal sense in English: Judas was not a priest, and there was no such character as Jiminy Cricket before Disney came along (they named their character after the expression, rather than the other way around). However, each expression bears a striking resemblance to another popular exclamation, *Jesus Christ!*, which expresses roughly the same range of meanings, though with slightly more force. In fact, both *Judas Priest* and *Jiminy Cricket* are what we call **taboo deformations** of *Jesus Christ*. What does this tell us about the history of English? We can't infer anything about the grammatical structure of the language from these taboo deformations, but we can develop a slightly better idea of the semantics of *Jesus Christ* and the interface between social mores and linguistic taboos during the period in which these expressions were formed and used.[52] More specifically, we can tell that then—as now—there existed a line between what could be said and what couldn't; furthermore, *Jesus Christ* fell on the bad side of this line, whereas today it no longer does (for most speakers of English). (Many similar developments

---

[52] Deformation in fact plays a major role in historical linguistics in precisely those areas of the lexicon which are "sensitive".

can be seen in the history of English, such as *dadgum(med)* and *goldern(ed) < god damn(ed)*, or *tarnation < eternal damnation.*)

2.4. Age-based variation revisited

We've seen thus far that forms and expressions which no longer make synchronic sense can be used to look into the past of the language you're studying. The story doesn't end there, however. As we mentioned briefly in section 1, it is also possible to mine the historical memory of your informants for nuggets of linguistic history. In this subsection we consider how techniques and data drawn from the study of linguistic variation can be used for this purpose.

Historical fieldwork goes hand-in-hand with age-based linguistic variation of the sort we discussed in the previous chapter, specifically variation of types 1 and 2, where type 1 involves forms that are used by older people, but are lost or disappearing among younger people, and type 2 involves forms that are tied to disappearing technologies and other evanescent phenomena. Forms such as *davenport* and *fanny* are examples of type I. One can cite further examples such as the exclamation *my word* or the use of *start* in the sense of "fright", as in *you gave me an awful start, Bert Richard!*, which I remember my grandparents saying. A nice example of type 2 age-based variation is found in my paternal grandfather's continued use of *icebox* to refer to refrigerators, reflecting the fact that in his youth the only devices available for storing food were literally large boxes in which one put ice. (*Icebox* continued to be learned by children for a while after the electrically-refrigerated metal container replaced the ice-filled container—we know someone born after World War II who uses *icebox*, for example—but it is not used by today's younger generations.)

You should be careful when collecting this type of information, though, because the differences that you notice in your elders' speech are not always the result of age-based variation. For example, my father's father also says things like *them boxes*, where the oblique personal pronoun *them* is used for the demonstrative adjective *those*. In this case, the difference between my grandfather's speech and standard English does not result from the fact that he belongs to an older generation, but rather is due to the fact that he was raised in a different dialect area (the Appalachian region of western Pennsylvania), and preserves many Appalachian dialect features in his speech (though the *them X* construction is not limited to Appalachia).

2.5. Dialects again

This brings us to our next point: the study of historical linguistics of the sort we have been outlining in this chapter is also related to dialectology, since older forms can often be found in related dialects of the language you are studying. For example, one can still find dialects in the United States that preserve the old three-way deictic system (*here : there : yonder*; *this : that : yon(der)*; etc.) that has disappeared in standard English. In fact, any dialect that you study is likely to preserve some linguistic features that other dialects don't. To illustrate this point, we randomly took up a brief list of dialect words from Newfoundland, and sure enough we found a number of interesting archaisms, including the following (data from Devine 1937):

- *oxter* **'armpit'**. This is still the word used for 'armpit' in the traditional dialects of Ireland and the extreme north of England, as you can see in the map below. (Interestingly, its Old English ancestor, *ocusta*, was also confined to the same part of England! The Old English form also shows that the *r* in *oxter* results from hypercorrection.)

- ***gossip* 'godfather or godmother'.** This word now means 'person who habitually spreads intimate or private rumors or facts' in modern English. However, this sense only appeared in the sixteenth century; the word, derived from *god + sib* 'blood relative' (cf. Old English *godsibb*), originally referred to the sponsor at a baptism, a meaning which is preserved intact in Newfoundland.

- ***homely* 'inclined to stay at home'.** This is the original meaning of the word, which is also preserved in parts of Great Britain. *Homely* of course later came to describe a plain and unattractive person or object in standard American English.

Bear in mind that it is not always the case that the nonstandard dialect is conservative relative to the standard dialect. In the case of the Gujarati word for 'small knife' that we mentioned in chapter 11, for example, the standard dialect's form tʃʰʌɾi is older than the dialectal form sʌɾi.

Finally, it is often useful to be aware that gender-based variation can also reveal linguistic history. The English word *hussy*, for example, reveals stages in the phonological development of English that are lost in its re-formed modern cognate, *housewife*.

The upshot of our discussion in this section is that it is often useful to combine one's dialectal and historical fieldwork, as the two areas each provide morsels of information for the other. Now that we have some idea of the sort of material to collect, let us turn to the problem of how to collect it.

Words for 'armpit' (Trudgill 1990:109)

3. How to collect it

As far as the collection of forms that don't make sense goes (cf. sections 2.1-2.3), there are no special procedures involved. In this situation, you simply take the data you have collected and look for forms, expressions, and so on that don't make sense given your knowledge of the structure of the language you're studying.

Collecting data on age-based variation, archaic usages, and so forth is much more challenging, in the sense that you have to ask the right questions and have your informants in the right frame of mind to get the sort of answers you want. We recommend that you start with the direct approach: ask your informants if they can think of any ways in which their parents'/grandparents'/elders' speech is or was different from their own. You need to give your informants a lot of time to answer this sort of question, because the information you're looking for won't just pour out instantaneously in a nicely packaged bundle. Different memories will come back in different situations, and the more time you give your informants to stew over these questions (and we mean days, weeks, and months here, not minutes!), the more likely they are to recall the desired kind of information. We've found it helpful to lightly encourage our informants to note down any relevant memories that pop into their heads outside of our sessions, just in case they forget them in the meantime.

There are a few other tricks that you can use to trigger your informants' memories if they're having trouble thinking of anything particular about their elders' speech patterns. First of all, it's always helpful to give them examples of the sort of information you're looking for. You should preferably give them examples from their own language, of course, but if these are lacking you can give some examples from your own language, such as the *davenport* case we mentioned earlier in this chapter. Secondly, ask your informants for any anecdotes or other bits of general lore that they remember about their parents, grandparents, and so on. Reminiscing about the past often gets people in the right mood to recall linguistic memories, and the specific tales that your informants recount may even contain older linguistic forms without them being aware of it. Thirdly, if it's possible with the language you're working on, you should find some older texts and go over them with your informants. Note down any differences that you come across between the language of the text and that of your informants, and try to get their reactions to these differences: "I've never heard this construction", "my parents might use this word, but I never would", "only old people say this", and so on. Be sure to ascertain for each linguistic difference whether it is completely incomprehensible to your informants, or if it is unclear but they can make a good guess, or they know it but don't use it, etc. Finally, you can try asking your informant to imitate an old person talking. This technique can be useful—if your informant is willing and able to carry out such an imitation—because people often produce things when "performing" that they would not otherwise think of.

4. Traps and pitfalls

Now that you have in hand all the basics required to begin collecting data conducive to historical reconstruction, we'd like to issue a few brief warnings about problems and pitfalls that you might encounter when carrying out this sort of work. First of all, we must reiterate that you should take with a grain of salt everything that your informants say about the history of their language. Speakers often know various things about the history of their language, in part because they've internalized some of what they heard from their elders, but sometimes their historical notions are wrong, especially if they're school-trained and/or nationalistic. To take a simple example, Armenians claim that an Armenian named Mesrob invented both the Armenian and the Georgian alphabets, but the Georgians insist that the Georgian alphabet (and perhaps some others as well) was created by a Georgian! Whenever you hear assertions with such obvious nationalistic ties being made, you should be on your guard and make sure to double-check all of the relevant information at a later date. A similar phenomenon that you're likely to encounter is the "primacy myth": informants tend to think that their language is the oldest in its family. No matter which Indo-European language you take, for example, the average man on the street who speaks that language is liable to mention that he read somewhere that it is the most archaic and conservative of the Indo-European languages. A popular variant of this is the speaker of a nonstandard dialect who states that his dialect is the most archaic of all varieties of his language, and certainly much more archaic than the standard language.

This brings us to our final warning: *beware of hearsay.* Anything that your informant "read somewhere" or heard from "a friend of a friend" should be treated with extreme caution. Verify information of this sort whenever possible; when it isn't possible to do so, make sure that you mention the exact source of your information, together with your assessment of its degree of reliability. Just so you know the sort of thing to look out for, here are some typical examples of hearsay regarding the histories of individual languages:

- **Elizabethan English is still spoken in the Appalachians.** This popular myth is bound to pop up anytime you mention at a cocktail party that you're a linguist. Unfortunately, it's entirely untrue!
- **Sicilian is Latin.** We once heard this from an Italian-American graduate student at Harvard.
- **The Zoks are half-Jewish Armenian merchants, and they intentionally altered their language so that no one outside of their community could understand it, thereby enabling them to discuss business matters in absolute secrecy.** This is the standard party line that one hears from anyone who has heard of the Zoks, an ethnic group closely related to the Armenians who lived in Nakhichevan until they were exterminated in 1919. In fact, they simply spoke a language closely related to Armenian,

which due to centuries of isolation had ceased to be mutually intelligible with it. The one Zok speaker that we met confirmed, before he died at the age of 96 in 1995, that the half-Jewish legend was entirely unfounded.

The last of these cases demonstrates that you should go straight to the horse's mouth whenever possible. All sorts of hearsay and half-truths arise in the absence of hard facts[53], but many of these falsehoods can be dispelled when you consult the actual people involved.

Once you've avoided all of the traps and pitfalls that inevitably arise and you have your linguistic data in hand, your next task is to use these data to begin reconstructing the history of your language. This is the domain of *internal reconstruction*, which is discussed in most historical linguistics textbooks. We recommend to interested readers the discussions of internal reconstruction in Bynon 1977:89-98; Crowley 1992, ch. 6; and Fox 1995, chapters 7 and 8.

Suggested Readings
Ehlich, Konrad. 1981. The Native Speaker's Heritage: On the Philology of "Dead" Languages. In Florian Coulmas, ed., A Festschrift for the Native Speaker, 153-165. The Hague: Mouton.

---

[53] Those who are interested in this phenomenon should consult Jerry Lembcke's *The Spitting Image: Myth, Memory, and the Legacy of Vietnam*, which deals with the origins of the (false) tradition that Americans spit on Vietnam veterans on their return from the war.

Labov, William. 1974. On the Use of the Present to Explain the Past. Proceedings of the Eleventh International Congress of Linguists, 825-851. Bologna: Società Editrice Il Mulino. Reprinted in Readings in Philip Baldi and Ronald Werth, eds., Historical Phonology, 275-312. University Park: The Pennsylvania State University Press.

Meillet, Antoine. 1967. The Comparative Method in Historical Linguistics. Translated by Gordon Ford. Paris: Librairie Honoré Champion.

Exercises

1. Identify five linguistic features (such as a word, phrase, or pronunciation) that you consider to be archaic in your native language. Before looking them up, discuss any intuitions that you have about these features: when they date from, in what situations they would be used today, when they became archaic, and so on. Next, look up these features in an etymological dictionary or historical grammar of your language, and compare the information given there to the impressions that you had beforehand.

2. Collect five features in your informants' language that they consider to be archaic. Before looking up these features, collect from your informants any intuitions that they have about these features: when they date from, in what situations they would be used today, when they became archaic, and so on. Next, look up these features in an etymological dictionary or historical grammar of your informants' language, and compare the information given there to the impressions that your informants had beforehand.

3. Repeat problem 1, but with features characteristic of old people's speech rather than archaic speech.

4. Repeat problem 2, but with features characteristic of old people's speech rather than archaic speech.

5. Discuss how you might go about conveying to your informants the distinction between old people's speech and archaic speech.

6. We know that the productive plural formation process in English involves adding -*(e)s* to the singular form of a word. We also

know that the -*s*- plural ending has been in our language since Indo-European times. If we find a modern English word that takes the -*(e)s* plural, can we assume that it took the ancestor of this plural form in Indo-European? Why or why not?

Appendix 1 The International Phonetic Alphabet (IPA)

As of this writing, the most up-to-date version of the IPA can be downloaded from http://www.arts.gla.ac.uk/IPA/images/ipachart.gif.

THE INTERNATIONAL PHONETIC ALPHABET (revised to 2005)

CONSONANTS (PULMONIC)   © 2005 IPA

	Bilabial	Labiodental	Dental	Alveolar	Postalveolar	Retroflex	Palatal	Velar	Uvular	Pharyngeal	Glottal
Plosive	p b			t d		ʈ ɖ	c ɟ	k ɡ	q ɢ		ʔ
Nasal	m	ɱ		n		ɳ	ɲ	ŋ	ɴ		
Trill	ʙ			r					ʀ		
Tap or Flap		ⱱ		ɾ		ɽ					
Fricative	ɸ β	f v	θ ð	s z	ʃ ʒ	ʂ ʐ	ç ʝ	x ɣ	χ ʁ	ħ ʕ	h ɦ
Lateral fricative				ɬ ɮ							
Approximant		ʋ		ɹ		ɻ	j	ɰ			
Lateral approximant				l		ɭ	ʎ	ʟ			

Where symbols appear in pairs, the one to the right represents a voiced consonant. Shaded areas denote articulations judged impossible.

CONSONANTS (NON-PULMONIC)

Clicks	Voiced implosives	Ejectives
ʘ Bilabial	ɓ Bilabial	ʼ Examples:
ǀ Dental	ɗ Dental/alveolar	pʼ Bilabial
ǃ (Post)alveolar	ʄ Palatal	tʼ Dental/alveolar
ǂ Palatoalveolar	ɠ Velar	kʼ Velar
ǁ Alveolar lateral	ʛ Uvular	sʼ Alveolar fricative

VOWELS

Where symbols appear in pairs, the one to the right represents a rounded vowel.

OTHER SYMBOLS

ʍ Voiceless labial-velar fricative
w Voiced labial-velar approximant
ɥ Voiced labial-palatal approximant
ʜ Voiceless epiglottal fricative
ʢ Voiced epiglottal fricative
ʡ Epiglottal plosive

ɕ ʑ Alveolo-palatal fricatives
ɺ Voiced alveolar lateral flap
ɧ Simultaneous ʃ and x

Affricates and double articulations can be represented by two symbols joined by a tie bar if necessary. k͡p t͡s

SUPRASEGMENTALS

ˈ Primary stress
ˌ Secondary stress   ˌfoʊnəˈtɪʃən
ː Long   eː
ˑ Half-long   eˑ
̆ Extra-short   ĕ
| Minor (foot) group
‖ Major (intonation) group
. Syllable break ɹi.ækt
‿ Linking (absence of a break)

DIACRITICS   Diacritics may be placed above a symbol with a descender, e.g. ŋ̊

̥ Voiceless	n̥ d̥	̤ Breathy voiced	b̤ a̤	̪ Dental	t̪ d̪	
̬ Voiced	s̬ t̬	̰ Creaky voiced	b̰ a̰	̺ Apical	t̺ d̺	
ʰ Aspirated	tʰ dʰ	̼ Linguolabial	t̼ d̼	̻ Laminal	t̻ d̻	
̹ More rounded	ɔ̹	ʷ Labialized	tʷ dʷ	̃ Nasalized	ẽ	
̜ Less rounded	ɔ̜	ʲ Palatalized	tʲ dʲ	ⁿ Nasal release	dⁿ	
̟ Advanced	u̟	ˠ Velarized	tˠ dˠ	ˡ Lateral release	dˡ	
̠ Retracted	e̠	ˤ Pharyngealized	tˤ dˤ	̚ No audible release	d̚	
̈ Centralized	ë	̴ Velarized or pharyngealized	ɫ			
̽ Mid-centralized	e̽	̝ Raised	e̝	(ɹ̝ = voiced alveolar fricative)		
̩ Syllabic	n̩	̞ Lowered	e̞	(β̞ = voiced bilabial approximant)		
̯ Non-syllabic	e̯	̘ Advanced Tongue Root	e̘			
˞ Rhoticity	ɚ a˞	̙ Retracted Tongue Root	e̙			

TONES AND WORD ACCENTS

LEVEL		CONTOUR	
e̋ or ꜛ	Extra high	ě or ꜛ	Rising
é ꜓	High	ê ꜔	Falling
ē ꜕	Mid	e᷄ ꜖	High rising
è ꜗ	Low	e᷅ ꜘ	Low rising
ȅ ꜙ	Extra low	e᷈ ꜚ	Rising-falling
↓ Downstep		↗ Global rise	
↑ Upstep		↘ Global fall	

382

Appendix 2 Sample answers to selected problems

Chapter 1, #4
The only available speaker of the language you are interested in is female, and you are male. Unfortunately, it is not acceptable in her culture for women to speak with foreign males. How might you get around this problem without seriously violating her cultural mores?

If possible, read an ethnography of the people and culture in question to familiarize yourself with the social dynamics of the taboo (i.e. discover what types of social relations between natives and foreigners are permitted and under what circumstances). What you want to find out here is whether any and all interactions between her and a foreign male are disallowed, or rather if it is just one-on-one interactions that offend. In one student's experience, members of host families and friends can often help with situations where culturally unacceptable male-female interaction in theory is in practice fairly innocuous. So, one could first ask members of a host family or friends about the culturally acceptable ways to bend the rule in question.

IF IT IS A "SOFT" TABOO:
Ask a female colleague (or friend, depending on the situation) to accompany and assist you in all meetings with the informant.
If you are a (heterosexual) married man, indicate that your wife will be accompanying you for each meeting. (It can be tricky to reveal that you have a non-heterosexual partner, depending on the particular beliefs in the woman's culture; we welcome your suggestions on this point.) If you are not married, wear a wedding ring to indicate that you are not on the market. (There are of course some ethical problems with this latter strategy.)
Encourage the informant to bring a male family member, friend, or spouse to each session.

Offer to conduct the sessions in an area where the informant feels safe (e.g. in public in the company of native males or in her home in the presence of her family). Warning: this may backfire, since the informant may not want the violation to be public.

Make every effort to manage your personal appearance in a way that is modest/appropriate for your informant's culture. Fortunately, people often excuse foreigners/outsiders from fully inhabiting the roles of their own culture.

Stting behind a screen may do the trick, as it did for one of Vaux's students when she visited her aunt, a cloistered Carmelite nun.

IF IT IS A "HARD" TABOO:

Try to conduct the interviews over the telephone. Email may also work, depending on how their culture construes "speaking" with a foreign male.

Arrange for a female colleague or male insider to conduct the sessions, with you interacting with the interviewer from a distance in real time if possible, either by phone, over an intercom or walkie-talkie (preferably as unobtrusive as possible), or perhaps even by computer. Perhaps with time and an intermediary the informant might be persuaded (watch out— don't push too hard) to accept first a male's presence during the elicitation sessions, and then his sharing the work.

If the consultant is currently living away from her home (and if she is truly the only available speaker of this language—the situation does sound exogamous), it might make a difference to her if she could be guaranteed anonymity in any published account of the work.

If this isn't possible, try to prepare a list of questions in advance designed in such a way that you obtain the maximum amount of reliable data that you need, despite that fact that you won't be able to shape the interview on the spot. Have your stand-in record everything, of course, preferably also with video equipment (to get some idea of the meta- and extra-linguistic goings-on during the interview). Crucially, be sure that your friend is properly prepped so that (s)he does not offend or otherwise put off the informant.

Be sure to credit your helper appropriately.

Chapter 2, #3

Transcribe the following text into the IPA, based on your pronunciation or that of a native speaker if you are not one.

wʌr 'ɪz ənd 'entʰ ɡɹə'mærəkəl

baj deɪv 'bɛɹi

aj kʰæ'nat ˌovəɹ'ɛmfəˌsajz ði ɪm'pɔɹrəns əv ɡʊd 'ɡɹæməɹ. wʌr ə kʰɹak. aj kʰʊd 'izəli ˌovəɹ'ɛmfəˌsajz ðə ɪm'pɔɹrəns əv ɡʊd 'ɡɹæməɹ. fɔɹ əɡ'zæmpəl, aj kʰʊd seɪ: " bæd 'ɡɹæməɹ ɪz ðə 'lidɪŋ kʰʊz əv slow, 'pʰɛɪnfəl deθ ɪn nɔɹθ ə'mɛɹɪkə," ɔɹ "wɪ'θawt ɡʊd 'ɡɹæməɹ, ðə ju'najɹəd steɪts wʊd hæv lɒst wəɹəld wɔɹ tʰuw." ðə tʰɹuθ ɪz ðæt 'ɡɹæməɹ əz nat ðə most ɪm'pɔɹrənt θɪŋ ɪn ðə wəɹəld. ðə 'supəɹ bol ɪz ðə most ɪm'pɔɹrənt θɪŋ ɪn ðə wəɹəld. bʌt 'ɡɹæməɹ əz stɪl ɪm'pɔɹrənt.

fɔɹ əɡ'zæmpəl , sə'pʰoz ju aɪ 'biɪŋ 'ɪntəɹˌvjud fɔɹ ə dʒab æz ən 'ɛɹˌpʰlɛɪn 'pʰajlət , ənd jɔɹ pʰɹə'spɛktəv əm'pʰlɔjəɹ æsks juw ɪf juw hæv ɛni əks'pɪɹiəns, ənd juw 'ænsəɹ : "wɛl, aj ɛɪntʰ nevəɹ 'ækʃəli flajd no 'ækʃəl 'ɛɹˌpʰleɪnz əɹ 'nʌθɪŋ, bʌt aj ɡat 'sevɹəl 'pʰajlət stajl hæts ənd 'sevɹəl fɹendz hu aj lajk tʰə tʰak ə'bawt 'ɛɹˌpʰleɪnz wɪθ ."

ɪf juw 'ænsəɹ ðɪs weɪ, ðə pʰɹə'spɛktəv əm'pʰlɔjəɹ wɪl ə'miɹiətli 'ɹiˌlajz ðət ju hæv 'ɛndəd jɔɹ 'sentəns wɪθ ə ˌpʰɹɛpə'zɪʃən . (wʌt ju ʃʊd hʌv sed, əv kʰɔɹs , ɪz "sevɹəl fɹendz wɪθ hu aj lajk tʰə tʰʊk ə'bawr 'ɛɹˌpʰleɪnz.") so ju wəl nat ɡet ðə dʒab, bə'kʰʌz 'ɛɹˌpʰleɪn 'pʰajləts hæf tə juz ɡʊd 'ɡɹæməɹ wen ðeɪ ɡet ɒn ðə 'ɪntəɹˌkam ənd əks'pleɪn tə ðə 'pʰæsəndʒəɹz ðət, bə'kʰʌz əv haj wɪndz, ðə pʰleɪn ɪz ɡoɪŋ tʰə tʰeɪk ɒf 'sevɹəl 'awəɹz leɪr ənd lænd ɪn pʰi'ɛɹ, sawθ də'kʰoɹə, ɪn'stɛr əv ˌlɒs 'ændʒələs .

Chapter 7, #2
You have decided to create an orthography for your informant's language, which currently has none. Discuss the merits of using a system that conveys allophonic distinctions, versus a system that conveys only phonemic distinctions.

The choice of a system of orthography for a language should be based on the purpose(s) it is intended to serve. It is one thing to develop a system for academic purposes, linguistic or otherwise. (N.B. It is also often necessary to make distinctions even within academia, e.g. between linguistic use and that of history, anthropology, literary studies, etc.) It is another to develop the system to serve speakers of the language as a literary device, which is what I am interested in here.

Speakers' preferences should be considered first and foremost. It is the speakers who will utilize their writing system; they own their language and should be able to make any and all decisions which concern it. I would add to this that it is almost as important to design the orthography in such a way that the speakers will like it and want to use it; if they refuse to use it, it doesn't matter how considerate you've been on other fronts, because the system will die.

ADVANTAGES OF THE ALLOPHONIC SYSTEM:
An allophonic system conveys more phonetic and phonological detail, therefore strictly speaking more accurate. It is conceivable that this greater faithfulness to the actual pronunciation would help children learn the orthography in some situations, though this would have to be verified first by experimentation. One case of allophony in orthography that comes immediately to mind is Turkish, which (generally) writes final devoicing (kitap 'book' : kitab-ım 'my book'). Rumor has it, though, that Atatürk told Hagop Dilaçar (the Armenian in charge of designing the Roman-based Turkish orthography) to convey devoicing in the system not because he wanted to convey allophony, but rather because he wanted the renditions of the words to differ from those of the old Ottoman system.
Perhaps the community is interested in archiving the exact pronunciation of their language—the community may believe, for example, that their language will soon be confined to religious contexts and they believe moreover that pronouncing

things correctly keeps the user safe, and also ensures the efficacy of the ritual being performed. (This was the case with Sanskrit, which I think is why they have such a highly allophonic system. The priests in fact went to great lengths to ensure that the texts would survive the passage of time unaltered, including the memorization of multiple versions of each text, some with dummy syllables inserted, some without, etc.) In such cases an orthography that conveys allophonic distinctions would be a better choice, though the texts in the archive should be tape-recorded (and ideally videotaped) as well.

One must consider the extent to which native speakers are aware of allophonic alternations in their language. Uri cites the example of a Turkish speaker who couldn't understand why the bare form of 'book' in Turkish is written <kitap> rather than <kitab>, since he apparently was unaware of the final devoicing rule.

A more general concern is the number of characters needed to accommodate all of the allophones. If the language is highly allophonic, it makes no sense to come up with numerous special characters and diacritics, which are only bound to complicate the learning process and discourage speakers from using the orthography. It is thus only practical to represent allophones in cases where there are only a few such distinctions. At any rate, it does not seem wise to represent in any practical orthography *all* minor phonetic nuances and conditioned alternations.

ADVANTAGES OF THE PHONEMIC SYSTEM:

Fewer symbols required.

For that reason, easier to match up with an existing limited system, such as the Latin alphabet.

May reflect speakers' conscious understanding of their language more directly. (For example, English speakers typically believe that the p's in *pit* and *spit* are identical because they derive from the same phoneme, though they are not identical phonetically.)

For both of these reasons, it is more appropriate for use by communities trying to maintain or revitalize their language via pedagogical materials, newspapers, etc.

Much easier for humans who are not phonologists or phoneticians.

Other possibilities are a system that conveys *fewer* distinctions than are found in the phonemic system, or *more* distinctions than are

Linguistic Field Methods

found in the allophonic inventory. The former type is common in languages that borrow their orthographic system from a language that has fewer contrasts, as was the case with English borrowing from Latin. (It is no coincidence that the Latin phonemic system has five vowels—*a e i o u*—and so does the English spelling system, even though English has many more vowel phonemes than that.) Perhaps the most striking case is Pahlavi (a middle Iranian language), which has no more than ten letters, but approximately 25-30 phonemes. A particularly amusing example is the Pahlavi word for the vina (an Indian instrument), *vin*, which is written | | |. (The symbol | represents *w*, *n*, *r*, and Ø in the Pahlavi orthography; here it is read wn' from right to left, with the short *i* not written, and the final pipe functioning as an "otiose stroke", in other words representing nothing.)

Many writing systems of South and Southeast Asia convey more distinctions than are found in the allophonic system of the language. This is typically for historical reasons, such as the language having lost a phonemic contrast after its orthography was developed. A particularly notorious example is Tibetan, in which the seat of the Panchen Lama, written as <*Bkra-shis-lhun-po*>, is pronounced [ʈʂáxiɫynbo] . Cape Verde, too, has opted for an etymologically-based orthography, in part because of the ties that this establishes with its prestigious lexifier Portuguese, and perhaps also partly because it makes it easier for speakers to treat in a unitary fashion all of the varieties of the Portuguese-Cape Verdean continuum that they control.

Food for thought: Is an alphabet-based transcription scheme better than one that is syllabic or based on some other non-western scheme? How or why not?

Chapter 7, #7

You are having trouble deciding whether or not your informants are inserting an epenthetic vowel in word-initial clusters. For example, given a word written <kra> in their orthography, you cannot tell whether they are pronouncing it as *[kra]* or *[kəra]*. Discuss some ways in which you might ascertain which of these two forms they are actually saying.

You can begin by asking your informants if they feel they are pronouncing (and/or inserting) a vowel between the two consonants in question. This can also be approached by asking the speakers how many syllables the word contains, but this raises a new problem, because the question expects a whole number in response, whereas the speakers may feel that [kəra] has "one and a half" syllables, for example. (This is the case in Armenian, where half syllables are enshrined in the pantheon of linguistic elements by Armenian linguists.)

Note, though, that the language described in the question has an orthography; if your informants are familiar with the conventions of this system, it may interfere with their judgements. This is the case for example with speakers of minority languages in Turkey, because the Turkish spelling system systematically inserts <y> between consecutive vowels. When a speaker interprets a vowel sequence as –iyo-, for example, it is therefore not clear whether (s)he is doing so because there actually is a y there, or rather because the orthography would render the sequence that way.

Bear in mind also that native speaker intuitions are not always reliable anyway, even if one removes the orthography problem.

Ask your informants to pronounce the relevant words as slowly as possible. Sometimes interesting phonological revelations turn up this way. (Beware, though, that these revelations may reflect a phonological system belonging to a register other than the one you are trying to study.)

Try to find minimal pairs I: between [kra] and [kəra].

Try to find minimal pairs II: in this case, where the same cluster appears, but with one of the two consonants different.

Maybe the language uses poetic alliteration involving entire initial clusters.

Make good recordings and test the duration of the putative vowel. If possible, also do X-rays, palatograms, etc.

Beware that *r* is very tricky to pin down.

Look for phonological evidence for the presence or absence of the schwa:

- Stress: if the language has initial stress, see if the putative schwa is stressed or not.
- Syllable structure: see what the inventory of syllable types is in the language as a whole. If for example it becomes clear that syllable-initial clusters are not allowed outside of this sequence, then it may well have a schwa.
- See if the language has any rules that refer to syllable count. (These are fairly common cross-linguistically; e.g. in Armenian monosyllables take one plural suffix, and polysyllables take another.) Do the same for feet.
- If possible, test language games on the words. Games that reverse the phonemes or insert fixed segmental material after each onset or nucleus would be best.
- See how the words behave with respect to partial reduplication and truncation phenomena.
- Test the words in different phonological contexts, e.g. in connected speech after vowel- vs. consonant-final words. If the language allows phrasal resyllabification, this may clarify whether there is an epenthetic vowel in isolation or not.
- Beware that epenthetic vowels are often inserted at the very end of the phonological derivation, and therefore may not participate in any phonological rules.

References

Abbi, Anvita. 2001. A manual of linguistic field work and structures of Indian landuages. Munich: Lincom Europa.

Agar, Michael. 1996. The Professional Stranger: An Informal Introduction to Ethnography, second edition. Academic Press.

Allen, Harold. 1971. Principles of informant selection. American Speech, 1971, 46, 1-2, Spr-Sum, 47-51.

Allen, Harold. 1989. New or old-fashioned? Informant awareness of chronological status. American Speech 64.1:3-11.

Ammon, U., N. Dittmar, and K. Mattheier, eds. 1988. Sociolinguistics, vol. 2, ch. 8, Elicitation methods. Berlin: De Gruyter.

Anderson, Loretta and Doris Cox. 1970. Learning Candoshi monolingually. In Alan Healey, ed., Translator's field guide, 306-310. Ukarumpa: Summer Institute of Linguistics.

Aronson, Elliot, Timothy Wilson, and Robin Akert. 2004. Social Psychology. Garden City, NJ: Prentice Hall.

Australian Institute of Aboriginal Studies. 1967. Linguistic materials for fieldworkers in Australia. Canberra.

Avanesov, R. and V. Orlova. 1964. Russkaja Dialektologija. Moscow: Nauka.

Bach, Emmon. 2003. Postcolonial(?) Linguistic Fieldwork. Massachusetts Review 44.1/2:167ff.

Bailey, Guy and Jan Tillery. 1999. The Rutledge Effect: the impact of interviewers on survey results in linguistics. American Speech 74.4:389-402.

Bailey, Guy and Margie Dyer. 1992. An Approach to Sampling in Dialectology. American Speech 67.1:3-20.

Bakker, Peter. 2001. Review of Vaux and Cooper, Introduction to Linguistic Field Methods. Anthropological Linguistics 43.1:108-110.

Ballmer, Thomas. 1981. A Typology of Native Speakers. In Florian Coulmas, ed., A Festschrift for the Native Speaker, 51-67. The Hague: Mouton.

Bard, Ellen Gurman, Dan Robertson, and Antonella Sorace. 1996. Magnitude Estimation of Linguistic Acceptability. Language 72.1:32-68.

Barnwell, Katharine. 1998. Preparing to be a consultee: How to get the best help from your consultant. Notes on Translation 12.4:42-45.

Bastian, J., P. Eimas, and A. Liberman. 1961. Identification and Discrimination of a Phonemic Contrast Induced by Silent Interval. The Journal of the Acoustical Society of America 33:842.

Beck, David. 2003. Review of Newman and Ratliff. Anthropological Linguistics 45.3:343-346.

Beekman, John. 1968. Eliciting vocabulary, meaning, and collocations. Notes on Translation 29:1-11.

Beekman, John. 1980. Three focuses of consultation procedures. Notes on Translation 81:2-14.

Bender, Byron. 1995. Lend Me Your Ears! Oceanic Linguistics 34:1.

Bendor-Samuel, John. 1974. Towards a grammatical model suited for field work / Propositions pour un modèle grammatical approprié aux travaux sur le terrain. In Les langues sans tradition écrite: Méthodes d'enquête et de description, 307-26. Actes du Colloque International du CNRS, Nice 28 juin à 2 juillet, 1971. Paris: Société d'Études Linguistiques et Anthropologiques de France.

Bird, Steven. 1999. Multidimensional exploration of online linguistic field data. NELS 29:33-50, Pius Tamanji et al., eds.

Birdsong, David. 1989. Metalinguistic Performance and Interlinguistic Competence. Berlin: Springer.

Blackwell, A., E. Bates, and D. Fisher. 1996. The time course of grammaticality judgment. Language and Cognitive Processes 11.4:337-406.

Bloch, Bernard. 1935. Interviewing for the Linguistic Atlas. American Speech 10.1:3-9.

Bouquiaux, Luc and Jacqueline Thomas. 1992. Studying and describing unwritten languages. Dallas, Texas: The Summer Institute of Linguistics.

Bradburd, Daniel. 1998. Being There: The Necessity of Fieldwork. Washington: Smithsonian Institution.

Brame, Michael. 1987. Ungrammatical Notes, 13: A Taller Man Than My Mother. Linguistic Analysis 17.1-2:99-109.

Breen, Gavan. 1981. The Mayi languages of the Queensland Gulf country. Canberra: Australian Institute of Aboriginal Studies.

Brewster, E. Thomas. 1982. Language Acquisition Made Practical: Field Methods for Language Learners. Pasadena: Lingua House.

Briggs, Charles. 1995. Interview. In Verschueren et al. 1995, 601-606.

Bryant, Margaret. 1945. Proverbs and How to Collect Them. Greensboro, North Carolina: American Dialect Society.

Burling, Robbins. 1984. Learning a field language. Ann Arbor: The University of Michigan Press. Prospect Heights, IL: Waveland Press. Second edition 2000. [Reviewed in Language 77.4:852-853, 2002.]

Bynon, Theodora. 1977. Historical Linguistics. Cambridge: Cambridge University Press.

Cameron, Deborah, et al. 1998. Researching language: Issues of power and method. London: Routledge.

Carr, Philip. 1993. Phonology. New York: St. Martin's Press.

Carroll, John, Thomas Bever, and Chava Pollack. 1981. The Non-Uniqueness of Linguistic Intuitions. Language 57.2:368-383.

Carstairs-McCarthy, Andrew. 1992. Current morphology. London: Routledge.

Cassidy, Frederick, and Audrey Duckert. 1970. A method for collecting dialect, second edition. Greensboro, North Carolina: American Dialect Society.

Cassidy, Frederick, ed. 1985-. Dictionary of American Regional English. Cambridge: Belknap Press.

Catford, J. C. 1974. Phonetic fieldwork. In Thomas A. Sebonk, ed., Current Trends in Linguistics, Vol. 12: Linguistics and Adjacent Arts and Sciences, 4. The Hague: Mouton.

Chafe, Wallace. 1965. Review of Grammar discovery procedures: A field manual, by Robert Longacre. Language 41:640-47.

Chaudron, Craig. 1983. Research on Metalinguistic Judgments: A Review of Theory, Methods, and Results. Language Learning 33:343-377.

Chomsky, Noam. 1964. The Logical Basis of Linguistic Theory. In Horace Lunt, ed., Proceedings of the Ninth International Congress of Linguists, 914-1008. The Hague: Mouton.

Chomsky, Noam. 1965. Aspects of the theory of syntax. Cambridge: MIT Press.

Chomsky, Noam. 1968. Language and mind. New York: Harcourt, Brace, and World.

CNRS. 1974. Les Langues sans tradition ecrite: methodes d'enquete et de description. Paris: S.E.L.A.F.

Cochran, Anne. 1976. Linguistic patterns in languages of Irian Jaya and Papua New Guinea: A manual for beginning field workers—preliminary report. In Ignatius Suharno and Kenneth Pike, eds., From Baudi to Indonesian, 38-40. Jayapura: Cenderawasih University and Summer Institute of Linguistics.

Comrie, Bernard and Norval Smith. 1977. Lingua Descriptive Studies: Questionnaire. Lingua 42:1-72.

Comrie, Bernard. 1981. Language Universals and Linguistic Typology. Chicago: University of Chicago Press.

Comrie, Bernard. 1988. The role of the field linguist. Notes on Linguistics 41:4-6.

Coulmas, Florian, ed. 1981. A Festschrift for the Native Speaker. The Hague: Mouton.

Cowan, George. 1970. The monolingual approach to studying Amuzgo. In Alan Healey, ed., Translator's field guide, 300-305. Ukarumpa: Summer Institute of Linguistics.

Cowart, Wayne. 1989. Illicit Acceptability in picture NPs. In C. Wiltshire, R. Graczyk, and B. Music, eds., Papers from the 25th Annual Meeting of the Chicago Linguistic Society, Vol. 1: The General Session. Chicago, 27-40.

Cowart, Wayne. 1989a. Illicit Acceptability in picture NPs. In Caroline Wiltshire, Randolph Graczyk, and Bradley Music, eds., Papers from the 25th Annual Meeting of the Chicago Linguistic Society, vol. 1: The General Session, 27-40. Chicago.

Cowart, Wayne. 1989b. Notes on the Biology of Syntactic Processing. Journal of Psycholinguistic Research 18.1:89-103.

Cowart, Wayne. 1994. Anchoring and Grammar Effects in Judgments of Sentence Acceptability. Perceptual and Motor Skills 79.3:1171-1182.

Cowart, Wayne. 1997. Experimental Syntax: Applying Objective Methods to Sentence Judgments. Thousand Oaks, CA: Sage Publications.

Craig, Colette. 1979. Jacaltec—field work in Guatemala. In T. Shopen, ed., Languages and their speakers, 3-57. Cambridge, MA: Winthrop.

Crowley, Terry. 1992. An Introduction to Historical Linguistics. Oxford: Oxford University Press.

Cukor-Avila, Patricia & Guy Bailey. 2001. "The effects of the race of the interviewer on sociolinguistic fieldwork". Journal of Sociolinguistics 5,2:254-270.

Decker, Kendall. 1991. Strategy for data collection in bilingual communities. In Gloria Kindell, ed., Proceedings of the Summer Institute of Linguistics international language assessment conference, 243-248. Dallas: Summer Institute of Linguistics.

Dixon, Robert. 1984. Searching for Aboriginal Languages: Memoirs of a Field Worker. Chicago: University of Chicago Press.

Dixon, Robert and W. Ramson. 1992. Australian aboriginal words in English. Melbourne: Oxford University Press.

Dongoske, Kurt, T. Ferguson, and Michael Yeatts. 1994. Ethics of Field Research for the Hopi Tribe. American Anthropological Association Anthropology Newsletter 35(i):56.

Dooley, Robert. 1989. Suggestions for the field linguist regarding quotations. Notes on Linguistics 44:34-50.

Dorian, Nancy C. 1986. "Gathering language data in terminal speech communities". In J. A. Fishman, A. Tabouret-Keller, M. Clyne, Bh. Krishnamurti, & M. Abdulaziz, eds., The Fergusonian Impact, Volume 2: Sociolinguistics and the Sociolinguistics of Language. Berlin: Mouton de Gruyter.

Dumézil, Georges. 1967. Études Abkhaz. Documents Anatoliens sur les langues et les traditions du caucase V. Paris: Librairie Adrien-Maisonneuve.

Duval, S. and R. Wicklund. 1972. A Theory of Objective Self-Awareness. New York: Academic Press.

Ehlich, Konrad. 1981. The Native Speaker's Heritage: On the Philology of "Dead" Languages. In Florian Coulmas, ed., A Festschrift for the Native Speaker, 153-165. The Hague: Mouton.

Emerson, Robert, Rachel Fretz, and Linda Shaw. 1995. Writing Ethnographic Fieldnotes. Chicago: University of Chicago Press.

Finnegan, Ruth. 1992. Oral Traditions and the Verbal Arts: Guide to Research Methods. London: Routledge.

Foley, W. 1991. Field methods. In K. Malmkjaer, ed., The linguistics encyclopedia, 121-127. London: Routledge.

Forsberg, Vivian. 1984. On checking meaning. Notes on Translation 102:9-21.

Fox, Anthony. 1995. Linguistic Reconstruction. Oxford: Oxford University Press.

Frank, Paul. 1999. Report on LinguaLinks CD-ROM: Field guide to recording language data by Charles F. Grimes. Notes on Linguistics 2.1:37-39.

Franklin, Karl. 1969. Review of Field linguistics: A guide to linguistic field work, by William Samarin. Linguistics 48:125-28.

Freed, Barbara F. 1978: From the Community to the Classroom: Gathering Second-Language Speech Samples. Arlington, Va.: CAL.

Fuller, Janet. 2000. Language choice and speaker identity: the influence of a researcher's linguistic proficiency in interviews. Southern Journal of Linguistics 24.1:91-102.

Gade, Daniel. 2001. The languages of foreign fieldwork. Geographical Review 91.1/2:370-379.

Gala, L. R. [no date] Gala's Dynamic Dictionary, English-English-Gujarati & Gujarati-Gujarati-English Combined Dictionary. Ahmadabad: Gala Publishers.

García de Diego, Vicente. 1946. Manual de Dialectología Española. Madrid: Instituto de Culture Hispánica.

Geest, Ton van der. 1995. Over letterenonderzoek: de methodologie van het Neerlandistische onderzoek in het bijzonder de methodologie van de taalbeheersing. Assen: Van Gorcum.

Gibson, Edward and James Thomas. 1999. Memory Limitations and Structural Forgetting: The Perception of Complex Ungrammatical Sentences as Grammatical. Language & Cognitive Processes 14.3:225-48.

Gick, Brian. 2002. The use of ultrasound for linguistic phonetic fieldwork. Journal of the International Phonetic Association 32.12:113-122.

Gilliéron, Jules and E. Edmont. 1902-10. Atlas linguistique de la France. Paris, H. Champion.

Goodwin, C. 1993. Recording human interaction in natural settings. Pragmatics 3.2:181-209.

Gordon, Raymond. 1986. Some psycholinguistic considerations in practical orthography design. Notes on Literacy special issue 1:66-84.

Greenbaum, Sidney. 1973. Informant Elicitation of Data on Syntactic Variation. Lingua 31:201-212.

Greenbaum, Sidney. 1976. Syntactic Frequency and Acceptability. Lingua 40.2/3:99-113.

Greenbaum, Sidney. 1977a. Judgments of Syntactic Acceptability and Frequency. Studia Linguistica 31.2:83-105.

Greenbaum, Sidney. 1977b. The linguist as experimenter. In Fred Eckman, ed., Current themes in linguistics, 125-144. Washington: Hemisphere Publishing Corporation.

Grigoryan, Aharon. 1957. Hay Barbaŕagitut^{h}yan Dasənt^{h}ats^h. [Course in Armenian Dialectology], chapter 2, Barbaŕneri Usumnasirman Met^{h}odnerə [The Methods of Studying Dialects], 495-530. Erevan: State University Press.

Grimes, Charles. [n.d.] LinguaLinks. Dallas: Summer Institute of Linguistics. (Includes: Field guide to recording language data, by Charles Grimes; Language data collection guidelines for working with language associates; eliciting, organizing, and preserving data; sample elicitation questions; Studying and describing unwritten languages, by Luc Bouquiaux, Jacqueline Thomas, and James Roberts.)

Grimes, Charles. 1992. Field guide to recording language data. [Ambon] and Kangaroo Ground: Pattimura University and Summer Institute of Linguistics.

Grimes, Joseph. 1992. Calibrating sentence repetition tests. In Eugene Casad, ed., Windows on bilingualism, 73-85. Summer Institute of Linguistics and the University of Texas at Arlington Publications in Linguistics, 110. Dallas: Summer Institute of Linguistics and the University of Texas at Arlington.

Grimes, Joseph. 1995. Language survey reference guide. Dallas: Summer Institute of Lingistics.

Grimes, Joseph. 1997. Ethnographic questions for field workers. Notes on Anthropology and Intercultural Community Work 27:17-19.

Gudschinsky, Sarah. 1967. How to Learn an Unwritten Language. New York: Holt, Rinehart and Winston.

Guillaume, Gabriel. 1963-6. Atlas linguistique armoricain roman. Angers: the author.

Haggard, M. 1978. The devoicing of voiced fricatives. Journal of Phonetics 6:95-102.

Hale, Austin. 1998. Comments from an international linguistics consultant: Thumbnail sketch. Notes on Linguistics 81:5-8.

Hale, Ken, Michael Krauss, Lucille Watahomigie, Akira Yamamoto, Colette Craig, LaVerne Masayesva Jeanne, and Nora England. 1992. Endangered Languages. Language 68.1:1-42.

Hale, Ken. 1966. Review of Handling unsophisticated linguistic informants, by Alan Healey. American Anthropologist 68:807-8.

Hale, Ken. 2001. Ulwa (southern Sumu): The beginnings of a language research Project. In Paul Newman and Martha Ratliff, eds., Linguistic Fieldwork. Cambridge: Cambridge University Press.

Hancock, Ian. 2005. The Concocters: Creating Fake Romani Culture. In Nicholas Saul and Susan Tebbutts, eds., The Role of the Romanies: Images and Self-Images of "Gypsies"/Romanies in European Culture. Liverpool: University of Liverpool Press.

Hardman, M. and Syoko Hamano. 1995. Language Structure Discovery Methods, fourth edition. Gainesville, FL: Andean Press.

Hartman, James W. 1969. Some Preliminary Findings from DARE. American Speech 44.3:191-199.

Harris, Zellig. 1942. Morpheme Alternants in Linguistic Analysis. Language 18:169-180.

Headland, Thomas. 1973. A method for recording formal elicitation. Notes on Translation 50:22-27.

Headland, Thomas. 1985. On recording ethnographic field notes. Notes on Anthropology 1:11-12.

Healey, Alan, ed. 1975. Language learner's field guide. Ukarumpa: Summer Institute of Linguistics.

Healey, Alan. 1964. Handling unsophisticated linguistic informants. Linguistic Circle of Canberra Publications A, 2. Canberra: Australian National University.

Healey, Alan. 1968. Review of Field linguistics: A guide to linguistic field work, by William Samarin. The Bible Translator 19:178-181.

Healey, Alan. 1970. List of words suitable for monolingual eliciting. In Alan Healey, ed., Translator's field guide, 395-404. Ukarumpa: Summer Institute of Linguistics.

Healey, Alan. 1975. Obtaining linguistic data. In Alan Healey, ed., Language learner's field guide, 344-360. Ukarumpa: Summer Institute of Linguistics.

Healey, Alan. 1975. Testing the recognition of utterance pairs. In Alan Healey, ed., Language learner's field guide, 399-407. Ukarumpa: Summer Institute of Linguistics.

Heath, Jeffrey. 2002. Review of Newman and Ratliffe. Journal of African Languages & Linguistics 23.2:229ff.

Heine, Bernd and Wilhelm Mohlig, eds. 1980. Language and dialect atlas of Kenya. Berlin: Reimer.

Henderson, Julius and John Harrington. 1914. Ethnozoology of the Tewa Indians. Washington: Government Printing Office.

Hinds, John. 1981. The Interpretation of Ungrammatical Utterances. In Florian Coulmas, ed., A Festschrift for the Native Speaker, 221-235. The Hague: Mouton.

Hiramatsu, Kazuko and Diane Lillo-Martin. 1998. Children Who Judge Ungrammatical What They Produce. In Annabel Greenhill, Mary Hughes, Heather Littlefield, and Hugh Walsh, eds., Proceedings of the 22nd Annual Boston University Conference on Language Development, 337-47. Somerville, MA: Cascadilla.

Hockett, Charles. 1942. A system of descriptive phonology. Language 18:3-21.

Hofmann, Thomas. 1993. Realms of meaning: an introduction to semantics. London: Longman.

Hohulin, Richard. 1982. Questioning our questioning technique. Notes on Translation 91:28-32.

Holliday, Adrian. 2002. Doing and Writing Qualitative Research. London: Sage Publications.

Hollingsworth, Kenneth. 1999. The MiniDisc: a better way to do field recordings. Notes on Anthropology 3.4:56-63.

Holstein, James. 1995. The Active Interview. Thousand Oaks: Sage Publications.

Householder, Fred. 1973. On Arguments from Asterisks. Foundations of Language 10:365-376.

Howell, N. 1990. Surviving fieldwork. American Anthropological Association.

Hunt, Geoffrey. 1992. The indispensable tape recorder. Notes on Linguistics 56:5-9.

Hymes, D. 1978. The ethnography of speaking. In Joshua Fishman, ed., Readings in the sociology of language, 99-138. Mouton.

Itkonen, Esa. 1981. The Concept of Linguistic Intuition. In Florian Coulmas, ed., A Festschrift for the Native Speaker, 127-140. The Hague: Mouton.

Jackson, Bruce. 1987. Fieldwork. Urbana: University of Illinois Press.

Jakobson, Roman and Krystyna Pomorska. 1983. Jakobson-Pomorska Dialogues. Cambridge: MIT Press.

Johnson, Jeffrey. 1990. Selecting ethnographic informants. Qualitative Research Methods #22. London: Sage Publications.

Johnston, Raymond. 1980. Grammar and basic vocabulary in Oceanic Austronesian languages: A standard elicitation schedule. Ukarumpa: Summer Institute of Linguistics.

Karins, K. and N. Nagy. 1993. An Experimental Method for Determining Grammaticality. Penn Review of Linguistics 17. Center for Research in Language Newsletter, 6(1).

Kaye, Alan. 2001. Review of Vaux and Cooper, Introduction to Linguistic Field Methods. Word 52.1:121-125.

Kaye, Alan. 2002. Review of Newman and Ratliffe. Language 78.4:798-9.

Keller, Frank. 1996. How do humans deal with ungrammatical input? Experimental evidence and computational modelling. In Dafydd Gibbon, ed., Natural Language Processing and Speech Technology. Results of the 3rd KONVENS Conference, Berlin, 1996. Mouton de Gruyter.

Keller, Frank. 1999. Review of The Empirical Base of Linguistics: Grammaticality Judgments and Linguistic Methodology, Carson T. Schütze. Journal of Logic, Language and Information 8.1:114-121.

Keller, Janet. 2003. Review of Newman and Ratliff. American Anthropologist 105.4:857-8.

Kelly, John and John Local. 1989. Doing phonology: observing, recording, interpreting. Manchester: Manchester University Press.

Keltner, David and J.R. Robinson. 1997. Defending the status quo: Power and bias in social conflict. Personality and Social Psychology Bulletin 23:1066-1077.

Kenstowicz, Michael. 1994. Phonology in Generative Grammar. Oxford: Blackwell.

Kibrik, A. 1977. The methodology of field investigation in linguistics. The Hague: Mouton.

König, Werner. 1978. Dtv-Atlas zur deutschen Sprache: Tafeln und Texte. München: Deutscher Taschenbuch Verlag.

Kurath, Hans. 1968. The Investigation of Urban Speech. American Dialect Society 49.

Labov, William. 1971. Methodology. In W. Dingwall, ed., A survey of linguistic science. University of Maryland Linguistics Program, 412-97.

Labov, William. 1972. The Logic of Nonstandard English. In Labov 1972b.

Labov, William. 1972a. Some principles of linguistic methodology. Language in Society 1:97-120.

Labov, William. 1972b. Language in the Inner City: Studies in the Black English Vernacular. Philadelphia: University of Pennsylvania Press.

Labov, William. 1974. On the Use of the Present to Explain the Past. Proceedings of the Eleventh International Congress of Linguists, 825-851. Bologna: Società Editrice Il Mulino. Reprinted in Philip Baldi and Ronald Werth, eds., Readings in Historical Phonology, 275-312. University Park: Pennsylvania State University Press.

Labov, William. 1975a. Empirical foundations of linguistic theory. In Robert Austerlitz, ed., The scope of American linguistics, 77-134. Lisse: Peter de Ridder Press.

Labov, William. 1975b. What is a Linguistic Fact? Lisse: Peter de Ridder Press.

Labov, William. 1984. Field methods of the project on linguistic change and variation. In John Baugh and J. Sherzer, eds., Language in use. Readings in sociolinguistics, 28-53. Englewood Cliffs: Prentice-Hall.

Labov, William. 1987. Some observations on the foundations of linguistics. Manuscript, University of Pennsylvania.

Labov, William. 1996. When Intuitions Fail. In Lisa McNair, ed., CLS 32: Papers from the Parasession on Theory and Data in Linguistics, 77-105. Chicago: University of Chicago Press.

Ladefoged, Peter. 1993. A Course in Phonetics, Third Edition. Fort Worth: Harcourt Brace Jovanovich Publishers.

Ladefoged, Peter. 1997. Instrumental Techniques for Linguistic Phonetic Fieldwork. The Handbook of Phonetic Sciences, William Hardcastle and John Laver, eds. Oxford: Blackwell.

Ladefoged, Peter. 2003. Phonetic Data Analysis: An introduction to phonetic fieldwork and instrumental techniques. Oxford: Blackwell.

Larmouth, Donald W., Thomas E. Murray, & Carmin Ross Murray. 1992. Legal and Ethical Issues in Surreptitious Recording. Tuscaloosa: University of Alabama Press.

Larson, Richard and Gabriel Segal. 1995. Knowledge of Meaning: An Introduction to Semantic Theory. Cambridge: MIT Press.

Lasnik, H. and M. Saito. 1984. On the Nature of Proper Government. Linguistic Inquiry 15.2:235-289.

Lastra de Suárez, Yolanda. 1986. Las áreas dialectales del náhuatl moderno. Mexico: Universidad Nacional Autónoma de México.

Lawrence, Wayne. 2000. /str/ → /štr/: Assimilation at a Distance? American Speech 75.1:82-87.

Leaders, Marlin. 1991. Eliciting figures of speech. Notes on Translation 5.4:31-45.

Lee, Raymond. 1995. Dangerous Fieldwork. Qualitative Research Methods, vol. 34. Thousand Oaks, CA: Sage Publications.

Lembcke, Jerry. 2000. *The Spitting Image: Myth, Memory, and the Legacy of Vietnam.* New York: New York University Press.

Levelt, W. 1972. Some psychological aspects of linguistic data. Linguistische Berichte 17:18-30.

Levinsohn, Stephen. 1983. Pragmatics. Cambridge: Cambridge University Press.

Levinsohn, Stephen. 1994. Field procedures for the analysis of participant reference in a monologue discourse. In Stephen Levinsohn, ed., Discourse features of ten languages of West-Central Africa, 109-121. Dallas: Summer Institute of Linguistics and the University of Texas at Arlington.

Levinson, S. 1992. Primer for the field investigation of spatial description and conception. Pragmatics 2:5-47.

Linn, Michael. 1983. Informant Selection in Dialectology. American Speech 58:225-43.

Lodge, M. 1981. Magnitude Scaling: Quantitative Measurement of Opinions. Beverley Hills, CA: Sage Publications.

Lodge, Milton. 1981. Magnitude Scaling: Quantitative Measurement of Opinions. Beverley Hills, CA: Sage Publications.

Longacre, Robert et alii. 1978. The role of a consultant. Notes on Linguistics 5:23-29.

Longacre, Robert. 1964. Grammar Discovery Procedures: A Field Manual. The Hague: Mouton.

Lounsbury, Floyd. 1953. Field techniques and techniques in linguistics. In Anthropology Today: Selections, ed. by Sol Tax. Chicago: University of Chicago Press.

Loving, Aretta. 1962. On learning monolingually. Philippine Journal for Language Teaching 1.3/4:11-15.

Macaulay, Monica. 1998. Training Linguistics Students for the Realities of Fieldwork. Symposium on Practical Fieldwork, LSA, January 1998. [Available from the author, University of Wisconsin-Madison]

Makkai, Valerie. 1975. 'Pretty Damn Seldom......': On the Grammaticality of Ungrammatical Utterances. Columbia, SC: Hornbeam.

Malinowski, B. 1922. Argonauts of the Western Pacific. Routledge and Kegan Paul.

Marks, L. E. (1968). Scaling of grammaticalness of self-embedded English sentences. Journal of Verbal Learning and Verbal Behavior 7:965-967.

Matteson, Esther. 1976. Developing the lexicon of an unwritten language. Notes on Translation 59:18-27.

Matthewson, Lisa. 2004. On the Methodology of Semantic Fieldwork. International Journal of American Linguistics 70:369 415.

Maynor, Natalie. 1982. Grammatical Judgments in LANE. American Speech 57:228-231.

McDavid, Raven. 1985. Eliciting: Direct, Indirect, and Oblique. American Speech 60:309-17.

McKinney, Carol. 1995. Review of Fieldwork in developing countries, by Devereux, Stephen and John Hoddinott, eds. Notes on Anthropology and Intercultural Community Work 18:41-43.

Meillet, Antoine. 1924. La méthode comparative en linguistique historique. English translation The Comparative Method in Historical Linguistics by Gordon Ford, 1970. Paris: Librairie Honoré Champion.

Merrifield, William. 1968. Review of Field linguistics: A guide to linguistic field work, by William Samarin. International Journal of American Linguistics 34:217-19.

Mey, Jacob. 1981. Right or Wrong, my Native Speaker. In Florian Coulmas, ed., A Festschrift for the Native Speaker, 69-84. The Hague: Mouton.

Mey, Jacob. 1993. Pragmatics: An Introduction. Oxford: Blackwell.

Miller, James. 1973. A Note on So-called 'Discovery Procedures'. Foundations of Language 10:123-139.

Miller, V. 1953. Present-day use of the broad A in eastern Massachusetts. Speech Monographs 20.4:235-246.

Milroy, Lesley. 1987. Language and Social Networks, second edition. Oxford: Basil Blackwell.

Milroy, Lesley. 1987. Observing and analysing natural language. Oxford: Blackwell.

Morreau, Michael. 1993. Norms or Inference Tickets? A Frontal Collision between Intuitions. In Ted Briscoe, Ann Copestake, and Valeria de Paiva, eds., Inheritance, Defaults, and the Lexicon, 58-73. Cambridge, England: Cambridge University Press.

Mosel, Ulrike. 2002. Dictionary making in endangered speech communities. Proceedings of the International Workshop on Resources and Tools in Field Linguistics, Las Palmas. http://www.mpi.nl/lrec/2002/papers/lrec-pap-07-Dictionary_Endangered_SpComm.pdf

Mufwene, Salikoko. 1997. The ecology of Gullah's survival. American Speech 72.1:69-83.

Munro, Pamela. 2000. Field linguistics. In Mark Aronoff and Janie Rees-Miller, eds., The Handbook of Linguistics. Malden, MA: Blackwell.

Muradjan, H. et alii. 1977. Hajereni Barbaṙagitakan Atlasi Njut^heri Havak^hman Tsragir [Plan for Collection of Materials for a Dialect Atlas of Armenian]. Erevan: Haykakan SSH GA Hratarakč^hut^hjun.

Nagata, Hiroshi. 1987. Long-Term Effects of Repetition on Judgments of Grammaticality. Perceptual and Motor Skills 65.1:265-299.

Nagata, Hiroshi. 1989. Effect of Repetition on Grammaticality Judgments under Objective and Subjective Self-Awareness Conditions. Journal of Psycholinguistic Research 18.3: 255-269.

Nagata, Hiroshi. 1989. Judgments of Sentence Grammaticality and Field-Dependence of Subjects. Perceptual and Motor Skills 69.3:739-747.

Nagata, Hiroshi. 1989. Judgments of Sentence Grammaticality with Differentiation. and Enrichment Strategies. Perceptual and Motor Skills 68:463-469

Nagata, Hiroshi. 1989. Repetition Effect in Judgments of Grammaticality of Sentences: Examination with Ungrammatical Sentences. Perceptual & Motor Skills 68.1:275-282.

Nagata, Hiroshi. 1992. Anchoring Effects in Judging Grammaticality of Sentences. Perceptual and Motor Skills 75.1:159-164.

Nagy, Naomi. 2000. Fieldwork for the new century: working in Faeto, an endangered language community. Southern Journal of Linguistics 24.1:121-136.

Nespor, Marina, and Irene Vogel. 1986. Prosodic Phonology. Dordrecht: Foris.

Newman, Paul, and Martha Ratliff, eds. 2001. Linguistic Fieldwork. Cambridge University Press.

Ní Chasaide, Ailbha. 1995. Irish. Journal of the International Phonetic Association 25.1:34-39.

Nida, Eugene. 1946. Morphology: The Descriptive Analysis of Words, second edition. Ann Arbor: University of Michigan Press.

Nida, Eugene. 1947. Field techniques in descriptive linguistics. International Journal of American Linguistics 13.3:138-46.

Nida, Eugene. 1948. A System for the Identification of Morphemes. Language 24.4:414-41.

Nida, Eugene. 1981. Informants or colleagues? In Florian Coulmas , ed., A Festschrift for the Native Speaker. The Hague: Mouton Publishers.

Nunan, D. 1992. Research methods in language learning. Cambridge: Cambridge University Press: 1-23.

Onions, C., ed. 1966. The Oxford Dictionary of English Etymology. New York: Oxford University Press.

Opie, Iona, and Peter Opie, eds. 1951. The Oxford Dictionary of Nursery Rhymes. Oxford: Oxford University Press.

Otero, Carlos. 1972. Acceptable Ungrammatical Sentences in Spanish. Linguistic Inquiry 3:233-42.

Paradis, Claude. 1996. Interactional conditioning of linguistic heterogeneity. In Gregory R. Guy et al., eds., Towards a Social Science of Language; Volume 1: Variation and Change in Language and Society, 115-133. Amsterdam: Benjamins.

Paul, Benjamin. 1953. Interview techniques and field relationships. In Sol Tax, ed., Anthropology Today: Selections. Chicago: Chicago University Press.

Payne, Stanley. 1951. The Art of Asking Questions. Princeton: Princeton University Press.

Payne, Thomas. 1991. Handling language data: Excerpts from a field manual. Notes on Linguistics 53:35-42.

Payne, Thomas. 1996. Field manual for descriptive linguistics.

Payne, Thomas. 1997. Describing Morphosyntax: A guide for field linguists. New York: Cambridge University Press.

Pederson, Lee, et alii. 1974. A Manual for dialect research in the Southern States, second edition. University of Alabama Press.

Pederson, Lee. 1974. Tape/Text and Analogues. American Speech 49.1/2:5-23.

Perdue, Clive, ed. 1993. Adult language acquisition: cross-linguistic perspectives. Cambridge: Cambridge University Press.

Perdue, Clive. 1984. Second language acquisition by adult immigrants: a field manual. Cross-linguistic series on second language research. Rowley, Mass.: Newbury House Publishers.

Peterson, G. and H. Barney. 1952. Control methods used in a study of the vowels. Journal of the Acoustical Society of America 24.2:175-184.

Pierrehumbert, Janet. 1993. Prosody, Intonation, and Speech Technology. In M Bates and R. Weischedel, eds. Challenges in Natural Language Processing, 257-282. Cambridge: Cambridge University Press.

Pierrehumbert, Janet. 2003. Probabilistic Phonology: Discrimination and Robustness. In Rens Bod et al., eds., Probabilistic Linguistics, 177-228. Cambridge: MIT Press.

Pierrehumbert, Janet and D. Talkin. 1992. Lenition of /h/ and glottal stop. In G. Docherty and D. Ladd, eds., Papers in Laboratory Phonology II: Gesture, Segment, Prosody, 90-117, Cambridge: Cambridge University Press.

Pike, Kenneth. 1947. Phonemics: A Technique for Reducing Language to Writing. Ann Arbor: University of Michigan Press. Second edition, 1971.

Pike, Kenneth. 1982. Some questions for field linguists beginning language analysis. Notes on Linguistics 24:3-14.

Pillai, Mekkolla Parameswaran. 1983. Assissi Malayalam-English Dictionary, second edition. Changanacherry: Assissi Printing & Publishing House.

Pinker, Steven. 1994. The Language Instinct. New York: William Morrow and Company.

Pittman, Richard. 1970. A method for eliciting paradigmatic data from text. In Alan Healey, ed., Translator's field guide, 377-78. Ukarumpa: Summer Institute of Linguistics.

Pittman, Richard. 1970. On eliciting transformations in Vietnamese. In Alan Healey, ed., Translator's field guide, 379-390. Ukarumpa: Summer Institute of Linguistics.

Plénat, Marc. 1995. Une approche prosodique de la morphologie du verlan. Lingua 95:97-129.

Poplack, Shana. 1989. The care and handling of a megacorpus: the Ottawa-Hull French project. In Ralph Fasold and Deborah Schiffrin, eds., Language Change and Variation, 11-444. Amsterdam: Benjamins.

Postal, Paul. 1966. Review of Grammar discovery procedures: A field manual, by Robert Longacre. International Journal of American Linguistics 32:93-98.

Postal, Paul. 1974. On Raising: One rule of English grammar and its theoretical implications. Cambridge: MIT Press.

Pratt, T. 1983. A case for direct questioning in traditional fieldwork. American Speech 58.2:150-155.

Proteau, Lorenzo. 1996. La Parlure Québécoise. Boucherville: Les Éditions des amitiés franco-québécoises.

Pynte, Joel. 1991. The Locus of Semantic Satiation in Category Membership Decision and Acceptability Judgment. Journal of Psycholinguistic Research 20.4:315-335.

Quas, Jodi and Jennifer Schaaf. 2002. Children's memories of experienced and nonexperienced events following repeated interviews. Journal of Experimental Child Psychology 83.4:304-338.

Redard, G. 1960. Atlas linguistique de l'Iran: Questionnaire normale. Berne (no publisher mentioned).

Redden, James. 1982. On expanding the meaning of applied linguistics: A suggestion for training linguists and language teachers in field linguistics. Notes on Linguistics 22:19-23.

Ringen, Jon. 1977. On evaluating data concerning linguistic intuition. In Fred Eckman, ed., Current themes in linguistics, 145-162. Washington: Hemisphere Publishing Corporation.

Ringen, Jon. 1981. Quine on Introspection in Linguistics. In Florian Coulmas, ed., A Festschrift for the Native Speaker, 141-151. The Hague: Mouton.

Roberts, Taylor. 2000. Review of Vaux and Cooper, Introduction to Linguistic Field Methods. Language 76.2:485.

Robinson, Dow. 1970. Manual for analytical procedures in phonology. Huntington Beach: Summer Institute of Linguistics.

Ruoff, A. 1973. Grundlagen und Methoden der Untersuchung gesprochener Sprache. Tübingen: Niemeyer.

Rupp, James. 1974. On eliciting metaphors. Notes on Translation 53:17-22.

Samarin, William. 1967. Field Linguistics: A Guide to Linguistic Field Work. New York: Holt, Rinehart and Winston, Inc.

Sampson, Geoffrey. 1980. Schools of linguistics. Stanford: Stanford University Press.

Sampson, Geoffrey. 1987. Evidence against the 'Grammatical'/ 'Ungrammatical' Distinction. In Willem Meijs, ed., Corpus Linguistics and Beyond, 219-226. Amsterdam: Rodopi.

Sanjek, Roger, ed. 1990. Fieldnotes: The Makings of Anthropology. Ithaca: Cornell University Press.

Sankoff, David & Gillian Sankoff. 1973. Sample survey methods and computer-assisted analysis in the study of grammatical variation. In R. Darnell, ed., Canadian Languages in their Social Context. Edmonton: Linguistic Research, Inc.

Sapir, Edward. 1933. La réalité psychologique du phonème. Journal de psychologie normale et pathologique 30:247-265.

Saussure, Ferdinand de. 1916. Course in General Linguistics [original title Cours de linguistique générale]. English translation by Roy Harris. La Salle, Illinois: Open Court, 1986.

Schensul, Stephen, Jean Schensul, and Margaret LeCompte. 1999. Essential Ethnographic Methods: Observations, Interviews and Questionnaires, Vol. 2. Walnut Creek: AltaMira Press.

Schneider, Hans Julius. 1995. Intuition and introspection. In Verschueren et al. 1995, 606-608.

Schnelle, H. 1981. Introspection and the Description of Language Use. In Florian Coulmas, ed., A Festschrift for the Native Speaker, 105-126. The Hague: Mouton.

Schütze, Carson. 1996. The empirical base of linguistics: Grammaticality judgments and linguistic methodology. Chicago: University of Chicago Press.

Schwarte, Barbara. 1974. Intuitions of grammaticality and the 'law of contrast': A pilot study. Studies in the Linguistic Sciences 4:1:198ff.

Senft, Gunter. 1995. Elicitation. In Verschueren et al. 1995, 577-581.

Senft, Gunter. 1995. Fieldwork. In Verschueren et al. 1995, 595-601.

Seuren. 1966. Review of Grammar discovery procedures: A field manual, by Robert Longacre. Foundations of Language 2:200-212.

Shapiro, Michael. 1995. A Case of Distant Assimilation: /str/ → /štr/. American Speech 70.1:101-07.

Sheidlower, Jesse, ed. 1995. The F-word. New York: Random House.

Shopen, T., ed. 1979. Languages and their speakers. Cambridge, MA: Winthrop.

Shorey, Hazel. 1986. Some advantages and disadvantages of using mobile units for on-site preparation of vernacular materials. Notes on Literacy (special issue) 1:38-47.

Shuy, Roger. 1968. Field techniques in an urban language study. Urban language series 3. Washington: Center for Applied Linguistics.

Shuy, Roger. 1983. Unexpected by-products of fieldwork. American Speech 58.4:345-358.

Slobin, Dan. 1967. A field manual for cross-cultural study of the acquisition of communicative competence. Berkeley.

Smith, Greg. 1984. Sampling Linguistic Minorities: A Technical Report on the Adult Language Use Survey. London: Linguistic Minorities Project.

Snyder, William. 2000. An Experimental Investigation of Syntactic Satiation Effects. Linguistic Inquiry 31.3:575-582.

Sobin, Nicholas. 1994. An acceptable ungrammatical construction. In Susan Lima, Roberta Corrigan, Gregory Iverson, eds., The Reality of Linguistic Rules, 51-66. Amsterdam: John Benjamins.

Sorace, Antonella. 1995. Acquiring linking rules and argument structures in a second language: The unaccusative/unergative distinction. In Lynn Eubank, Larry Selinker, and Michael Sharwood Smith, eds., The Current State of Interlanguage, 153-175. Amsterdam: John Benjamins.

Sorace, A. 1996. The Use of Acceptability Judgments in Second Language Acquisition Research. In William Ritchie and Tej Bhatia, eds., Handbook of Second Language Acquisition, 375-409. Malden, MA: Blackwell.

Spencer, Andrew. 1991. Morphological Theory: An Introduction to Word Structure in Generative Grammar. Oxford: Blackwell.

Spencer, Andrew. 1996. Phonology. Oxford: Blackwell.

Spencer, N. 1973. Differences Between Linguists and Nonlinguists in Intuitions of Grammaticality-Acceptability. Journal of Psycholinguistic Research 2.2:83-98.

Starks, Donna. 1998. An alternative type of rapid and anonymous survey. In Claude Paradis, Diane Vincent, Denise Deshaies, and Marty Laforest, eds., Papers in Sociolinguistics; NWAVE-26 à l'Université Laval, 11-18. Québec City: Nota bene.

Stevens, Ken. 1998. Acoustic Phonetics. Cambridge: MIT Press.

Stokoe, William and Rolf Kuschel. 1979. A field guide for sign language research. Silver Spring, MD: Linstok Press.

Stone, Maureen. 1997. Laboratory Techniques for Investigating Speech Articulation. The Handbook of Phonetic Sciences, William Hardcastle and John Laver, eds. Oxford: Blackwell.

Suharno, Ignatius. 1976. Monolingual data eliciting: Some local constraints on workable analytical procedures with reference to Baudi. In Ignatius Suharno and Kenneth Pike, eds., From Baudi to Indonesian, 1-10. Jayapura: Cenderawasih University and Summer Institute of Linguistics.

Sutter, Judith and Cynthia Johnson. 1990. School-Age Children's Metalinguistic Awareness of Grammaticality in Verb Form. Journal of Speech and Hearing Research 33.1:84-95.

Swadesh, Morris. 1934. The Phonemic Principle. Language 10:117-129.

Tillery, Jan. 2000. The reliability and validity of linguistic self-reports. Southern Journal of Linguistics 24.1:55-68.

Troike, Rudolph and Muriel Saville-Troike. 1987. Video recording for linguistic fieldwork. Notes on Linguistics 37:44-51.

Trudgill, Peter. 1990. The Dialects of England. Oxford: Blackwell.

Ulvestad, Bjarne. 1981. On the Precariousness of Linguistic Introspection. In Florian Coulmas, ed., A Festschrift for the Native Speaker, 245-261. The Hague: Mouton.

Upton, Clive, Stewart Sanderson, and John Widdowson. 1987. Word Maps: A Dialect Atlas of England. London: Croom Helm.

Vaux, Bert and Justin Cooper. 1998. Introduction to Linguistic Field Methods. Munich: Lincom Europa.

Vaux, Bert, Sergio LaPorta, and Emily Tucker. 1996. Ethnographic Materials from the Muslim Hemshinli with Linguistic Notes. Annual of Armenian Linguistics 17.

Verschueren, Jef, Jan-Ola Östman, and Jan Blommaert, eds. 1995. Handbook of pragmatics: manual. Amsterdam: John Benjamins.

Voegelin, Charles. 1960. Guide for Transcribing Unwritten Languages in Field Work. Manuscript, Harvard University.

Ward, Ida. 1937. Practical Suggestions for the Learning of an African Language in the Field. London: Millbank House.

Wardhaugh, Ronald. 1985. How Conversation Works. Oxford: Blackwell.

Warren, Richard. 1970. Perceptual restoration of missing speech sounds. Science 167:392-393

Wells, John. 1982. Accents of English. Cambridge: Cambridge University Press.

Wells, John. 2002. [Untitled autobiography]. In Keith Brown, Vivien Law, and R. Robins, eds., Linguistics in Britain: Personal Histories. London: Philological Society.

Werner, Oswald. 2000a. How to Reduce an Unwritten Language to Writing I. Field Methods 12.1:61-71.

Werner, Oswald. 2000b. How to Reduce an Unwritten Language to Writing II: Consonants. Field Methods 12.3:239-250.

Werner, Oswald. 2001. How to Reduce an Unwritten Language to Writing III: Phonetic similarity, suspicious pairs, and minimal pairs. Field Methods 13.1:97-102.

Werner, Oswald. 2002a. How to Reduce an Unwritten Language to Writing IV: Complementary distribution. Field Methods 14.2:217-227.

Werner, Oswald. 2002b. How to Reduce an Unwritten Language to Writing: V. Problems with Phonemes. Field Methods 14.3:337–342.

Whaley, Lindsay and Lenore Grenoble, eds. 1998. Endangered Languages: Current Issues and Future Prospects. Cambridge: Cambridge University Press.

Wilson, George. 1944. Instructions to collectors of dialect. Greensboro, North Carolina: American Dialect Society.

Wittgenstein, Ludwig. 1958. Philosophical Investigations. Translated by G. Anscombe. New York: Macmillan.

Wolcott, Harry. 1995. The Art of Fieldwork. Walnut Creek: Altamira Press.

Wolff, Hans. 1969. A Comparative Vocabulary of Abuan Dialects. Evanston: Northwestern University Press.

Wolfram, Walt, and Ralph Fasold. 1974. Field methods in the study of social dialects. In Walt Wolfram and Ralph Fasold, eds., The study of social dialects in American English. Englewood Cliffs, NJ: Prentice-Hall.

Wolfram, Walt. 1986. Good data in a bad situation: Eliciting vernacular structures. In Joshua A. Fishman et al., eds., The Fergusonian Impact; Volume 2: Sociolinguistics and the Sociology of Language, 3-22. Berlin: Mouton de Gruyter.

Wolfram, Walt. 1998. Scrutinizing linguistic gratuity: Issues from the field. Journal of Sociolinguistics 2.2:271-9.

Wolfson, Nessa. 1976. Speech events and natural speech: Some implications for sociolinguistic methodology. Language in Society 5:189-209.

Wright, Joseph. 1905. The English Dialect Grammar. Oxford: Henry Frowde.

Wurm, S. 1969. Linguistic fieldwork methods in Australia. Canberra: Australian Institute of Aboriginal Studies.

Zaliznjak, Andrej. 1967. Russkoe imennoe slovoizmenenie. Moscow: Nauka.

Zurif, E., Caramazza, A., & Myerson, R. 1972. Grammatical judgments of agrammatic aphasics. Neuropsychologia 10:405-417.